P9-CLD-797

Modernization and Political-Tension Management: A Socialist Society in Perspective

Dennis Clark Pirages
foreword by
Jan F. Triska

The Praeger Special Studies program—utilizing the most modern and efficient book production techniques and a selective worldwide distribution network—makes available to the academic, government, and business communities significant, timely research in U.S. and international economic, social, and political development.

Modernization and Political-Tension Management: A Socialist Society in Perspective
Case Study of Poland

HN 537.5
.P53

PRAEGER SPECIAL STUDIES IN INTERNATIONAL POLITICS AND PUBLIC AFFAIRS

Praeger Publishers   New York   Washington   London

INDIANA
PURDUE
LIBRARY

WITHDRAWN

FORT WAYNE

PRAEGER PUBLISHERS
111 Fourth Avenue, New York, N.Y. 10003, U.S.A.
5, Cromwell Place, London S.W.7, England

Published in the United States of America in 1972
by Praeger Publishers, Inc.

All rights reserved

© 1972 by Praeger Publishers, Inc.

Library of Congress Catalog Card Number: 70-180850

Printed in the United States of America

This study of the effects of industrialization on Polish society is an important contribution to the growing body of empirical literature in comparative politics. Using contemporary Poland as his laboratory, Dennis Pirages examines facets of hypotheses advanced by Seymour Lipset, Phillips Guttright, Gabriel Almond, Sidney Verba, and others on the relationship between modernization and societal decision-making. Is there indeed an overall tendency for modernizing societies to move toward more open forms of government? Testing the hypotheses against the date he began collecting while enrolled in the University of Warsaw's Department of Sociology, Dennis Pirages concludes that, indeed, in Poland modernization is one of the major variables creating pressures for new forms of political authority. The social consequences of rapid economic development do call for changes in the structure of decision-making. However, the author recognizes the necessity of incorporating the crucial intervening variable of foreign ties and influence. No political system is an island unto iteslf, and the presence of the Soviet Union, ally and sponsor of the Polish People's Republic, is another important factor shaping political outcomes in Poland.

Professor Pirages' study is one product of a collective research effort, the Stanford Studies of the Communist System, which covers a decade. In 1962, sponsored and assisted by the Ford Foundation as a part of the expansion of the International Studies at Stanford University, we were awarded funds to undertake a long-range study of communist states. We decided to make our starting point the international communist movement, chiefly because the activities that the members of the movement have historically displayed have produced important effects on the members as well as on the movement. It would be difficult, we thought, to understand the structure and operation of communist states without understanding the communist parties, the original members of the movement. And, indeed, this initial approach has permitted us to relate activities to effects in a theoretically meaningful way. We began by delving into issues such as the origin, proliferation, and development of communist parties; decision-making and political change in, associational theory, and organization of those parties; and the transformation of communist parties from non-ruling to ruling parties.

To make our framework more precise, systematic, and comprehensive than was the case in the past, we approached the complex of national communist parties as an international political system. We found this approach useful for several reasons. First, it permitted description, ordering, and classification of interacting units--the communist parties--according to their changing functions in the system; gradually we were able to reach generalizations about functions, and on this basis to construct analytical models. Second, the comparative politics field has developed a set of functions which offer uniform categories for comparison; these as well as the hypotheses and theories produced by studies of political development offered us the opportunity to apply and test such hypotheses and theories in the complex real world of communist parties. Third, our approach permitted us to understand and better explain the structures of communist states, as here the communist parties perform basic political functions: They support communications within a common culture, provide unifying operational concepts, legitimize the rule, and so on. And fourth, while communist states could not exist without communist parties, communist parties could and did in fact exist without the states. For this reason, communist parties appeared to us to deserve particular attention, and thus we approached them as an international political system.

This initial period in our research undertaking produced a series of papers written by faculty and students at the Institute of Political Studies.

These studies, in turn, led to further research and publications. Collectively, our research efforts signalled an attempt to develop and build the theory and methodology of the social sciences into the study of communist affairs. In particular, many authors applied and tested hypotheses and models developed by theorists in the fields of comparative politics and international relations. As a consequence, systems analysis, game theory, computer content analysis, integration theories, quantitative trans-action analysis, coalition theory, survey research, factor and regression analysis, and other theoretical frameworks, research techniques, and methodologies have been brought to bear by the authors on the research and study of communist affairs.

Recently we have begun to focus our attention increasingly upon that part of the world which, from the point of view of both comparative and inter-national politics, as well as the possibility of cooperation with local social scientists, seems the most interesting and challenging: namely, Eastern Europe. The changes in political climate in Eastern European communist party-states that are responsible for changing relations with the Soviet Union and with each other; and the fact that Eastern European societies are, comparatively speaking, less closed to observation and field studies than they were in the past, make these societies increasingly attrac-tive as laboratories for empirical political scien-tists. A new propensity toward openness and offi-cially sanctioned field studies, survey research, and other forms of empirical research appears to be on the upswing in Eastern Europe.

Professor Pirages is the first in our group to come up with a full-length study of an Eastern Euro-pean society conceived and carried out along these lines and under these more favorable auspices. He tested the new conditions in Poland and found them indeed more conducive to empirical research than was the case in the past. Moreover, he succeeded in finding interested Polish social scientists willing

to help him with advice, data, and facilities. We
had hoped to be able to couple our research interests
with those of Eastern European colleagues. We had
heard of the young and articulate professionals and
academics in institutions of higher learning associated with social science organizations, including
political science associations in some Eastern European countries; and grouped around newspapers and
periodicals, TV and radio stations, and similar organs of mass communication in other Eastern European
countries. Dennis Pirages' experience and study was
helpful and useful. Indeed, since then we have started several joint research undertakings with Eastern
European social scientists. The major thrust in
this direction is our survey research project in
Yugoslavia and Hungary (and possibly in Romania) on
citizens' participation in community decisions on the
local level, in which our collaboration with local
social scientists is supported by their governments,
the Ford Foundation, and the National Science Foundation.

Jan F. Triska

Looking back to 1966, when serious work on this
study began, the most striking observation seems to
be how little initial perceptions need to be modified
as a result of the events of the last five years.
The problems faced by today's political leaders are
much the same as they were. The cast of characters
is a bit different, and there have been a few minor
incidents--even a bit of bloodshed. But Poland is
an industrial society, and large-scale social and
political change does not come about easily under
such conditions.

Even with the wisdom of hindsight I do not feel
that any of the conclusions growing out of this study
need modification. Admittedly, the sudden ouster of
Gomulka came as a bit of a surprise, but the incred-
ible political blunders that preceded this period
were even more surprising. For example, it simply
isn't intelligent to substantially hike prices on
consumer goods during the Christmas season. Had
these miscalculations not been made, Gomulka might
still be in power today. In any industrial nation,
incumbent political leaders bent on maintaining
power usually have the resources to do so.

It remains to be seen whether Edward Gierek
will initiate new policies capable of bridging the
gap between the realities of an industrial society
and the rigid demands of socialist doctrine. There
are indications that he may be doing just that. As
with all fundamental policy shifts, however, they
can only take place silently lest conservative critics
regain the upper hand. It is clear that the next
decade in Poland will be a fascinating period as a
maturing socialist society attempts to alter the
decisional model that has brought so much progress
but has become outmoded by the industrial society
it fostered.

CONTENTS

Chapter

LIST OF TABLES

Modernization and Political-Tension Management: A Socialist Society in Perspective

1

MODERNIZATION AND
POLITICAL-TENSION
MANAGEMENT:
THE SOCIALIST
SOCIETY

In 1967, two Polish sociologists lamented in an essay that the socialist experience has been systematically excluded from efforts to construct theories of social change. They claimed that this was due to ethnocentrism among Western scholars and that the "process of social change taking place in the Polish countryside presents a rich field for the construction of theory."[1] Although the ethnocentric bias charge is not well supported by evidence, it is true that socialist countries have, until very recently, been ignored in most studies dealing with social and political change. This exclusion has been partially due to circumstances beyond the control of Western theorists--circumstances that have been slowly changing since the Twentieth Party Congress in the Soviet Union.

Empirical studies of political and social change in socialist countries have been few in the past because of lack of information and research opportunities.* Due to the de-Stalinization events

---

*The term "socialist" currently has a variety of meanings. We usually describe the Scandinavian

after the Twentieth Party Congress, a gradual return
to the empirical study of social questions in socialist societies has become possible. In the less
liberal socialist countries--East Germany and the
Soviet Union, for example--empirical research has
continued to lag far behind that being done in other
countries.[2] Fortunately Poland experienced a re-
surgence of her sociological tradition in the late
1950's, and, despite some setbacks a decade later,
important behavioral data have been gathered that
is not readily obtained in other socialist countries.

This should not be taken as a blanket excuse
for Western social and behavioral scientists who
have neglected this potentially rich field of study
for other reasons. For a long period, the study of
socialist politics and society was dominated by an
emphasis on the "totalitarian" model of control.[3]
If one accepted the relevance of this model, there
was really no reason to study the whole socialist
organization--all important social and political
changes were regarded as taking place at the top of
the hierarchy. The study of socialist politics was
dominated by those dedicated to ferreting out subtle
changes at the very top, and little attention was
paid to what was taking place in other sectors.
With few exceptions, those trained in the social
and behavioral sciences were not especially interested in the modernization of socialist society;
those trained in political analysis contented themselves with elite studies.[4] Only most recently has

---

countries as well as China as socialist. None of
the countries in the Communist Bloc claims to really be communist in social, political, and economic
terms. Instead the term socialist is preferred to
describe the stage that has been reached in the
struggles for utopia. In keeping with this usage,
the socialist countries referred to in this study
are those states dedicated to the building of communism as an ultimate goal as opposed to the great
number of countries that could be referred to as
socialist.

there been a real effort to begin to gain understanding of the socialist social organization, modernization and social change within the socialist
framework, and the role of the political system in
socialist decision-making.[5]

It is with these observations in mind that the
present study has been undertaken. It represents
an attempt to reconcile the growing body of theoretical literature dealing with modernization and
society with some of the empirical data recently
made available in one socialist country. Although
each individual socialist country presents a unique
case, what can be learned from the intensive study
of one country, where appropriate data are available, has many applications in the study of similar
phenomena in less open socialist societies.

DECISIONS AND SOCIAL ORGANIZATION

In studying societies, we are really looking
at organizations of human beings who originally
banded together to take advantage of various aspects
of economies of scale. Disregarding the complex issues of what actually sparked the development of
primitive societies, it is clear that early humans
discovered that through cooperation in larger groups
they were able to reach goals that they as individuals or extended families could not otherwise obtain.
Social organization has permitted man to survive in
a world for which he was not otherwise competitively
suited. Man's greatest asset in confronting a hostile environment has been his ability to conceptual-
ize and communicate and thus cooperate in a division
of labor.

Societies have historically varied in size from
the very small primitive tribe to our very large and
complex contemporary nation-states. Man's first cooperative efforts were small by contemporary standards and limited to banding together to seek food
and shelter and to provide for the common defense
against hostile elements. The development of modern
communication systems and the use of machines in an

increasingly complex division of labor have made
very large-scale social organization feasible if
not desirable. In our contemporary world, cooperation in societies is most frequently embedded within
the boundaries of nation-states. The size and com-
plexities of the societies in which we live often
lead us to forget the rationale that underlies social organization and we take the cooperative organization of humans within the national society
for granted.

Even in the small primitive tribe, the allocation of tasks and responsibilities in the division
of labor occasioned the emergence of a system for
making decisions. Most frequently one man or a
small group made the major decisions for the society
and criteria for inclusion in the decision-making
process were simple, such as age or blood ties. As
people began to take advantage of the economies of
scale associated with the industrial revolution,
making decisions became increasingly complex. The
allocation of values and rewards as well as the distribution of responsibilities in today's societies
are no longer simple tasks that can be carried out
on a face-to-face basis.[6] The management of society
has become too complicated to be handled by one man
or a very small group. New decision-making schemes
have emerged ranging from those in which a small
group tries to make most of the important decisions
on the basis of information provided by coopted
technocrats to those in which representative institutions have been established to attempt to imple-
ment the belief that the best decisions are made by
polling the will of the majority.

In addition to allocative functions--distribu-
ting values, rewards, and responsibilities--the
political decision-makers also decide future societal goals and legitimate certain patterns of behavior. Societies need a core of normative order
through which social behavior can be collectively
organized.[7] The core of normative order, or Durk-
heim's "collective conscience," is codified and explicated in the political arena. The establishment

of law and order means deciding which patterns are
or ought to be accepted by the majority, making the
enforcement of this behavior legitimate by vote,
and enforcing these decisions. The more complex a
society becomes, the more difficult it is to determine what patterns are most functional or even acceptable to the majority of citizens.

The political system is not only a conservative codifying body but also acts as the initiator
of new patterns through goal-setting responsibilities.[8] In this respect, the political decision-
makers are the "managers" of society. Their decisions greatly influence the lives of all those in
the social organization--they manage the distribution of tasks and rewards, and they set the organizational goals. One of the most interesting differences between socialist and capitalist or monist
and pluralist societies is the emphasis on future
goals found in socialist politics as opposed to the
"muddling through" characteristic of pluralistic
systems feeding on the reconciliation of diverging
interests.[9]

The distribution of decision-making authority
within the social organization is different in each
society. The scope and pervasiveness of decisions
made by top-level managers--elected officials in
democracies and representatives of controlling interests in more authoritarian systems--varies with
each type of social organization. In monist or col-
lectivist societies, top-level management has great
responsibilities in making detailed societal decisions. In more pluralist societies, a greater
variety of groups influence the decisions affecting
the common interest. In a socialist or monist society, very few important decisions are made outside of a tightly controlled party-management hierarchy; it is, therefore, not difficult to pinpoint
the centers of decision-making. In a pluralist society, on the other hand, the portion of decisions
affecting the whole social organization taken by
political management at the very top is much smaller than in the monist counterpart and consequently

it is much more difficult to affix decision-making responsibility.

In reality, no society can be described as completely monist in decision-making structure; even in the most tightly controlled society, many important decisions are made outside the official hierarchy. The most monist of societies must transfer into political decisions subtle pressures from all sectors.

Perhaps the most powerful variable discriminating among managerial systems in different societies is the ability of those outside the formal policy-making arenas to influence the decisions made therein. A. S. Banks and P. M. Gregg empirically factor analyzing the structure of the world's political systems found this to be the strongest descriptive dimension and labeled it the degree of "access" given to those outside the political arena. Access comes close to describing what is usually thought of as democracy. The main components of this dimension according to Gregg and Banks are "hierarchical as opposed to competitive bargaining processes, consolidated as opposed to distributed authority and force, and totalitarian restrictions as opposed to institutionalized openness of political channels."[10]

Socialist societies differ considerably from others along this dimension because of restricted citizen access to political decision-making. There is much more emphasis on planning future goals at the expense of reconciliation of current group interests. This mobilization type of decisional model was initiated by Stalin in meeting awesome post-revolutionary problems and was most successfully employed in industrializing and reconstructing Eastern Europe from the ashes of World War II. This hierarchical and rigid model of decision-making was adopted by dependent party leaders in most of the socialist countries and maintained even after Stalin's death, because of both inertia and self-interest among the party managers. It has worked most efficiently, however, in societies

where resources must be mobilized to meet pressing
economic goals and has been considerably less successfully employed in more affluent societies.

MODERNIZATION AND DECISION-MAKING

Industrialization is the core of the modernization process that has aided the development of modern large-scale societies. Modernization has received its greatest impetus from the economies of
scale in factory production made possible by the
introduction of machine labor. Since the late Middle Ages, the size of basic social units has been
altered from the old self-sufficient units of production (the tribe, estate, or village) into much
larger units more able to rationally exploit the
efficiencies of mass production techniques. This
has been accompanied by the freeing of individuals
from their old primordial ties and loyalties and
regrouping them or "mobilizing" them in more urban
areas where they are available for integration into
the more highly organized and centralized production and distribution system.[11]

Today, modernization is still universally
sought. Political managers in the monist as well
as pluralist, the industrial as well as agricultural, countries are nearly unanimous in their professed desire to seek more material goods for citizens.[12] In the socialist countries, political leaders have made great progress in their efforts to
industrialize their nations in the aftermath of the
War and continue to make great political capital
from high rates of economic growth, pointing to
them as major factors legitimating their rule. Indeed, growth of all kinds is interwoven in the core
of all socialist political programs; material abundance seems as important to socialist political
leaders as to their capitalist counterparts.

The socialist bloc is today composed of countries that have attained varying levels of modernization ranging from East Germany and Czechoslovakia,

highly industrialized countries as a result of sustained efforts over the past two decades, to Albania
and Bulgaria, countries that have just commenced the
long struggle to attain the fruits of industrial development. The Stalinist organization of society
was effective in all these countries in mobilizing
resources needed for industrial growth in the post-
war period, but recent events in Czechoslovakia and
Poland attest to the problems of maintaining rigid
control once the great mobilization efforts have
waned.[13]

Although it is clear that all countries are industrializing or modernizing, it is important to
note that no one knows exactly where the more complex future organization of production and distribution will lead. It is very likely that some of the
most industrialized countries will soon no longer
be able to profit from an increasingly complex division of industrial labor or from the economy of
scale and that future advances will be tied to a
division of decision-making labor. Unlike the industrial revolution, which depended upon innovation
and novelty in combining humans and machines to make
the production of goods more efficient, the new
cybernetics revolution will depend on the development of information storage and retrieval techniques. Greater satisfactions are likely to come
from insights into social problems derived from information collection and storage rather than from
better organized production of material goods. The
basis for social stratification will undoubtedly
shift from possession of economic resources to intellectual abilities during this period of increasing emphasis on knowledge and skill in the division
of decision-making labor.[14]

It is fortunate that the socialist societies
are all still at levels of development where the
organization of productive forces and the exploitation of economies of scale are yet very important
in the modernization of society. Far from having
exhausted the possibilities of utilizing larger
scales in mass production, an increasingly complex

division of labor and organization into larger aggregates is a most important part of modernization
in all the socialist countries. Previous social
and political effects of machine-based modernization in other countries can be effectively employed
to generate hypotheses concerning the bounds of efficient decision-making and tension management in
the industrializing socialist societies. Although
these countries will not slavishly follow the examples of their more pluralist counterparts, judgments and hypotheses generated on the basis of available evidence from other societies can be extremely
relevant for the study of socialist modernization.

Modernization in any society implies massive
changes in social organization. These include increasing urbanization, higher levels of average educational attainment, increasing scope of mass communications, and increasing levels of personal
wealth.[15] As individuals are mobilized into industrial society, their orientations toward the world
around them shift from local, conservative, traditional patterns to more universal, secular, and rational evaluations.[16] Belief in the efficacy of collective action soon follows. These industrialization-
related changes in the social fabric, discussed in
more detail in Chapter 2, have important impacts on
the efficiencies of various models of political
decision-making.

Seymour Martin Lipset was among the first to
deal with the question of modernization and changes
in decision-making structure. He found a strong
correlation between indicators of modernization and
what he defined as democracy. Concomitant with the
increasing division of labor in the industrialization process, a middle class having a stake in continued political stability emerges as a defender of
the political order. Lipset argued that this results from increasing societal wealth, education,
and urbanization, all factors that tend to amelio-
rate social struggles and thus enhance political
stability and democratic potential.[17]

In the same research tradition, Philips Cutright claimed that political development, defined
in terms of complexity and specialization of nations'
political institutions, is closely related to socioeconomic characteristics. His data illustrate a
clear tendency for modern societies to cluster at
the politically developed end of his scale; the less
modern countries are grouped at the politically
less-developed end. Cutright's measures are much
better described as indicators of political democracy and stability than anything that might be
called political development. In short, he duplicated Lipset's findings that there is indeed a tendency for more highly industrialized countries to
move toward representative institutions in government as well as political stability.[18]

More recently, G. Almond and S. Verba have
found that cooperation and social trust are most
important in fostering attitudes supporting democracy. Democracy survives best in an atmosphere of
compromise where no important issues are left un-
reconciled over a long period of time. Education
and other modernization-related social factors are
found to be most important in development of the
attitudes and skills required for compromise and
cooperation.[19] Close analysis of the Almond and
Verba data reveals that for the sample of five countries functional position in the division of labor
is very important in determining political attitudes.
Those possessing more education, more interpersonal
contacts, heavier occupational responsibilities,
and more opportunities to consider political matters
are those who most demand political responsiveness
on the part of the policy-makers regardless of
country.[20]

The literature indicates that the organization
of decision-making in society tends to naturally
change as the division of labor becomes more complex. Political stability and access to the
decision-making arena for a greater portion of the
citizens are associated with industrialization for
a variety of reasons. An educated citizenry is

aware that political managers control the allocation of values, rewards, and responsibility and set
societal goals. Functionally speaking, a modern society requires a delegation of responsibility because the hierarchical or custodial model where all
decisions are made by a few at the top is extremely
inefficient in solving the more complex problems
associated with modern society. The scope of decisions that can be made successfully by political
managers, often far removed from the problems, nar-
rows as the number of decisions that must be made
multiplies. As the allocation of responsibility is
broadened, so is the allocation of rewards. One of
the most important perceived rewards is access to
the decision-making arena.

One can thus visualize a "normal" curve tracing
the relationship between industrialization and the
form of the decision-making structure. There is a
tendency for more modern societies to be managed by
decision-makers working within a democratic decision-
making structure. Regardless whether we use the
term access, democracy, or any equivalent, taken as
a whole, the more modern a society the greater the
chances that the average citizen can influence decisions, has an opportunity to become a decision-
maker, and has a voice in determining who shall
make key decisions.

It is important to remark that this rule holds
only in the aggregate and that there are many devia-
tions. Differing historical experiences, characteristics of national political cultures, and social
homogeneity are key factors that influence the relationship between modernity and political access.
In addition, there is evidence that as countries
become extremely modern by conventional standards,
they reach a threshold beyond which they no longer
are characterized by more accessible decision-making
systems. Using a very sophisticated definition of
democracy, D. E. Neubauer has found that for the
most industrial societies, economic development
ceases to be highly correlated with advances in
levels of democracy.[21] The socialist countries are

far below the level at which this threshold effect
becomes important, however, and we can safely assume
that these access pressures found in the general
sample of societies are operational in socialist
countries.

The most striking feature of this curve is the
extent to which the socialist societies deviate
from it. Using almost any measure of access or
democratization devised, these countries offer much
less of it to their citizens than do more pluralist
societies. Thus, returning to the observation made
at the beginning of the chapter, in this area of research the socialist countries have been convenient-
ly overlooked. Both Lipset and Cutright ignored the
fact that some of the socialist levels of industrialization exceed those of some of the more democratic capitalist states.

In this respect, these societies represent a
group of very deviant cases. The reasons that they
deviate so far from this hypothetical curve are not
mysterious. Hierarchical, custodial decision-making
models were imposed on all the socialist countries
that fell under Soviet domination after World War II
without consideration of national differences in
level of modernization or political culture. At the
time of imposition, these models were efficient in
reconstructing societies that had been severely dam-
aged by the War. Now the socialist societies have
been totally reconstructed and new levels of modernization have been reached. The decision-makers in
the ruling parties, however, have in many cases been
loathe to give up their tight control over allocations of power and privilege. The only clear socialist exception is Yugoslavia, a country in which
socialism developed without the help of Soviet arms,
where citizen participation in politics is more
than commensurate with that which would be predicted
by recourse to universal standards.[22]

The pressures for more meaningful political
participation and more representative institutions
has recently been most apparent in Czechoslovakia.

Novotny was rebuffed in his attempts to maintain the
rigid Stalinist formulas in the face of pressures
generated by an industrial economy and liberal political traditions. Faced with slowdowns in production and lagging worker productivity, he was backed
against the wall even within the Party as demands
for liberalizing the political process met with his
stern rebuff.

The Dubcek liberalization followed Novotny's
ouster, but this more sensible turn of events was
cut short by Soviet leaders fearful that these moves
would feed back to their own restless citizens. The
Czech events were not isolated incidents in the socialist bloc; almost all Party leaders have been
hesitant to experiment with more liberalized decisional structures in the face of new citizen and
even Party demands. They have relied on a variety
of tactics designed to control the most threatening
aspects of widespread citizen discontent and have
suffered loss of prestige, authority, and even political office as a result.

HOLDING SOCIETIES TOGETHER

All forms of organization use a variety of
pressures to keep their members in line. In large
and complex societies, political managers possess a
variety of powers and use different types of tactics
to keep citizens compliant and the system functioning. Societal decision-makers can enforce their decisions by applying utilitarian, coercive, or persuasive techniques. Citizen compliance is maintained
because of fear, self-interest, or moral commitment
to social goals.[23]

Coercive power is at the base of all social organization. Without ultimate recourse to physical
sanctions against extreme deviants, society would
be at the mercy of those deciding not to comply
with decisions taken in the political arena. Coercive power must be utilized when citizens will
not subscribe to the commonly accepted norms and

beliefs. But it is not only extreme deviants who
comply out of fear of sanctions; many laws in every
society are obeyed only out of fear of the consequences and not because the rules are held to be
logical.

Inasmuch as political managers control the
allocation of rewards and values, they also can employ utilitarian power or economic benefits in maintaining compliance. One of the major reasons people
obey laws is that they know that compliance is associated with economic rewards. Those in charge of
reward distribution can use their powers to induce
those who would rather not comply to modify their
positions. Although citizens do not ordinarily
make a daily calculation of the advantages they receive from their support of political regimes, evidence indicates that commitment to regime goals is
strongest among those who experience a steady im-
provement in economic situation in relation to their
reference groups.[24]

The strongest pressure maintaining social cohesion is persuasive power. Based on the development of moral commitment, this type of power is
easiest to exercise and most effectively employed.
All societies are to some extent held together by
these invisible moral bonds often rooted in less
than rational sentiments and beliefs. Parents,
peer groups, and religious leaders are all responsible for inspiring commitment to accepted goals and
values among the young. When leaders can maintain
citizen compliance by appealing to these commonly
held values, little coercion need be used. Therefore, political leaders work to change the core of
accepted values to correspond to their own vision
of the world because the gulf separating citizen
values and those of societal managers is a measure
of the limits of potential for effective employment
of persuasive power.[25]

The use of any type of power has costs and
limitations. Societal managers desire to enforce
their decisions by persuasion and hope to develop a

moral commitment to social norms among citizens.
Persuasive power is cheap because few resources
must be used to encourage desired citizen behavior.
If the citizen can be shown that the expected behavior is in keeping with the interests of society
as a whole or with commonly accepted principles, he
is likely to be more willing to comply. It is unfortunate for political leaders that most people no
longer comply with decisions for moral reasons. In
contrast to the feudal society, where authority was
buttressed by the Church's recourse to ultimate
sanctions, contemporary citizens comply for more
materialistic reasons.

As political man has become more analytic,
utilitarian or economic power has been much more
successfully employed in holding societies together.
A greater proportion of the population refuses to
base compliance on allegiance to absolute principles
and unquestioningly accept authority. Instead, the
new political compliance is based on self-interest
in the benefits that continued support of the
decision-making structure will bring. This type of
compliance is costly to decision-makers because it
requires the "buying off" of more demanding segments
of society through rechanneling values and rewards.
Limits are thereby placed on the prerogatives of
societal managers.

Coercive power is by far the most expensive
tool to employ in cementing the social organization.
Although it is most basic and available for use in
a crisis, its successful employment is limited to
those situations in which a majority is clearly not
committed to societal goals. Coerced personnel can
only be forced to perform menial tasks amenable to
easy quantification. Tasks requiring motivation or
initiative cannot be assigned to the coerced and
alienated citizen because, unless there can be
quantification of effort, there is no way to accu-
rately gauge performance. Not only does the coercive leadership expend resources to maintain a coercive apparatus, but this approach to maintaining
social organization discourages maximal citizen productivity and innovation.[26]

Traditional societies are cemented by a normative involvement on the part of the vast majority
of the citizens. Whether discussing the feudal societies of the Middle Ages or contemporary African
tribal societies, a feature that all have in common
is an unquestioning commitment among the members.
The citizen never questions the decisions made and
complies with them for fear of upsetting the order
established by supernatural powers. The rationality
aspects of the increasingly complex division of
labor, however, militate against this simplistic
traditional type of political compliance. People
now ask what their own interests are in complying
with these decisions in an increasingly secular
world. Societal managers must more often legitimate
their performance with hard economic results rather
than by recourse to mysterious absolute principles.
If their performance does not live up to citizen expectations, they are more frequently removed from
office.

The socialist countries represent examples of
societies in which coercion has been freely used by
party managers to maintain political and social order during past periods of turmoil. It could be
argued that the heavy reliance on hierarchical
decision-making and mobilization politics following
the War had to be buttressed by reliance on force
to be successful. It can't be denied that the party
managers made tremendous progress in creating societies of relative abundance from the War's ruins.
Coercive force was most functional in squeezing
largely agrarian masses into new economic roles in
the industrializing societies. There were excesses
during this period, but, on balance, a difficult
and arduous task was completed in an extremely
short period of time.

The Twentieth Party Congress in the Soviet
Union represented a first step in moving socialist
societies away from reliance on force and toward
more utilitarian or normative compliance structures.
In more industrial socialist societies, the economic costs of maintaining an old hierarchical

decision-making system buttressed with the heavy reliance on coercion have become prohibitive. These
changes have not been easy or trouble-free. Conservative elements in all the socialist societies
resist these pressures for change and prefer the
proven techniques of societal control. Developing
moral or utilitarian commitment requires politicians
to give up a portion of their privilege and a good
share of their arbitrary power. The older and more
conservative elements in most party leaderships
"would rather fight than switch" and have clung desperately to the old coercive models that have maintained them in power for the last twenty years.

SOCIALIST TENSION MANAGEMENT

     Having made a decision to retain the old coer-
cive and hierarchical models of control as far as
possible, the conservative elements in the socialist
countries are faced with special management problems.
Resisting natural pressures for more citizen access
to decision-making requires a heavy investment of
talent and resources in the management of political
tensions. Many among top-level politicians fear
that loosening tight controls means loss of political office and are willing to expend any effort
necessary to maintain control over a semi-alienated
citizenry.

     Political-tension management is not unique to
the socialist countries but it is most apparent and
easiest to study in these countries because it is
there that pressures for change are most intense.
Inasmuch as the need to manage new pressures on
decision-makers has been an integral part of socialist industrialization, especially during periods of
intense mobilization, coercive force has been frequently used as emergency social cement. The required resource investment in tension management
has been heavy and the objective costs in wasted
productivity have been high, but to ideologically
or selfishly motivated politicians the costs have
appeared much smaller. Costs have only become more

apparent since the rigid inefficient decisional models have caused problems reflected in measurable losses in economic productivity. This has been clearly demonstrated in the economic misfortunes causing Novotny's downfall in Czechoslovakia and Gomulka's demise in Poland.

Industrialization and the accompanying moderni-zation of socialist societies have put new resources into the hands of the political managers and en-hanced control possibilities. Changing citizen ex-pectations, however, are creating new management problems. These more complex industrial societies represent a radically different type of organiza-tion to manage and the managerial rules have dras-tically changed. There are a greater number of citizens whose opinions now need to be taken into account in making new policies. Tension management activities in these more complex societies requires knowing where pressures for change are likely to arise and developing methods to deal appropriately with them.

Socialist political leaders can no longer rely on the crude management tactics characteristic of the past. The numbers that now must be controlled are too large for summary measures and the costs of citizen discontent are becoming more prohibitive. Resources provided by the industrial revolution per-mit more complicated and subtle types of societal management, and prevention of political decay by recourse to force is reserved for extreme periods of stress.[27]

An increase in persuasive powers used to build commitment to socialist regime norms has been one of the important changes in socialist tension management weaponry concomitant with increased in-dustrialization. Socialist political managers con-trol an expanding educational system to which a greater number of youths are exposed for an increas-ing period of time each year. Control of informa-tion flow through an expanded media is another

important management tool. These are combined with
attempts to downgrade the authority of family and
Church and replace it with that of the less traditional youth group under the auspices of the ruling
party. A new picture of reality more in keeping
with the Party's view of the world is hopefully
created in the minds of the young, thus enhancing
the managers' persuasive powers.

The most obvious change in management capabili-
ties has taken place in the economic sphere; a judi-
cious distribution of increasing economic abundance
is used to build calculative involvement among citizens with growing expectations. People seldom bite
the hand that feeds them and in this case those who
feel they are receiving at least a fair share of
economic benefits relative to others are not likely
to revolt against Party leadership. Dependence on
this type of power is fraught with danger, and
periods of depression and recession obviously must
be avoided at all costs. It is also not always
easy to convince the upwardly mobile that they are
receiving a fair share of the available economic
benefits.

Although terror in its most blatant forms has
been removed from the socialist tension management
arsenal, fear remains an important psychological
weapon that can be readily employed. The midnight
knock on the door, death, and long prison terms
were largely eliminated after the Twentieth Party
Congress, and now, with the exception of the sacri-
fice of an occasional scapegoat, they have been replaced by more subtle pressures emanating from
state control of job and promotion opportunities.
Although fears of losing a job or promotion cannot
be equated with the ultimate penalty, Party control of the distribution of privilege and prestige
is used as an effective weapon in insuring loyalty
to the party line. This is especially important
when replacement of key personnel becomes common-
place as a method of keeping high-level officials
off balance.[28]

POLAND: A MANAGED SOCIETY

Socialist societies offer the best opportunities to study tension management because they deviate so far from the normal curve in terms of access offered to citizens. Political tensions arise from demands that citizens perceive as not being met. The restraints placed on active and meaningful political participation in socialist societies are an important source of political tensions and friction. The price paid by the parties for holding citizens at arm's length is a heavy investment in tension management activities. Tensions must be managed in other societies also, but with a few significant exceptions the socialist societies far exceed others in terms of investment in tension management.

Poland is a country worth studying intensively for several reasons, both practical and theoretical. Aside from the surge of interest in recent events, the student demonstrations in 1968, and the more recent shift in political leadership, the Polish United Workers' Party has spearheaded an intensive modernization campaign begun with the seizure of power and ideological mobilization more than two decades ago. During this period, the Polish people have been transformed from peasants and villagers (only 27 percent of the population lived in urban areas in 1931) to city dwellers sustained by a moderate and growing industrial base.[29] Major cities have been swollen by migrating peasants, and towns and cities have sprung up in the fields to replace the small villages. In 1931, 60 percent of the people were in agriculturally oriented occupations; only 38 percent remained in these areas in 1960.[30]

Contemporary Poland offers an exciting blend of the traditional with the modern. The countryside is still untouched by modernity in many parts. The horse remains an important source of power in the countryside as well as a symbol of peasant defiance of Party-directed mechanization programs. Unlike other socialist countries, land ownership in Poland is still largely confined to small private

holdings as collectivization has really never been
successful. Attempts at politicizing the peasantry
have met more apathy than resistance. Throughout
Polish history, the succession of different masters
has cautioned the peasant against becoming involved
in political affairs and the contemporary farmer remains apolitical.

In contrast to the unchanging countryside,
Poland's larger cities are alive with industrial
activity. Housing for the expanding urban population is being constructed everywhere. Traffic jams
are more common as private automobile ownership is
expanding more quickly than plans for new streets.
Shops and stores are stocked with goods that may
not be luxurious by Western standards but are certainly welcomed by prospective buyers who have en-
dured twenty years of austerity in economic affairs.
Although the industrial cities often appear somber
and grey, beneath the surface large-scale social
and economic changes have been taking place.[31]

The Polish United Workers' Party (PUWP), in
cooperation with the United Peasant Party and the
Social Democrats acting as its auxilliaries, has
presided over this transformation of Polish society.
While the society has been changing, however, the
Party has been transformed much less rapidly. In
Warsaw, for example, 1961 figures revealed that
nearly two thirds of PUWP membership had joined the
Party before 1948.[32] Figures for the rest of the
country were not so extreme, but as a whole nearly
half of the Party membership in 1961 had been recruited before the Twentieth Party Congress in the
Soviet Union. Thaw and liberalization movements
beginning in 1956 restored Wladyslaw Gomulka to a
position of power as First Secretary of the Polish
United Workers' Party, but his more recent performance left many followers bitterly disillusioned.
Under Gomulka, the Party clung to increasingly more
orthodox standards and refused to transform itself
into a truly democratic and representative institution, a situation partially responsible for his replacement by Edward Gierek.

In today's industrializing society, the Polish masses have become "demassed" and the Party's authoritarian approach to decision-making is increasingly coming under fire from young technocrats with important responsibilities in the ever-growing industrial establishment. Poland has entered what has been referred to as the second round of industrialization, in which the old hierarchical models of decision-making meet with less than cordial acceptance from the increasingly expectant society.[33] The Party, determined to maintain political control on its own terms, has until recently been forced to use most of the weapons in the tension management arsenal.

In addition to these reasons for studying Poland, the availability of data is another important factor. In most of the socialist countries, the social sciences are in an embryonic state. Poland has a respected sociological tradition that enjoyed a rebirth with the thaw in the mid-1950's. Consequently a wealth of empirical data relevant to the study of political-tension management has become available in the last decade. Although recent political transitions have disturbed the initiation of new studies, the legacy of research built up in the 1960's is most impressive.

Availability of data is still restricted in Poland, as in other monist societies, but it is available to the resourceful. The largest share of empirical data has been gathered by the Public Opinion Research Center and reported in fragmentary form in the Polish Sociological Bulletin, published in English, and Studia Sociologiczne, a Polish publication. The chapters that follow make use of data and studies reported in the formal journals, the most interesting reports published by the Public Opinion Research Center, collections of relevant statistical data, and personal experience gained during a year spent at the University of Warsaw.

NOTES

1. Krzysztof Ostrowski and Adam Przeworski, "A Preliminary Inquiry into the Nature of Social Change: the case of the Polish Countryside," Studies in Polish Political System, ed. Jerzy J. Wiatr (Warsaw: Ossolineum, 1967).

2. The best examples of recent socialist research are outlined in the summary article by J. Shippee, "Empirical Sociology in the East European Party-States," Communist Party States: Comparative and International Studies, ed. J. Triska (Indianapolis, Ind.: Bobbs-Merrill, 1969).

3. This model was most extensively developed in Z. Brzezinski and C. Friederick, Totalitarian Dictatorship and Autocracy (New York: Frederick A. Praeger, Inc., 1961).

4. One of the outstanding exceptions was R. Bauer and A. Inkeles, The Soviet Citizen (Cambridge, Mass.: Harvard University Press, 1959).

5. For an excellent summary of movement in this direction, see F. J. Fleron, "Toward a Reconceptualization of Political Change in the Soviet Union: The Political Leadership System," Comparative Politics, Vol. I, No. 2 (1969).

6. This definition of political activity corresponds closely to that suggested by D. Easton, A Framework for Political Analysis (Englewood Cliffs, N.J.: Prentice-Hall, 1965).

7. T. Parsons, The Social Systems (New York: The Free Press of Glencoe, 1951), p. 10.

8. See K. Deutsch, "Integration and the Social System: Implications of Functional Analysis," The Integration of Political Communities, eds. P. E. Jacob and J. V. Toscano (New York: J. B. Lippincott, 1964), pp. 179-209.

9. The term monist is employed here closely following its use by G. Fischer, The Soviet System and Modern Society (New York: Atherton Press, 1968). See pp. 1-18.

10. A. S. Banks and P. M. Gregg, "Dimensions of Political Systems: A Factor Analysis of a Cross-Polity Survey," American Political Science Review, Vol. LIX, No. 3 (1965), pp. 602-14.

11. See K. Deutsch, "Social Mobilization and Political Development," American Political Science Review, Vol. LV, No. 3 (1961), 493-514. Also C. Geertz, "The Integrative Revolution: Primordial Sentiments and Civic Politics in the New States," Old Societies and New States, ed. C. Geertz (New York: The Free Press, 1963).

12. See J. F. Triska (ed.), Soviet Communism: Programs and Rules (San Francisco, Calif.: Chandler Publishing Co., 1962), pp. 68-97.

13. This corresponds to views on cybernetics and human nature expressed by L. Von Bertalanffy, Robots, Men, and Minds (New York: George Braziller, 1967), pp. 29-43, 55-69.

14. A. Etzioni, The Active Society (New York: The Free Press, 1968), pp. 198-203.

15. See D. Lerner, The Passing of Traditional Society (New York: The Free Press of Glencoe, 1958), Ch. 2; S. M. Lipset, Political Man (Garden City, N.Y.: Doubleday, 1960), p. 32 ff. For precise correlations between developmental variables of this nature, see B. M. Russet et al., World Handbook of Political and Social Indicators (New Haven, Conn.: Yale University Press, 1964), p. 261 ff.

16. Lerner, op. cit., pp. 47-52.

17. Lipset, op. cit., Ch. 2. Also "Some Social Requisites of Democracy," American Political Science Review, Vol. LIII, No. 1 (1959), pp. 69-105.

18. P. Cutright, "National Political Development: Its Measurement and Social Correlates," Politics and Social Life, ed. N. W. Polsby, R. A. Dentler, and P. A. Smith (Boston, Mass.: Houghton Mifflin Co., 1963), pp. 569-82.

19. G. Almond and S. Verba, The Civic Culture (Princeton, N.J.: Princeton University Press, 1963), Ch. 15.

20. N. Nie, B. Powell, and K. Prewitt, "Social Structure and Political Participation I and II," American Political Science Review, Vol. LXIII, Nos. 2 and 3 (1969).

21. D. E. Neubauer, "Some Conditions of Democracy," American Political Science Review, Vol. LXI, No. 4 (1967), pp. 1002-9.

22. For a more detailed discussion of these points, see D. Pirages, "Modernization and Political Change in the Communist System," Communist Party States: Comparative and International Studies, ed. J. F. Triska (Indianapolis, Ind.: Bobbs-Merrill, 1969).

23. A. Etzioni, A Comparative Analysis of Complex Organizations (New York: The Free Press, 1961), pp. 4-16.

24. See R. E. Lane, Political Ideology (New York: The Free Press, 1962), pp. 91-92, for insight into the relationship of economic incentives and support for American democratic values.

25. Etzioni, The Active Society, pp. 357-59.

26. Etzioni, A Comparative Analysis of Complex Organizations, pp. 33-39, for a more detailed discussion of incentives and compliance in different organizational settings.

27. S. Huntington describes political decay
as the breakdown of political order in the face of
intense social mobilization. For more details, see
"Political Development and Political Decay," World
Politics, Vol. XVII, No. 3 (1965), pp. 386-430.

28. See D. Pirages, "Modernization and Political Organization: Pressures for New Decisional
Models in Socialist Society," Leadership Change in
Eastern Europe and the Soviet Union, ed. R. Farrell
(Chicago, Ill.: Aldine Publishing Co., 1969), for
a more complete discussion of how these techniques
have been used in Poland.

29. Rocznik Statystyczny 1966 (Warsaw: Glowny
Urzad Statystyczny, 1966), p. 24.

30. Ibid., p. 35.

31. Among the most interesting and relevant
recent works dealing with Polish politics and society are H. Stehle, The Independent Satellite (New
York: Frederick A. Praeger, Inc., 1965); A. Bromke,
Poland's Politics (Cambridge, Mass.: Harvard University Press, 1967); J. Szczepanski, Polish Society
(New York: Random House, 1970); and relevant sections of P. Lendvai, Anti-Semitism without Jews
(Garden City, N.Y.: Doubleday, 1971).

32. PZPR w 1961 (Warsaw: Polish United Workers' Party, 1962), pp. 3-5 (restricted circulation).

33. See J. Triska, "Political Response of
One-Party States to Economic Affluence and Social
Complexity: Eastern Europe" (paper presented to
the American Political Science Association meeting
in Chicago, Ill., September, 1967).

2

INDUSTRIALIZATION AND POLITICAL DEVELOPMENT: A THEORETICAL PERSPECTIVE

Modernization is a process centered around changes in society linked with increasingly higher levels of industrial organization. The dimensions of modernization in contemporary societies have yet to be precisely explicated, but there is clearly a cluster of economic, political, and social phenomena all related to changes in industrial organization. The shifts in social and political organization that accompany the increasingly sophisticated division of labor and the utilization of machine power in the economies of scale need to be spelled out in greater detail to understand more clearly the relationship between modernization and problems of political-tension management.

Only in the most modern or advanced societies has the exploitation of the economies of scale begun to approach its limits. Most contemporary nation-states are still "modernizing" or moving in a direction defined by increasing economic complexity. In this respect, industrial modernity is a condition toward which all nations are aspiring but which can best be defined only by reference to the world's most complex industrial societies. More modern societies are universally desired by

political managers because of the material benefits
the more productive industrial establishment puts
in their hands for distribution. In emphasis on
economic growth and continued industrialization,
there is little difference between the Program of
the Communist Party of the Soviet Union and the
platforms of the Republican or Democratic parties
in the United States.[1]

Modernization, when more precisely defined,
acts as a universal anchor upon which can be based
predictions about future effects of the industrial
and cybernetics revolution on the nature of existing social and political organization. The most
general relationships between level of modernity
and the structure of decision-making have been outlined in the preceding chapter. There are many
other important relationships that can be gleaned
from contemporary and historical analyses of the
modernization process. Aspects of social and political change that can be isolated in this manner
are important in understanding political-tension
management in a changing world.

MODERNIZATION AND THE SOCIAL FABRIC

One of the most important aspects of modernization is the reorganization of society from largely
self-sustaining local groups with limited ties to
the larger nation-state into an integrated and industrialized whole with greatly increased interaction between the center and the peripheral areas.
In traditional society the extended family, the
village, or the tribe represents a miniature, self-
contained unit having very little interdependence
with the larger social and political whole. The
larger nation-state is rarely significant for the
village dweller, with the possible exception of tax
collection time. Industrialization turns the
nation-state into the basic unit; central governments in most nations now penetrate even the most
peripheral areas of society. Economies of scale
require the mobilization of human resources for the

factory and the integration of peripheral areas into the mainstream of society.

Traditional society is a stable society. The
child in peripheral areas is socialized in an environment nearly duplicating that in which his an-
cestors were raised.[2] Social mobility is minimal,
and the child soon learns his designated place in
the social structure. No rationale is given for
existing stratification other than that things have
always been the way they are perhaps bolstered by
occasional recourse to a deity or foundation myth
that links the privileged with the supernatural.
Based largely on stratification arising from land
ownership, village society is characterized by a
rigid and unquestioned system of reciprocal social
and economic obligations. Power, privilege, and
prestige are closely linked in primitive societies
and are tied to ownership of the means of production essential to the existence of the miniature
societies.[3]

Daniel Lerner used the term empathy to describe one of the most important qualities that
differentiates the inhabitants of the isolated village or tribe from more urban counterparts.[4] The
tradition-bound villagers rarely come in contact
with individuals from outside their village and
consequently have little impetus to question the
existing state of affairs. There is little motivation for developing empathy skills involving
abilities to understand people and events in the
outside world. Life is predetermined for the village dweller in that tradition dictates life styles
and manner of living. Innovation comes about slowly in this environment and the villagers have great
difficulty comprehending new ideas.

The industrial revolution has struck and continues to strike mortal blows to these more dis-
persed types of social organization. With the
implementation of economies of scale involving mass
production techniques, it is no longer justifiable
or logical in the eyes of the political managers to

permit the existence of small-scale peripheral
agrarian societies when other possibilities exist.
Development strategies dictate that human resources
be freed from primordial local ties and mobilized
in close proximity to the industrial enterprises
that are the key to production of politically important material benefits.[5]

Profound social reorganization takes place
during the early stages of industrialization as
people, mainly the young, move from isolated villages to developing urban areas where they discover a completely different world beyond the confines
of the village. As great numbers of migrants come
together in the cities, they discover others who
share similar life situations. Exposure to newspapers, the radio, the and movies increases the individual's psychic mobility or empathy as well as
economic, social, and political expectations.[6]
Greater consciousness of numbers, increased contact
with the media, and the resulting increase in all
types of expectations significantly change problems
of political-tension management.

In the early stages of industrialization, it
takes time for attitudes to change as illiterates
learn to read and as the village mentality gives
way to a more cosmopolitan orientation toward life.
The peasant may remove his robe, substituting a
pair of cover-alls, but this does not necessarily
signify a basic change in mentality. Stalin proved
in the Soviet industrialization drive that basic
heavy industry can be established with minimal
change in citizen attitudes or expectations. His
successors, however, are finding that to advance a
society beyond primitive industrialization requires
active and innovative minds that have thrown off
more traditional backgrounds.

Concomitant with continued development of an
industrial establishment, a need for educated
specialists to direct it arises. The educational
system expands to produce manpower to fill an increasing number of highly important technical roles.

Literacy rates and educational enrollment climb in
response to societal needs. As skills required for
occupying important roles increase, so do citizen
expectations, and normally societal wealth is re-
distributed in deference to new demands. No political managers have yet been able to avoid increasing demands for privilege from groups assuming
heavier responsibilities. This is evidenced by the
fact that even in the most egalitarian societies
specialists receive many times the average compensation for the gainfully employed.[7]

Other modernization-related processes with
less direct links to the factory are important in
changing social expectations. Leaders in industrial societies are naturally concerned with a
manageable and efficient mass media which requires
the talents of other types of educated specialists.
Media personnel form part of a middle level of command and can use their potential power to act as a
buffer between citizens and political leaders in
the modernizing society.

In addition to the development of "mass" media,
programs of cultural enrichment encourage the development of literacy, art, film, and theatrical
talents as parts of "cultural" media. The emerging
cultural and educational intelligentsia performs
vital social criticism, develops self-consciousness,
and represents another segment of society that can
act as a check on more arbitrary powers of political managers.

Citizen movement into more demanding functional positions in society is accompanied by changes
in the distribution of political expectations.
Increasing levels of individual responsibility are
closely linked to interest in political affairs,
citizen understanding of the impact of government,
demands for access to the decision-making arena,
and feelings that individuals can or should be able
to influence their governments.[8] Additional data
indicate that these tendencies are magnified in
modern societies by increasing propensity to join

organizations.[9] Organizational membership brings
people together in situations where they compare
their expectations with those of others and act
jointly with others to bring pressures on political
leaders. In societies for which data are available,
there is a high correlation between socioeconomic
status, a very rough measure of an individual's
functional importance in society, and possession of
political information, feelings of subjective com-
petence, and political participation, whether meaningful or not.

Thus, the atmosphere within which political
decision-making takes place is heavily conditioned
by the technological revolution with its accompanying changes in social organization. Primitive
agrarian social systems are fast disappearing and
new relationships are developing between the periphery and the political managers of the industrializing nation-states. Social organization is
becoming much more complex and of necessity the number of specialists who make decisions important for
the whole society is increasing. Those in the more
important managerial positions are increasingly
distant from the decisions made by those at the
middle level of command and must delegate added decisional responsibility to them.[10] The delegation
of responsibility to lower levels leads directly to
delegation of political power as an increasingly
greater portion of decisions regarding societal
goals, allocation of responsibility, and allocation
of rewards is affected by decisions made by subordinate personnel.[11]

MODERNIZATION AND POLITICAL DEVELOPMENT

In addition to shifts in the social structure,
modernization involves many changes of a more political nature. Political leaders not only direct
the modernization of society, but are also embedded
in society and thus affected by the shifts they
help direct. Changes in the modernization-related
political rules are referred to as political

development. Exactly what political development
means is not clear.

The simplest but most ethnocentric attempt to
define political development equates it with institutions and participatory guarantees most similar
to those found in England and the United States.
According to those who proffer this view, these institutions have emerged from conditions stemming
from industrialization and natural pressures will
eventually lead other industrial societies to adopt
similar decision-making systems. The biases inher-
ent in this approach are quite clear and stem from
the belief that because the institutions developed
in these two countries have proven stable and responsive there is something inherently more "advanced" about them.[12] Those defining political development in these terms give little attention to
alternate forms of political decision-making that
might be preferable and ignore the potential weak-
nesses of these two systems, which have infrequently been tested by destabilizing political events.

A second broad category of definitions of political development relies heavily on direct effects of industrialization. Political systems are
defined as developed if there are heavy citizen demands for political participation, a movement toward national integration, or increasing institutional rationalization.[13] Political stability and
increasing institutionalization are also favored by
many approaching political development in this manner. A political system is considered developed if
there are few revolutionary threats or if sufficient
administrative capacity to maintain law and order
is available.[14] The more developed political system is characterized by universalistic criteria for
political recruitment, specified tasks for political institutions, and achievement instead of as-
cription as a criterion for public office.[15]

A third and somewhat different approach to development focuses on attitudinal and personality
characteristics. The developed polity is staffed

by decision-makers who have solved their personal psychic and identity problems, learned to trust their fellow man, and thus are capable of making rational and efficient decisions.[16] Perceived political efficacy, the belief that one's own actions are important in influencing decisions, and development of civic cooperation among citizens are isolated as conditions necessary for the construction of a viable and stable political management system.[17] Citizens living in developed political cultures have internalized a set of norms that permit political struggles to take place in an atmosphere of compromise, essential for political stability and eventually representative institutions.[18]

Perhaps the most useful approach to a definition of political development is one that concentrates on political development as a ratio or relational phenomenon, balancing the number of problems created by industrialization against the power of political institutions to deal with them. The developed polity is one with few social problems and well-developed political institutions defined in terms of adaptability, complexity, autonomy, and coherence.[19] Polities don't always develop linearly; it is possible for a decision-making system to decay when it is no longer able to adequately deal with citizen demands. A society with very weak political institutions can be beset with chronic political instability caused by personal, group, or parochial demands flooding directly into the political arena.

Almost all attempts to define political development, with the exception of the last, are closely linked to industrialization and modernization and either implicitly or explicitly recognize political development as a linear phenomenon. Stripped to essentials, these approaches all recognize that the more modern nation-state has a more participant citizenry, more resources available to the political managers, more complex political institutions, and more stable and legitimated patterns of political behavior. The citizens are more demanding of

the decision-makers, realize their stake in the
system, band together in organizations, and voice
demands for political and economic equality. All
of these factors are illustrated as militating for
the adoption of representative democratic institutions in industrial societies. The penchant for
these types of approaches among theorists is under-
standable in that most contemporary nation-states
present confirmation of predictions that could be
made from these models.

Recent history, however, offers several cases
where these explanations don't fit. Germany, at
the time of the Nazi take-over, was industrially
one of the world's most highly developed countries.
Yet, the citizens slipped most comfortably into a
system of political management antithetical to the
definitions of political development outlined above.
Contemporary France is a modern country but is
shaken periodically by rebellions that fall just
short of civil war. These outbreaks have been muffled by iron-handed rule but frequently surface in
student revolts and labor disputes.

The contemporary universe of nation-states offers many other examples of political systems that
haven't been behaving in accordance with these
linear models. Belgium is beset with internecine
warfare between the Flems and Walloons, and Canada
is increasingly forced to deal with a growing lin-
guistic problem among its French minority. In both
cases, political stability seems to be slowly declining along with many traditional democratic lib-
erties. Nor is the United States, the world's most
modern country, free from obvious signs of political decay. Riots in the ghettoes, student revolts
on college campuses, and the rash of political
assassinations and gun hoarding can only lead to
the conclusion that the United States is moving
away from political stability and perhaps to restrictions of traditional freedoms. Adding to the
evidence the socialist cases of modernization--
moderately to highly economically developed countries with less than democratic decisional systems

--makes it clear that there are many exceptions to
the linear relationship between industrialization,
stability, and democracy.

All these attempts at defining political development contain many valid and important points,
but there are numerous examples that don't clearly
fit into any one model. Each of these approaches
contains parts of the truth, but there are enough
problems to suggest the desirability of a somewhat
different approach to the ordering of available information. S. Huntington's observation that political systems decay as well as develop would seem
most relevant in this respect; the major problem
with the existing definitions is that they fail to
account for normatively unfavorable political
changes in more developed societies.

The view of political development that evolves
in this study stresses that political development
is not necessarily linear but that the industrial
revolution and the concomitant social and economic
modernization of society have been and are currently outlining parameters for political development.
Without social and economic change in society,
there is no impetus for political change. This
view of political development recognizes that the
nation-state has been and will continue to be the
basic unit within which political modernization
takes place. The economies of scale have greatly
increased the optimum size of the decisional unit
and have given political managers access to the
resources required to effectively govern larger
amounts of territory.

Political development, as discussed here, consists of three tendencies, aspects, or stages--
mobilization and community building, industrialization and rising expectations, and conservative
stabilization. The decision to discuss development
in this manner doesn't represent a commitment to
clear-cut distinctions between aspects but rather
recourse to an analytic division of the developmental process into segments that are useful in

describing shifts in political development occurring concomitantly with the modernization of society.

MOBILIZATION AND COMMUNITY BUILDING

The first phase of political development could be labeled mobilization and community building. As mentioned above, the pre-industrial society is based on a local organization of society into small villages, estates, or tribes. For all practical purposes, the larger nation-state or society, as we understand the terms, was nonexistent for most citizens before the impact of the industrial revolution. Political decision-making was considered by the masses to be the exclusive province of the chief or king and his representatives on the local level. The common people were hard worked, underfed, and traded or taxed as the nobility saw fit. Largely immobile and ignorant of the wider world, they had little concern for the affairs of state. War and taxes, frequent and heavy burdens, were considered inevitable.[20] In pre-industrial society, the social order was cemented by custom and clergy. Under most feudal arrangements common in Europe in the pre-industrial period, society was believed ordered by God into an unchangeable hierarchy of occupational groupings ascending to the ruler, assumed closest to the "eternal legitimator." Within this system, each of the classes owed obeisance to the decisions passed by those above in the system of respect shaped by God's hand. The peasants were created to till the earth, the clergy to minister to souls, and the nobility to cultivate order and maintain virtue in society.[21]

Although few completely pre-industrial societies remain in the contemporary world, recent history confirms the existence of similar types of social and political arrangements. In the emerging African and Asian states, the kings or chiefs have held unquestioned authority and have been the source of all power and privilege with the possible exception of the shaman or witch doctor.[22] The miniature

society or tribe is clearly divided into the few
who monopolize power and the many who dare not even
imagine themselves in the role of the more favored.[23] These societies are politically rigid,
and power has been jealously guarded by the few and
passed out according to traditionally sanctioned
primordial ties such as kinship, religion, language,
or social deportment.[24]

Mobilization and community building involves
the destruction of these politics of localism and
the creation of bonds directly linking the citizen
in the periphery with central decision-makers representing the larger nation-states. Mobilization
begins with the destruction of local primordial
ties and the absorption of the citizen into the
larger political whole. The ideological loyalties
of the village dweller are transferred from local
officials to central authorities backing programs
of development and industrialization. The village
social system crumbles as the younger citizens are
socialized into a system based on more universal
values.

Community building in nation-states historically became a reality with the crumbling of the
feudal empires in the late Middle Ages. It was
aided by the advent of production for profit and
the economies of scale accompanying the industrial
revolution. C. Black refers to this aspect of political development as the consolidation of modernizing leadership and traces its development back
to 1650 in England, where he claims it was not
basically completed until well into the nineteenth
century. France, the United States, and Canada
followed with the emphasis on consolidation coming
in the early part of the nineteenth century and
taking fifty to one hundred years to complete.[25]
Many contemporary developing nations have recently
embarked on campaigns of community building, most
frequently using the doctrine of nationalism to
penetrate the sleeping countryside. In India, for
example, large areas of the country still remain
unpenetrated and under the control of local

officials; New Delhi is not a reality for the
masses.

Mobilization is an aspect of politics found
in even the most modern nation-states. It is very
similar to political socialization. In any industrial society, people vary greatly in their attachments and allegiance to political leaders. Political managers have an interest in socializing all
children and disenchanted citizens into patterns
supportive of the political system. In this respect, mobilization as an aspect of politics is
always taking place as less committed citizens in
the periphery come into contact with the political
managers' ideas and children are taught appropriate
political values in the schools. During periods of
stability in modern societies, comparatively few
resources are invested in this type of activity and
its manifestations are less conspicuous.

Following major revolutions, victorious political leaders are faced with penetrating pockets of
resistance, a task that closely resembles the initial mobilization involved in nation building.
This type of ideological penetration takes a great
deal of time because the forces of resistance normally remain steadfastly loyal to the goals of the
old leaders. The Bolshevik Revolution in the Soviet Union is a good example of revolutionary
ideological penetration. The ideology of nationalism had been largely spread to the periphery by the
Czars, but the Bolsheviks combined nationalism with
economic development and socialism in their mobilization of the periphery. In Eastern Europe, the
new ideology proffered by the Communist parties
since World War II has been tied to new forms of
economic and social organization. Resistance has
come from those with vested interests in the old
regime as well as tradition-bound peripheral leadership.

The desire for mobilization has been triggered
by a shift in power from more traditional political
leaders to new groups proffering new goals.

Historically most challenges to the traditional
order have come from "modernizing" elites who have
been uncomfortable within the established social
order. They have often been the marginal men of
traditional society, close enough to the centers of
decision-making to understand the machinations that
were taking place but yet denied opportunities for
power and privilege. The composition and motivations of the emergent political managers has been
identified as among the most important factors in
determining economic growth potential as well as
probabilities of the development of more representative decision-making institutions.[26]

     Contemporary modernizers are in many respects
still marginal men although they have somewhat different motivations for seeking political change and
represent a different type of challenge to the traditional sources of power. Most contemporary nations engaged in mobilization have been first
stirred from their traditional lethargy by contacts
with more modern societies. Either through colon-
ialism or other contacts, important segments of the
population have been exposed to the glamour of
technologically advanced society and have been
moved to challenge the traditional social and economic order.

     The proponents of contemporary efforts at pen-
etration and community building are recruited from
the small stratum of the highly educated, often
sent abroad for higher education by their traditional families. Having returned from their experience in more modern societies, they have been
unable to adjust to domestic conditions. Frequently allied with "home-grown" intellectuals from the
few universities existing in the developing areas,
they challenge the traditional leaders in the name
of the people. Rapid economic development and the
redistribution of privilege are key items in their
programs. This coalition of the intelligentsia has
in common the forsaking of primordial ties, and political activity represents an outlet for unmet
affiliative and expressive needs.[27]

Although not all socialist revolutions have
occurred in countries in which conditions are analogous to those in the developing Asian and African
countries, there are many similarities. Nation
building has not been an issue of importance in the
socialist revolutions, as even in the Soviet case
the traditional authorities had been able to penetrate the periphery and cement some loyalty to the
nation-state. The exceptions are the Asian members
of the socialist system, where problems of national
identity are still very much intertwined with the
ideological struggle. In the Soviet Union and
Eastern Europe, however, mobilization occurred
fairly quickly as opposition to the revolutionary
leadership has been ruthlessly suppressed. Thus,
management energies have been quickly switched to
other goals such as industrialization and economic
and social reorganization. This is not to claim
that the political leadership in any socialist
country has been completely freed from the necessity of waging periodic campaigns to cement citizen
ties with the nation and its political leadership.

During the period of community building, the
leaders' goals are conditioned by the unstable conditions following the seizure of power. The primary goal is to complete the destruction of the old
social, economic, and political order and to cement
citizen allegiance with the new political leadership. The building of community and order, whether
it involves nation building and primitive industrialization or consolidation of a revolutionary
movement, depends heavily upon coercive force as a
cement that binds the society together in compliance with the dictates of the newly established
leadership.[28]

This aspect of development is accompanied by
the mobilization of human and natural resources
for the industrialization emphasis that follows.
Coercive force is not the only source of power;
apathy among a substantial portion of the population helps in the consolidation of authority. In
addition, upwardly mobile manpower from peripheral

areas, when rewarded, develops a stake in the maintenance of the new leadership. Unless the representatives of the traditional order receive help
from outside forces, they normally cannot muster a
major threat to the new leaders and at most have
the power to act as a check on programs of change
that are too rapid or radical.

A major impetus for the transition taking
place in the period of political mobilization and
community building is a rise in citizen expectations accompanying the penetration of the periphery.
The tension management tasks are somewhat eased by
the fact that these expectations can normally be
met with small quantities of resources. Emerging
from an environment of scarcity, the peripheral
citizen normally cannot help but be favorably im-
pressed by the government when he compares his new
status with that which he formerly held in the traditional village. Although the necessity for retaining investment capital limits the amount of
benefits that can be distributed to the newly expectant citizens, the beginnings of mass production
and redistribution of existing resources permit
some new allocations along with a moderate investment rate.

The removal of individuals from traditional environments, where order has been maintained by dependence upon primordial ties and rigid life styles,
is potentially dangerous. The transfer of loyalties to the modernizing leadership often takes place
in a revolutionary atmosphere culminating in the ex-
pulsion of the old authorities and their replacement
by charismatic leaders with whom the transitional
citizen can identify and to whom he can transfer
primordial attachments.[29] Although this more primitive or religious type of identification with the
new leadership is an important resource to use in
legitimating the new managerial system, the intense
politicization accompanying it can easily lead to
serious instability. Just as periods of great religious fervor produced saints and heretics, so
also the intense religio-politicization of the

periphery produces equivalents in the form of political heroes and villains.[30]

Demands for participation in the management of
societal affairs and access to decisional councils,
however, are learned only through increased social
communication and education. The first-generation
immigrant to the urban area or the newly recruited
citizen in the periphery have not been socialized
in cultures that encourage demands on political
leaders. The new decision-makers are therefore
forced to meet only minimal access·demands. Political decision-making is largely divorced from the
masses during the period of mobilization, and in
the absence of challenges rising within the managerial stratum itself there are few other serious
problems of political-tension management related to
access demands.

In Eastern Europe and the Soviet Union, the
greatest part of the mobilization of peripheral regions with doctrines of national unification was
accomplished before the socialist revolutions. In
the Asian socialist states, in Cuba, and in the
less-developed Eastern European countries, the penetration of the periphery by the combined ideology
of Communism and nationalism continues as the most
important aspect of political development. Only in
highly industrial countries, such as East Germany,
is the penetration aspect of political development
beginning to draw to a close.

In Poland, though the economy is moderately
developed by universal standards, the ideological
mobilization of the villages and countryside continues. The antisocial and apolitical peasant,
having little interest in the affairs of the state
and even less interest in the doctrines of socialism, is still encountered in many of the less accessible areas of the country. Although Poland has
definitely passed the peak of mobilization, it remains an important aspect of development as leaders
continue their attempts to integrate the peripheral
areas into the mainstream of socialist modernization.

INDUSTRIALIZATION AND RISING EXPECTATIONS

Once political leaders feel secure with the mobilization and ideological loyalties of a majority of citizens, they are free to turn their talents to industrialization and economic management. The original motive behind social mobilization is to combine people in larger aggregates so that the nation can profit from industrialization and the economies of scale. Once it is complete, a smooth industrialization program produces tangible benefits that can be used to build new citizen commitment.

In social and economic terms, the transition from politics of unification to politics of industrialization means shifting power from the hands of revolutionaries, ideologues, and marginal men to the modernizing managerial elite and technocrats. The intensive development of industry necessitates a continued influx of people to urban centers where their labor is used by the newly established industries. Agricultural organization in the countryside becomes more efficient so that fewer people are needed there to serve the needs of the growing cities.

Intensive industrialization can be a period of social and psychological stress for those most affected. The citizen is likely to change occupation, place of residence, life style, and beliefs about the nature of the world in which he lives. At the same time, due to the necessity of keeping consumption low while building up capital for heavy industry, the standard of living cannot increase rapidly enough to pacify expectations.[31]

Historically there has been a great deal of time available for gradual programs of industrialization and economic transformation. Pressures for change have been limited and have come mainly from the political leaders and their associates.[32] Contemporary industrialization takes place in a much different atmosphere. Political managers no longer

have the luxury of long periods of time to wait for
industrialization programs to bear fruit. The
masses have been mobilized and expectations have
been raised as old ties and values have been destroyed by mobilization activities. Population
pressures caused by phenomenal increases in natural
growth rates set very restrictive parameters within
which political managers can act in industrializing
societies.[33]

Accommodations must be worked out between
decision-makers and the masses limiting the rate of
consumption if industrial growth is to succeed.
Demands from citizens are frequently too great to
permit the expected response as the necessity of
accumulating investment capital puts stringent limits on consumption.[34] Many factors are important
in determining the political compromise reached between citizens and political leaders--the ideology
professed by the political managers, the time pressures for industrialization, isolation from other
societies, the natural resource base available for
exploitation, and the political culture context
within which the modernizers are working.

One of the most important of these factors is
the motivation and ideological background of the
decision-makers coming to power early in the period
of intense industrialization. In the beginning,
officials are prone to emphasize old order and community building goals. As a shift is made from
order to economic goals, there is a similar shift
in the basis for citizen compliance. Access to the
political arena is often increased in attempts to
build calculative and normative citizen involvement.
Those demanding access have normally been the economically more privileged, but they have been joined
in their demands by the many specialists upon whom
the central decision-makers become increasingly re-
liant as the economic, social, and political organization of society becomes more complex. Even if
the "establishment" refuses to yield to formal demands for access, the specialists maintain a negative decisional power by virtue of their important

positions in the increasingly complex society. Although basic decisions can be made by those at the top, implementation and modification takes place at the middle level of command and it is difficult for central decision-makers to adequately police implementation of their edicts.

Considerable broadening of the political structure is a requisite for movement to advanced stages of modernization. Although the military, traditional bureaucrats, and ideologically motivated intellectuals serve an important function in unifying a country and beginning a program of industrialization, they become increasingly expendable once ideological unification has been achieved and industrialization has begun. Gathering accurate information and formulating intelligent programs requires increased broadening of responsibility. As the economic transformation of society proceeds, the bevy of planners and specialists becomes increasingly important and expects a greater share of power and privilege in return for societal contributions.[35] If the benefits are not forthcoming, specialists can be forced to perform their functions in a perfunctory manner but innovation lags as everyone concentrates on doing just enough to get by without getting caught.

Although pressure for increased broadening of decision-making is a universal concomitant of movement to advanced stages of industrialization, political managers' responses are not always most functional for economic growth. The constant but slow demise of the Stalinist model of decision-making in Eastern Europe is illustrative of the problems that can be involved in broadening decision-making responsibility. Order goals and coercion have been stressed, and entrenched party bureaucrats regard the admission of new elements to the decision-making arena as a direct threat. Economic waste and stagnation has been one apparent result of continued reliance on this model, and each of the socialist countries has been forced to experiment with new economic models featuring some acceptance of wider sharing of responsibility.

The increased specialization of function required in industrial society leads to social, economic, and political differentiation of a middle
class whose interests are somewhat at variance with
those of the workers. Although demands of a new
urban working class are basically economic and only
become political and a potential source of trouble
when they aren't met, the functionally more important strata have typically made a greater investment in education or development of skills and expect concomitantly greater rewards. The industrial
revolution has been responsible for a reversal of a
trend toward greater inequality largely because of
greater numbers of people occupying critical positions in society who feel entitled to greater
shares of power, privilege, and prestige.[36]

The industrial transformation of society presents political managers with both the greatest
challenge to their power and the greatest potential
for support building among citizens. The promise
of better conditions is the economic "carrot" that
lures the labor supply to industrializing areas and
excites increasing expectations and demands. Industrialization provides increasing concrete benefits to be distributed in meeting these expectations, and the increased benefits in the well-
functioning economy serve as a legitimating mechanism. Political leadership is very rarely questioned in periods of prosperity; threats arise only
when the economic system fails to work.

The major challenge to political managers no
longer comes from within their own ranks; with increasing concentration on industrialization, the
expectations of the various mobile strata pose
threats. Urbanization, education, and increasing
interpersonal and mass communication serve as cata-
lysts for group formation. Awareness of the demands and expectations of others is important in
reinforcing economic and political desires. The
newly formed linkages between individuals and
groups calibrate the expectations of large segments
of society and increase the problems of managing
political tensions.

During the early stages of industrialization, an unequal distribution of economic and political resources can be rationalized as a necessity in pressing for the development of capital-intensive heavy industry. Eventually a point is reached where this argument is less valid to the concerned sectors of society. Over time, decisions are made on whether to open society to new demands or to increase investments in coercion and propaganda. Factors most important in determining the direction of development at this point are the ideological as well as selfish or selfless orientation of the leadership, the level of industrialization that has been attained, the potential for future economic development as assessed by the political managers, and the strength of demands for change coming from the citizens. A decision to forestall the opening of access to decision-making and a redistribution of privilege can mean a delay in entering the "second round of industrialization."[37] Modernizing leadership often refuses to broaden decisional responsibility and the distribution of privilege, and this has led to media censorship, terror tactics, the arrest of dissident elements, and the dissolution of threatening social organizations.[38]

Although retaining a closed type of decision-making system might seem efficient for some political leaders, there are many hidden costs. It is highly ineffective to use coercive force to attain economic and cultural goals requiring citizen innovation and commitment. In the early stages of development, characterized by simple order goals, the number of politically sensitive individuals is small and the demands they make are relatively insignificant. In a more complex society, the number of individuals who find repressive measures distasteful and resist them increases greatly and the cost of maintaining an effective control apparatus spirals accordingly. Very little innovation takes place in societies where important personnel are alienated by managerial methods.[39]

Industrialization and intensive economic development is critical for any society because of

the close link between patterns of political stability and the continued economic development of
society.[40] The industrializing socialist societies
have arrived at a point where the problems of maintaining a high rate of economic growth suggest political solutions that are ideologically unaccept-
able to political managers. The Twentieth Party
Congress in the Soviet Union was a watershed event
marking the end of the era of intense ideological
order building in the bloc and a shift to emphasis
on industrialization goals. Although the socialist
emphasis for the future is supposedly on development
of industry, the traditional party leadership in
all the socialist countries is on unfamiliar ground
when channeling energies into the industrialization
of society and frequently falls back on seeking
order goals.

CONSERVATIVE STABILIZATION

A third tendency in political development in
historical and contemporary experience represents
an end of the broadening of social and political
participation and is akin to Huntington's political
decay. It is a factor in all societies regardless
of level of modernization. It is certainly not a
necessary stage of political and social development,
but it is a tendency increasingly found in the most
advanced industrial societies. "Societies tend to
bureaucratize, decline in responsiveness, weaken
their commitments and give rise to oligarchies and
privileged collectivities."[41] Marx historically
inveighed against the owners of the means of production as forces blocking social change and reform,
but it is not only they who periodically resort to
the political arena to hamstring programs of reform
and franchise broadening. Those possessing just a
modicum of greater privilege than their neighbors
often turn into the staunchest defenders of the established order if they feel their positions of
relative superiority are threatened.

Huntington speaks of political decay as resulting from challenges presented by the rapid

social mobilization of society that cannot be met by available political institutions. He hints that political decay is of greatest interest to the student of developing areas as "corruption by the oligarchy inflames the envy of rising groups. Conflict between the oligarchy and the masses erupts into civil strife."[42] Although it is true that modernization and social mobilization place extremely heavy loads on the institutions in developing areas, too much attention has been paid to new demands created by modernization and very little focused on the concomitant problem of political responsiveness and intelligence. Political managers can and do become rigid. Institutions crystallize and represent only the interests of privileged strata. Whether demands outrun institutional ability to cope with them because of increasing numbers or because of increasing institutional rigidity, political decay results.

It is unfortunate that the dynamics of conservative stabilization have never been described in great detail. There are many reasons for this. It is much more acceptable to study the genesis of democratic tendencies in less industrial societies than to stir up trouble by studying conservative stabilization and political decay in advanced societies. Few governmental agencies or research organizations are likely to invest substantial amounts in potentially unpopular activities.

Societal goals are decided and privileges and responsibilities assigned through negotiations in the political arena; powerful groups flex their muscles there to cement their interests. During periods of rapid industrialization, privileged groups need worry little about maintaining their high standards of living as growing abundance leaves enough surplus to be distributed to the masses. When threats to the sanctioned distribution are perceived, whether in the form of a depression or in the rise of an expectant class, those possessing power don't hesitate to use it to block possible losses.

   Put in slightly different perspective, in all
societies there is a tendency for people in positions of power to cement their gains by rigid reliance on sanctioned and familiar patterns. The
sets of social and economic rules by which they or
their fathers acquired their fortunes take on the
air of absolutes and are staunchly defended against
encroachments by the less privileged groups wishing
to alter them. Risk and innovation are characteristic of young and active societies where the distribution of power and privilege is broadening.
Conservative retrenchment and the consolidation of
gains occurs when a large portion of the privileged
feels threatened by emerging groups.[43] These conservative tendencies are not restricted to the most
privileged segments of society, but are found in
almost all people as each seems to be more than
willing to defend his stake in the existing system
if he perceives his position as better relative to
his reference groups.[44] Although this tendency
should not be equated with mere greed, it seems
that humans can develop the most profound ideological justifications for their beliefs when threatened with loss of an increment of power or privilege

   Political managers are not much different during periods of stabilization and decay although
goals, motives, and personality types are changed.
During the first round of industrialization, the
decisions are made from the top down with little
resistance or difficulty from subordinate strata.
It is only in the second round of industrialization
that the middle level of command becomes more important and the much needed technocrats win an increasingly large share of power and privilege. As
the middle level of command swells in size and the
pace of industrialization slows, decision-making
procedures become routinized and each individual
technocrat is no longer vital to the decision-
making system. They are easily replaced with new
crops of university graduates eager to prove themselves in a slowing economy. The successful executive is no longer the bright young innovator but
rather the organization man who conforms to the

established rules and works within the increasingly powerful bureaucracy.*

In this situation, political managers shift emphasis to the integration of society as social frustration and anomie are indexed by rising crime rates and other indicators of social dislocation. The alienated citizen with no particular primary group ties and no stake in the system is a potential threat to the managerial elite.[45] An attempt is made to integrate the individual and make him feel a "primordial" type of attachment to the entire faceless society through impersonal contacts with the mass media and other vicarious social experiences. Continued innovation and creativity in this mass society is frowned upon and the instruments that liberated man from his traditional toil are turned against him to limit both his demands and his freedom. Using the educational system and the media, the modern stabilizing political manager concentrates on saturation attacks against the rise in expectations.

Thus, citizen expectations in the advanced industrial society diminish under the impact of political control of technology. "Under the conditions of a rising standard of living, non-conformity with the system appears to be socially useless, and the more so when it entails tangible economic and political disadvantages and threatens the smooth operation of the whole."[46] The revolution of rising expectations is dampened by managerial activity directed against the nonconforming upwardly mobile segments of the citizenry. Their alienation is lost in the faceless masses, apathetic in return

---

*In contemporary Poland, for example, in many fields the universities are turning out graduates having no positions waiting for them in the economy. In these circumstances, the removal of nonconformists can facilitate the entrance of upwardly mobile, and perhaps more loyal, young technocrats.

for slowly increasing standards of living. Political demands in the administered society are minimized because citizens know from experience that
the ruling coalitions or establishments will make
major concessions only in the face of revolutionary
violence. But the common man in mass society has
developed too great a stake in the existing system
of production and distribution to any longer be a
revolutionary threat.

In periods of conservative stabilization, it
no longer makes sense to talk about the management
of political tensions as only an aspect of politics.
Stability becomes a goal valued above all others
and politics becomes synonymous with tension management. Political decision-making is concerned with
the management of social conflicts regarded as normal and even functional as various groups quarrel
over the division of spoils.[47] Political managers
play one segment off against another in the pluralistic system and prevent threatening pressures for
an overhaul of the system from arising. Resources
are invested in insuring conformity to the demands
and values of "others" in the lonely crowd. The
system of decision-making is never questioned, especially as long as the flow of economic benefits
continues to pacify the vast middle class. The
managed masses are given a bland cultural and educational diet emphasizing adjustment at the expense
of critical thinking.[48]

SUMMARY AND CONCLUSIONS

The view of political development outlined
above does not pretend to be a developed theory but
is a realistic and useful way in which to analyze
the relationship between industrialization and politics. Whether to use the term tendency, stage, or
aspect of political development depends on the uses
one has for the paradigm. Historians would stress
that since the industrial revolution there has been
a temporal progression in modernizing societies
leading to conservative stabilization in the most

industrial societies. On the other hand, political
decision-makers concentrate varying amounts of resources and attention on each of these aspects
simultaneously in contemporary modernizing nations.

Modernization, whether historical or contemporary, changes the fabric of society and the nature
of the political system embedded in it. As social
goals change along with industrialization, so do demands for allocations and the problems of tension
management. The cycle of development portrayed
above is inevitable only because of the tendency
among politicians to seek the material rewards of
continued industrialization. Being so determined,
they face the prospect of contending with the
industrialization-generated political consequences.
It is likely, but not inevitable, that all societies
will move toward conservative stabilization unless
man is able to transform his privilege-seeking nature. As industrial societies become more mature,
the privileged elements strive harder to protect
their prerogatives and the less privileged have
more difficulty coping. It is rare to find an un-
selfish and future-oriented political leadership in
an advanced industrial society, but this is required
if political decay is to be prevented.

In Poland many regions are still being mobilized. The political leadership in these areas is
the socialist equivalent of the ideological uni-
fiers in other modernizing countries. Other regions must definitely be classified as industrializing and exhibit expected shifts in political
leadership. In the most urban areas, economic development is being less actively pursued as deliberate decisions have been made to decentralize investment. It is here that the expected switches to
tension management activities accompanied by shifts
in managerial composition and goals have taken
place.

The following chapters analyze the impact of
industrialization in terms of the resources made
available to Polish political leaders to help

dampen political tensions as well as the social and
political problems raised by socialist modernization. The problems faced by political modernizers
in Poland are in many ways indicative of those that
will inevitably have to be faced in other socialist
countries. As in other socialist countries, Polish
politicians have retained many aspects of the Stalinist model of decision-making that seems irrational and disfunctional in a modern industrial
society.

Although it may seem that political control of
the media, educational and economic systems, as
well as a monopoly of weapons creates unlimited
managerial possibilities, the extensive obvious use
of these instruments creates citizen resistance.
The limits of socialist political managers' power
to maintain outmoded decisional models and to manage citizen values are not clearly understood, but
they do exist and are the subject of analysis in
the following chapters. Chapter 3 evaluates the
success of attempts to mobilize and politically socialize youth into accepting regime values and beliefs. Chapter 4 evaluates the role of economic
incentives in creating citizen involvement and system stability. Chapter 5 evaluates the role of the
media in creating new social values and augmenting
political control over developing citizen demands.

NOTES

1. See the economic section of the Program of
the Communist Party of the Soviet Union for a direct comparison of socialist economic goals with
those that are sought in more capitalistic countries; J. F. Triska (ed.), Soviet Communism Programs and Rules (San Francisco, Calif.: Chandler
Publishing Co., 1962), pp. 68-96.

2. C. Black, The Dynamics of Modernization:
A Study in Comparative History (New York: Harper
and Row, 1966), pp. 24-26.

3. Lenski refers to this type of society as a horticultural society. See his description in G. Lenski, Power and Privilege (New York: McGraw-Hill, 1966), Chs. 6 and 7. Also E. E. Hagen, On the Theory of Social Change (Homewood, Ill.: The Dorsey Press, 1962), Ch. 8.

4. D. Lerner, The Passing of Traditional Society (New York: The Free Press of Glencoe, 1958), Ch. 2.

5. For a discussion of social mobilization and the breaking of primordial ties, see C. Geertz, "The Integrative Revolution: Primordial Sentiments and Civic Politics in the New States," Old Societies and New States, ed. C. Geertz (New York: The Free Press, 1963), pp. 105-57. Also see K. Deutsch, "Social Mobilization and Political Development," American Political Science Review, Vol. LV, No. 3 (September, 1961), pp. 493-514.

6. For a fuller discussion of these phenomena, see A. F. K. Organski, The Stages of Political Development (New York: Alfred A. Knopf, 1965), pp. 162-63.

7. Lenski, op. cit., pp. 308-12; and Black, op. cit., pp. 18-24.

8. In this respect, see the data in G. Almond and S. Verba, The Civic Culture (Princeton, N.J.: Princeton University Press, 1963), Chs. 3 and 7.

9. Ibid., pp. 302-3.

10. Lenski, op. cit., pp. 313 ff.

11. For explication of the meaning of "middle levels of command," see K. Deutsch, The Nerves of Government (New York: The Free Press of Glencoe, 1963), pp. 154-56.

12. R. A. Packenham, "Approaches to the Study of Political Development," World Politics, Vol. XVII, No. 1 (October, 1964), pp. 108-10.

13. See S. Huntington, "Political Development and Political Decay," World Politics, Vol. XVII, No. 3 (1965), pp. 386-430; and Political Order in Changing Societies (New Haven, Conn.: Yale University Press, 1968), Ch. 1 and references cited therein.

14. S. M. Lipset, Political Man (Garden City, N.Y.: Doubleday, 1960), Ch. 2. Packenham, op. cit. pp. 113-14. Huntington, Political Order in Changing Societies, pp. 12-23.

15. G. Almond and J. S. Coleman (eds.), The Politics of Developing Areas (Princeton, N.J.: Princeton University Press, 1960), pp. 532-33.

16. L. W. Pye, Politics, Personality and Nation-Building: Burma's Search for Identity (New Haven, Conn.: Yale University Press, 1962), pp. 42-56.

17. Almond and Verba, op. cit., Ch. 10.

18. For a discussion of the psychological attributes of "modern political man," see K. S. Sherrill, "The Attitudes of Modernity," Comparative Politics, Vol. I, No. 2 (1969), p. 184.

19. Huntington, Political Order in Changing Societies, Ch. 1, passim.

20. Organski, op. cit., p. 30.

21. J. Huizinga, The Waning of the Middle Ages (Garden City, N.Y.: Doubleday, 1954), pp. 57-59.

22. See Lenski, op. cit., pp. 168-79.

23. Lerner, op. cit., pp. 149-50.

24. Geertz, op. cit., p. 109.

25. Black, op. cit., p. 90.

26. See R. T. Holt and J. E. Turner, The Political Basis of Economic Development (Princeton, N.J.: D. Van Nostrand, 1966), Ch. 7, passim, for hypotheses about historical interaction between political regimes and the economic order in encouraging economic and democratic development. See also B. Moore, Jr., Social Origins of Dictatorship and Democracy (Boston, Mass.: Beacon Press, 1967), pp. 417-23.

27. E. Shils, "On the Comparative Study of the New States," Old Societies and New States, ed. C. Geertz (New York: The Free Press, 1963), pp. 1-26.

28. C. Johnson, Revolutionary Change (Boston, Mass.: Little, Brown, 1966), pp. 15-20, and references cited therein.

29. Geertz, op. cit., pp. 119-20.

30. D. E. Apter, "Political Religion in the New Nations," Old Societies and New States, ed. C. Geertz (New York: The Free Press, 1963), pp. 82-87.

31. Organski, op. cit., pp. 10-11; Black, op. cit., pp. 76-80.

32. See Moore, op. cit., Ch. 1, for a discussion of the role of gradualism in the comparatively peaceful British transition.

33. K. de Schweinitz, Jr., Industrialization and Democracy (New York: The Free Press of Glencoe, 1964), pp. 246-51. See also the model of civil strife based on relative deprivation in T. Gurr, "A Causal Model of Civil Strife: A Comparative Analysis Using New Indices," American Political Science Review, Vol. LXII, No. 4 (1968), p. 1104.

34. Organski, op. cit., pp. 10-11.

35. J. F. Triska, "Political Response of One-Party States to Economic Affluence and Social Complexity: Eastern Europe" (paper presented at

the American Political Science Association meeting in Chicago, Ill., September, 1967), pp. 16-19.

36. Lenski, op. cit., pp. 308-18.

37. Triska, "Political Response of One-Party States to Economic Affluence and Social Complexity: Eastern Europe," p. 13.

38. The type of society that can result when these atomization techniques are used is described in W. Kornhauser, The Politics of Mass Society (New York: The Free Press of Glencoe, 1959), Ch. 3.

39. A. Etzioni, A Comparative Analysis of Complex Organizations (New York: The Free Press, 1961), pp. 4-6.

40. See Holt and Turner, op. cit., passim, for a historical discussion of these relationships.

41. A. Etzioni, The Active Society (New York: The Free Press, 1968), p. 525.

42. Huntington, Political Order in Changing Societies, p. 86.

43. These power coalitions are analogous to the military-industrial complex or the power elite and are loosely chronicled in works such as G. W. Domhoff, Who Rules America? (Englewood Cliffs, N.J.: Prentice-Hall, 1967), and C. W. Mills, The Power Elite (New York: Oxford University Press, 1956).

44. The dynamics of conservative stabilization make a fascinating study. One of the most intriguing facts is that those who become most conservative or reactionary are not necessarily the extremely wealthy. In the United States, the back-bone of "law and order" movements and other conservative causes is the worried middle class striving to keep their allotted share of privilege unspoiled. The wealthy need not be so concerned as their position is fairly secure. In Poland, the most conservative or reactionary elements are found

in the higher echelons of the Party (self-made men
worried about the challenge presented by the emerging generation of technocrats) and the remnants of
the formerly wealthy private entrepreneurs who are
continually threatened by the Party leadership.
The most striking evidence of these dynamics is
found in France where the neofascists are recruited
from among the trapped petty bourgeoisie. The
lower-middle class, composed of small proprietors
and shopkeepers, is downwardly mobile in France,
and it is these people clinging desperately to
their privileges who provide fuel for the most extreme right-wing causes. Education is a variable
that has a unique relationship with right-wing
causes in France. Those with higher incomes than
their education would objectively warrant support
the extreme right; those making less than their
education would warrant support the left. This is
another example of those threatened by new definitions of fair exchange and equality clinging to
their positions of privilege by supporting right-
wing causes. See M. Dogan, "Political Cleavage and
Social Stratification in France and Italy," Party
Systems and Voter Alignments, ed. S. M. Lipset and
S. Rokkan (New York: The Free Press, 1967), pp.
154-59, 171.

45. Kornhauser, op. cit., pp. 43-51.

46. H. Marcuse, One-Dimensional Man (Boston,
Mass.: Beacon Press, 1968), p. 2.

47. Key examples of works by social scientists
clearly accepting the idea that conflict is inevitable or even functional are headed by L. Coser,
The Functions of Social Conflict (New York: The
Free Press, 1964), and R. Dahrendorf, Class and
Class Conflict in Industrial Society (Stanford,
Calif.: Stanford University Press, 1966). One
could also make a case that most contemporary literature in the social sciences is dedicated to
praising and further explicating the pluralist
struggle for spoils.

48. Black, op. cit., p. 81.

3

MOBILIZATION,
IDEOLOGY,
AND YOUTH:
STATE VS. SOCIETY

The development of a modern "new socialist
man" and a culture within which he will live are
priority goals among the world's ruling Communist
parties. Closely associated with this goal is an
emphasis on reshaping the sets of empirical beliefs,
expressive symbols, and values defining the situation in which political activity takes place.[1] Attempts to construct a new socialist political culture involve the mobilization of citizens in the
hopes that a commitment to leadership goals can be
created. The use of persuasive power is most effective or "congruent" in attempting to reach goals
of a cultural nature and is the cheapest and most
reliable way to hold societies together. When
moral involvement can be created among citizens,
political legitimacy is assured with little expense
to political leaders.[2]

Political socialization is important in developing a sense of community and lessening political
tensions. In most nation-states with established
and accepted institutions, political leaders have
the advantage that compliance with political decisions is taken for granted. The existence of a
state for a long period of time, the development of
trust relationships between important segments of

the citizenry and the decision-makers, and the continued productivity of the economy are all important factors in assuring support for political institutions. In the established society, few resources need be spent in encouraging citizens to
adopt desired patterns of beliefs and values; the
agents of political socialization do it very covertly. In the United States, this subliminal socialization starts in the home where most children in
the dominant political culture develop warm and diffuse reservoirs of support for the political leaders. This is followed by lessons reinforcing regime
norms in the schools.[3] Only poor performance by
political figures combined with increasing sophistication with age and education undermine this diffuse
support. In many cases this unquestioning support
for the political system continues uninterrupted
into adult life. Because in this case the socialization agents work willingly together in forming
the child's values, little active effort need be
made by political leaders to manage the role established institutions play in insuring continued respect for political leaders.

Not all political leaders are fortunate enough
to manage societies where political socialization
can take place so covertly. Societies in intense
flux, characteristic of the industrialization and
modernization process, have socialization problems
as change generates resistance. In the developing
areas of the world there is certainly no reservoir
of support available to the struggling new leadership, and its legitimacy is constantly being called
into question. Very few citizens are willing to
help insure continued political stability by forcing
leaders' norms on their fellow citizens. A similar
situation exists in the socialist countries where
old systems of social, economic, and political beliefs are being replaced by new programs. The pro-
jected changes encounter intense objections from
proponents of the old system and the legitimacy of
the new leadership is open to serious question.

When a political culture must be completely
remade, citizens are at best ambivalent about the

goals of the new leaders at the beginning. Political socialization must be overt and closely controlled by political leaders or children are likely
to learn the old values and patterns of behavior
instead of the new beliefs and values. The family,
for example, is one of the main traditional forces
in political socialization and is likely to teach
antiregime norms and values to the young unless its
power can be checked by political intervention.[4]
All other agents of socialization that can be utilized in any way are naturally seized upon by political leaders in attempts to overcome the negative
images of politicians learned in the home. Visibility of political control over socialization efforts
decreases their credibility, however, and only more
covert socialization is likely to remain deeply in-
grained.[5]

SOCIALIST POLITICAL SOCIALIZATION:
YOUTH GROUPS

        Political values are learned through both pri-
mary and secondary relationships. Primary groups
are those in which relationships are relatively un-
structured and members associate for other than
utilitarian reasons. Involvement in primary groups
is usually total, with few excluded dimensions of
activity. The family, peer groups, and to some extent the work group in industry are examples of primary groups characterized by affective relations
among group members. Members usually conform to
group norms willingly with only the pressure of
group censure acting to insure compliance. Member
orientation in the primary group is normative; one
remains a member and complies with the group's
wishes because of commitment to other members of
the group.[6]

        Secondary groups, by contrast, are character-
ized by a fragmented membership involvement. Although it is possible for a member of a secondary
group to develop a moral commitment, most secondary
relationships tend to be of a utilitarian nature.
Membership in voluntary associations such as the

PTA, affiliations with educational institutions, or
contact with political groups and the media are all
secondary relationships. The individual is involved
with the secondary group on relatively few dimensions. The involvement is sporadic, for limited
periods of time, and is considered less important
to the individual than relations with primary groups.
These relationships are characterized by few sanctions available for group use in enforcing norms relating to membership; the individual member is free
to accept or reject many of these norms with few
consequences.[7]

Primary groups play the most important role in
political socialization. Because of the importance
of primary relationships, people are most likely to
accept the political norms and values of primary
groups. Although only a small part of primary interactions are concerned with political affairs
under normal conditions, the acceptance of political norms that play an important role in primary
group interactions is almost complete. A political
leadership that desires to reconstruct a political
culture can do so most effectively by infiltrating
primary relationships where new norms and values
are most likely to be accepted. Unfortunately for
the proponents of social and political change, primary groups are also the most resistant to political infiltration.

Secondary relationships, on the other hand,
are most amenable to state infiltration but least
important in bringing about permanent changes in
beliefs and values. The state can control the
press and the educational system, and can restructure neighborhood and work groups, but the impact
thus obtained is minimal compared to the primary
group potential. If state influence is perceived
to pervade secondary relationships or if the values
championed by secondary agents are in sharp conflict
with those of primary groups, the individual re-
treats from secondary contacts into the safety of
primary groups where original beliefs are reinforced.
Thus, a separation between society and polity or

between primary and secondary institutions in society is observed when secondary institutions are politically controlled.[8]

Socialist leadership, faced with the problem of changing the political culture in a short period of time, has adopted special methods in attempting to negate the reactionary influence of primary groups. Realizing that primary groups and relations are not very amenable to ideological penetration, Soviet authorities set the pattern for other countries by attempting to upgrade the importance of secondary agents in political socialization and supplanting as many primary relations as possible. The power of the mass media has been stressed in all socialist countries in an attempt to exert maximum secondary influence on the socialist citizen. Attempts have also been made to use institutions of secondary and higher education to impress the norms and values of the modernizing political leadership on socialist youth.

Party attempts to create new primary relationships for children in the hope of eventually supplanting more conservative family influences are of even greater importance and theoretical interest. In the Soviet Union Octobrist, Pioneer, and Komsomol groups have been used to keep youths active in artificial peer groups from a very young age. Youth organizations are designed to exploit the youth collective in bringing moral pressure upon the child to conform to acceptable political and social norms. This is a direct attempt to remove the child from the influence of his parents and the neighborhood peer group composed of unsupervised schoolmates into the well-supervised youth collective.[9] In the checkered history of Soviet youth programs, there have been times when youths were removed from all family influence in state-operated boarding schools, but various problems have dictated downplaying of this strategy. The youth collective has not infrequently been used directly against the reactionary views of the family by encouraging children to report their parents' ideological deficiencies.[10]

The creation of controlled peer groups is not
without problems, however; political control and
supervision take their toll in organizational credibility. The young can most easily become involved
in organizations in which they perceive themselves
as playing a key role in shaping decisions. If the
collectivity is permitted to make its own decisions,
elect its own officers, and develop its own programs,
the members are most likely to be enthusiastic and
maintaining attendance and growing membership is no
problem. The political norms and values of the
group are most likely to be accepted willingly in
such an atmosphere. Too little control by the authorities is viewed with suspicion by the Party,
however, as leaders want to make certain that members accept the correct values and that organizational activities fall within the scope of programs
prepared by the Party. In many cases "overcontrol"
leads to membership apathy, lax attendance at meetings, and most certainly alienation from the norms
and values proffered by the organizers. The Party
is caught between the folly of permitting youth organizations to proceed in their programs unhindered
by supervision and the dangers of exercising too
much control over the groups' activities. The
Soviet youth program, emulated by the other socialist countries, has been noted for its policy of ex-
cessive control. In many of the other socialist
countries, however, the problem is one of lax discipline.[11]

In Poland the mobilization of both rural and
urban youth has been of great concern as over 40
percent of the population is under twenty years of
age. If the younger generation accepts socialist
norms and values, there need be little concern with
their elders; within the next two decades, youth
socialized within the system will form the majority
of adult citizens. Although concern with the ideological education of youth has been very great,
practical results have not been obvious, a matter
discussed at great length below. The formal structure of Polish youth organizations is not nearly so
elaborate nor effects so pervasive as in the Soviet

Union, largely a result of the fact that the program has met with less than enthusiastic reception.
Unlike the Soviet program, there is no organization
for very young children. The first contact the
child has with organized youth activity is when he
becomes eligible to join the Polish Scouting Union,
Zwianzek Harcerstwa Polskiego (ZHP), as a "regular
member" at the age of ten. The function of this
organization is somewhat akin to that of the Octo-
brists and Pioneers in the Soviet Union, but for a
variety of reasons the emphasis on ideological activities is small. Scouts are mainly concerned
with physical fitness, camping, and other typical
scouting ventures, and it is difficult to develop
ideological training programs compatible with these
activities. Second, although leading a group of
scouts might well earn Party accolades, the type of
individual who volunteers is not likely to be an
ideologically motivated person, at least no more
ideologically motivated than the typical scoutmaster.
Those dedicated souls interested in youth for ideological reasons are much more likely to forsake the
great outdoors for work in more advanced youth
groups. Finally, the age at which the youngster
joins the scouts is not one at which intense political indoctrination is very likely to be successful.

Composed of students aged eight to sixteen,
the scouts had 1,561,000 members in 1965, meaning
one of every four children in this age group was
enrolled in scouting ranks. According to the Political and Economic Yearbook, the aims of the organization are to cooperate closely with the
schools, develop close contacts with places of
work, and to encourage the universal development of
physical education, tourism, and concern for the
health and safety of children. Unlike their more
ideologically concerned Soviet counterparts, the
ZHP is really as politically harmless as the groups
of young scouts sporting their red and blue berets
on country outings would seem to indicate.[12]

Again departing from the Soviet model, the
Polish equivalent of the Komsomol is divided into

two branches. In the urban areas, the Union of
Socialist Youth, Zwiazek Mlodziezy Socjalistycznej
(ZMS), predominates and gears its programs to the
needs of the urban young. In the more rural areas,
the Union of Rural Youth, Zwiazek Mlodziezy
Wiejskiej (ZMW), operates a program geared to rural
problems and needs. In 1965, the combined membership in the two organizations stood at 1,715,000,
which represented about one quarter of those in the
relevant age categories. Unlike in the Soviet
Union, university student enrollment in youth organizations is far from complete even though there
is little doubt that youth organization membership
is becoming much more useful in obtaining university
admission as well as favored positions.

Based on these figures, the majority of the
membership of the more urban ZMS is between sixteen
and twenty years of age although a substantial portion are between twenty-one and twenty-six. There
is also a significant core of "old-timers" to super-
vise organizational affairs--one in every twenty
members of the "youth" organization is over twenty-
seven years of age. Composed mainly of high school
students, the membership also embraced 280,000
manual workers, 118,000 white-collar employees, and
55,000 university students to round out its total
membership of 901,000 in 1965.

The ZMS is assigned many functions, including
entertainment for youth, cooperating with industry
in easing the problems of the young person's transition to the work environment, and not least of all
helping shape the individual's ideological and political belief system. Its importance as a socialization agent has been largely undercut in Poland
both by the importance of the family in determining
moral conduct as well as by the fact that very few
of the basic circles have enough ideologically
motivated members to set the proper tone for the
rest of the group. With little ideological talent
available to the leadership, not much can be done
about ideological development for fear of completely losing the attention of the members. Both the

intensity of ZMS activities and its ideological impact are much smaller in Poland than in the Soviet
Union. Of the 37,000 circles, 13,000 are located
in places of work, which indicates that the role of
the ZMS is not so much geared to political education as it is to increasing production and insuring
that the young worker adjusts to the factory.[13]

The more rural ZMW does not differ substantially from the ZMS in form, but the goals of the organization are necessarily different in meeting the
needs of rural youth. Unlike the urban organization, which at least in theory can concentrate on
problems of work and ideology, the rural organization is dealing with farm youths who share very few
problems in common with the urban brethren. In
this environment, mobilization campaigns encouraging the development of many of the most rudimentary
forms of urban culture require a good deal of organizational effort. One of the main thrusts is
educational, and campaigns have been launched to
encourage the small portion of the membership that
hasn't finished seven years of schooling to do so
as well as to make information about further educational activities available to the 100,000 rural
youths who annually finish the seventh year of
schooling and fail to move on to schools offering
advanced education. In addition, the ZMW offers
programs of course work in rural areas and takes an
active interest in making educational materials
available in the countryside. Sports, tourism, and
recreational programs occupy much of the remaining
organizational effort. The ZMW suffers disadvantages similar to the urban group in that its tasks
are of such a rudimentary nature in such an unfer-
tile environment that little time can be spent sub-
jecting rural youth to intense doses of political
socialization.[14]

Taken together, the youth programs lack the
ideological emphasis of the Soviet program and membership in them often means nothing more than the
member insuring himself a spot in the university or
Party, or that the social and tourism program is

attractive. Thus, 13 percent of ZMW membership be-
longs simultaneously to one of the major political
parties. In a poll of ZMW members asked their reasons for joining the organization, 50 percent re-
plied that cultural activities, entertainment, and
social life were of primary importance.[15] The
Party excuses such responses by correctly pointing
out that such activities are necessary for youth
and even help "prevent scourges like drinking and
hooliganism, not to mention their importance in the
leveling of cultural differences between the rural
and urban milieux."[16]

Impressionistic data as well as a haphazard
sample of one university class strengthen this im-
pression of the attractions of the urban organization for the student. Among the thirty-three students questioned, only ten were members of the ZMS
or ZMW (nine ZMS); the rest belonged to the rather
innocuous Polish Student Union. When asked why
they joined youth organizations, only one person
said that it helped form moral character and three
claimed it served an educational function. The
rest of the sample listed either social or athletic
reasons, and no one felt that membership would be
important in shaping their careers.[17] Because of
the socialization efforts of both the family and,
in some cases, the Church and because the majority
of organization members are not ideologically committed, Party attempts to exploit youth organizations as agents of political mobilization and socialization have met with very limited success.

FAMILY, CHURCH, AND NEIGHBORHOOD

The strongest affective bonds and the source
of most important primary ties for most people are
found in the family. The family remains the single
most important force in shaping norms and values of
new generations in all cultures. While transmitting
other cultural attributes, the family also acts as
one of the most important agents in the transmission of a political culture from generation to generation. The more intense a child's relationship

with the family unit the more likely the family is
to shape his political views, but even in more
loosely knit families in highly industrialized countries parents are most important in politically socializing the young.[18] The family structure is most
efficient in transmitting political values to youth
because the socialization takes place covertly and
unconsciously. Parents don't usually consider it
one of their chief functions to inculcate regime
norms in the next generation. The acquisition of
parental values occurs when children are exposed to
seemingly innocent comments about political figures;
most of the important socialization experiences are
those parents have not really planned.

The family, as the basic unit in almost all
societies, is extremely resistant to penetration by
political forces. Only rarely in history, including isolated cases of child espionage in the Soviet
Union and China and a recent futile attempt by
former Superintendent of Instruction Max Rafferty
to form a youth corps of informers in California,
has the family ever been broken by political pressures. The family is the repository of the accrued
wisdom of past generations and is an extremely conservative institution. In the socialist countries,
the family acts as a major barrier to social and
political changes as the old systems of values ad-
vocated by most adults have been developed under
different social and political systems and are reactionary by contemporary political standards.
Socialist political managers have tried to discredit old family values and reduce the family as
an educational unit. The successes have been mixed
and have largely depended upon the strength of the
family unit in each society.[19]

The importance of the family has been particularly pronounced in Poland where it has often acted
as the last refuge in the face of the perils of
numerous wars and occupations. The turmoil surrounding the Communist seizure of power and the resulting period of political indecision and instability have accentuated family ties in spite of great
changes in family patterns resulting from the

industrialization of Polish society. Housing shortages keep children dependent upon parents for lodg-
ing until they are married, and in many cases the
first few years of married life are spent sharing
cramped quarters with the in-laws. Under these conditions, it is most difficult for political leaders
to discredit the family unit and lure young adults
away from parental values.

The rural family is most closely knit as is
the case in most other industrializing countries.
Although the industrial revolution is making itself
felt in all sections of Poland, living in rural
areas still means isolation from many of the "ameni-
ties" of urban civilization. In this environment,
the small villages and neighboring towns are the
horizons of an individual's world, and most face-to-
face interactions are with relatives. Newspapers
are frequently lacking in some isolated villages;
contact with the outside world is minimal. In the
country family, aunts, uncles, grandparents, and
others all take a vital interest in the child's
moral and political development. There are few
countervailing sources of values to which the child
can turn, and the weight of past generations comes
down heavily against Party attempts to inculcate
new socialist norms. It is "the Party" that currently threatens the existence of the independent
small farmer, and the attitudes the rural child in-
ternalizes in the all-embracing extended family environment are anything but cordial to political
authorities.[20]

The urban family in Poland remains an extremely tight-knit unit in the face of many adversities.
In the city, both parents normally work and the
young child begins his early life in a state-
operated nursery school. This is followed by
usual grade and secondary school education and,
for an increasing number, the university. Thus,
the child spends extremely little time out of the
grasp of state-run institutions. The family compensates by lavishing attention on the child during the time he is home, and as a result young

Poles are undoubtedly among the most sheltered children in modern industrial countries. In contrast
to his American counterpart, who begins to walk to
school unescorted at an early age and often plays
unsupervised within the parks, the Polish child is
seldom found apart from parents or state guardians
during his formative years.

During adolescence and the early years of
adulthood, the child remains in close contact with
the family in spite of state attempts to structure
his activities. The family plays an important role
in the acceptance or rejection of friends and ac-
quaintances. Most social life takes place within
the confines of the extensive network of close relatives. The tight housing situation and close parental supervision insure that rebellions against
parental values and authority are unlikely to escape detection. Making friends with children not
having the family stamp of approval is frowned upon,
and often at the university the young adult brings
new friends home for parental inspection. Thus,
the potential for rapid changes in religious or
political values is carefully screened.

One of the limited successes of state-directed
programs of mobilization is the diminishing influence of neighborhood peer groups. Childhood peer
groups are especially important in forming political and social attitudes in more industrial societies where they are increasingly replacing parental
authority. The peer group is particularly effective
in determining member values in that much time is
spent within it and strong emotional attachments
grow in peer group experiences. It isn't difficult
to understand why a young child would conform to
peer group norms in order to remain popular with
others given normal concern with maintaining the
favor of one's associates as an important motiva-
tional force. In societies with strong class-
oriented neighborhoods, the peer group acts with
the family as a conservative agent in maintaining
accepted political and social beliefs. In neighborhoods where parents share similar positions of power,

privilege, and sets of social and political values, children are encouraged to associate with each other; the parents know that the values proffered by other children are not likely to conflict with their own.[21]

One key side effect of the housing shortage in socialist society has been the destruction of the neighborhood as an integrated unit. Neighborhood life in rapidly growing urban areas now means living in a complex of new, hastily constructed high-rise apartment buildings. Although a wide variety of housing arrangements can be made in Poland, there is no way the character of neighbors can be ascertained in advance. Apartments are assigned by the appropriate governmental agency when available, and only a fool would turn down an assignment on the grounds that he wouldn't get along with the neighbors. Thus, one finds members of the working class occupying flats in the same building with young engineers, doctors, or even Party officials. This has, in many cases, nearly destroyed the cohesion of the neighborhood play group. Members of different occupational groups can be forced to live together, but no one can force parents to permit their children to play with children from "improper" backgrounds. With the exception of some flats in predominantly working-class areas, class-based value-cohesive neighborhoods are becoming increasingly rare in all the modernizing socialist societies. Political leaders accrue some benefits from this phenomenon as well as certain disadvantages. In one sense, the lack of natural neighborhood groupings makes the child more readily available for organized youth activities, but on the other it strengthens the already strong parental control over child contacts.

The Catholic Church also plays an important role in socializing Polish youth into traditional patterns. Although the Church is stronger in rural than in urban areas, it shapes many of the child's primary relationships in all cases. A nation-wide sample of youth aged fifteen to twenty-four produced 73 percent claiming to be Catholic and only 4 percent atheist.[22] In the countryside, the Church

exerts great pressure during the formative years in
the confessional as well as in more public displays
of attendance at Sunday mass, which often doubles
as antiregime indoctrination. The great ceremony
that accompanies the first communion and confirmation rites is designed to leave an indelible mark
on the political conscience as well as on the soul.
The commandment to "honor thy father and mother" is
strictly enforced by the Church and strengthens the
hold of the family over the child.

Among the more cosmopolitan in urban areas,
the Church does not have quite the influence that
it does in the countryside, but even in Warsaw the
influence of religion on the young is considerable.
Paradoxically, in many cases the antireligious
stand taken by the Party has prompted dissenters to
support religious institutions for political rather
than spiritual reasons. Many among the "fallen
brethren" realize the importance of the Church as a
political tool and support it for its political
value more than for the sake of their own spiritual
futures. Regardless of reasons for support, data
reveal that among Warsaw university students, 50 to
60 percent consider themselves to be religious or
adhering to religious traditions.[23] In many cases,
the primary ties with family and Church are so
strong and mutually reinforcing that the state-
directed socialization attempts account for very
little. Where religious faith is weak, the Catholic traditions, including strong emphasis on the
sanctity and importance of family ties, combine
with more pragmatic political attachments to the
Church to form large reservoirs of unpenetrable resistance to Party-directed political socialization.

STATE POWER: THE EDUCATIONAL SYSTEM

As the Party has seemingly failed in attempts
to penetrate and restructure the younger generation's primary relationships, the secondary agents
of socialization have been heavily exploited as a
supplement. The rapidly growing educational system

represents a state investment in the economic future of the country as well as in the socialization
potential of educational institutions. The child
in socialist countries spends a good portion of his
time in the care of state-operated institutions.
Because both members of the typical family hold
full-time positions in the modernizing socialist
economy, even the youngest children, from birth to
three years of age, spend eight hours a day in a
state-run ward for small children. Children from
age three to six attend neighborhood preschools;
older children attend primary and secondary schools.

The preschool is the first level at which any
kind of training with political significance is begun. Very few attempts at teaching political norms
are made at this level although emphasis on patrio-
tism and activities designed to create high levels
of need achievement are stressed. The preschool
creates a peer group for the child that develops
norms and standards of its own and helps substitute
for the destruction of the more loosely knit neighborhood groups. Children of all class origins are
intermingled in the nursery school, and the norms
developed among children represent a melting pot of
parental attitudes and values. In war games played
by children of this age, the Russians are frequently case in the role of the "Indians" in U.S. children's combat. In this manner some of the hatreds
of the older generation are successfully transferred to youngsters within the framework of state
institutions. It is not at all uncommon for children to come home from school after a day of contact with their comrades declaring that the Russians are bad people and asking why they want to
kill Poles.[24]

As an agent of socialization the preschool
clearly is a failure in that it can't really be
other than custodial in nature. Only very limited
political education programs can be attempted among
young children, and they learn more from other children than from the teacher. The values transmitted
by children in the preschool setting are nearly the

same as those absorbed within the family and precisely the types of values the political managers
would like to replace. Teachers are young females
with modest talent and can't be expected to undertake bold new ideological programs and indoctrinate
young children. The preschool teacher normally is
no more a convinced ally of the Party than are the
parents of the children she teaches and can hardly
be expected to be an important force in shaping the
political horizons of the young.

Elementary and secondary education offers a
much better opportunity to the leadership to present its case to the student. The school system is
under the tight control of the minister of education; textbooks and subject matter are easily controlled. The child spends six to eight hours each
day in the classroom--a captive audience for regime
propaganda. Ideally the heavy state investment in
education should pay handsome political dividends,
but in reality successes have been mixed at best.

The greatest difficulty in Party educational
plans is the problem of recruiting qualified personnel. In the early days immediately following
the Party take-over, teachers were given wholesale
dismissals on the grounds of political unreliabil-
ity. It was not long, however, before high-level
officials were sheepishly asking the dismissed
teachers to resume their original duties in the
face of a collapse of the educational system. This
problem has never really been solved--there are no
reasons why teachers should be more politically
aware or willing to act as instruments of the Party
than other citizens. Teachers are not particularly
well paid and have no great stake in the present
system. Although textbooks are outlined by the
state and the formal subject matter having political significance is prescribed, the state can exercise little jurisdiction over the individual classroom and innuendos or facial expressions, which are
often more potent than whole chapters of approved
political commentary.

The Party has not been unaware of this problem, and the ideological preparation of teachers
is being stressed throughout the country. Membership in youth organizations is encouraged in teacher's preparatory schools, and in 1961 25 percent of
future teachers were members of the ZMS as opposed
to a 16 percent average in other fields.[25] Despite
the Party's emphasis on the importance of teacher
ideological training, enrollment for grade and high
school teachers in the Party only inched upward
from 28 percent in 1961 to 31 percent in 1964.[26]
Considering that many join the Party for instrumental reasons or to stay out of trouble with superiors,
the political reliability of members of the teaching
profession is to be seriously questioned. If teachers as a group were a minority politically deviant
from society's norms, the Party could cope with the
problem by using student reports to weed out the
unfaithful. Because teachers' deviance from Party
norms is shared by society at large, however, very
little reliable information can be expected from
students in the classrooms. Even were it possible
to get the required attitudinal information, the
Party would still be faced with the problem of filling great numbers of vacancies left after the dismissal of the politically unreliable.

The Thirteenth Party Plenum devoted much of
its attention to the ideological preparedness of
students. Major changes implemented after the
Plenum included the creation of a department to co-
ordinate all educational problems from first grade
through the university and the introduction of
civic education courses in the eighth grade. In
addition, special departments were created in higher schools to offer courses in the foundations of
political science. The staffing of these new
courses presents the Party with another dilemma.
The students in them are generally intelligent
enough to challenge the unprepared party hack, and
the alert instructor is not likely to simply parrot
the party line, especially at the university level.[27]

The deficiencies in ideological preparation
among students coming from secondary schools have

been highlighted by polls dealing with political beliefs of high school graduates. A 1965 poll taken
at the Mining-Metallurgical Academy among first-
year students revealed that of 734 questioned students, 273 did not know the official position of
the "Head of State." In addition, twenty didn't
know the role Gomulka played in Polish politics and
sixty-seven did not know the name of the chairman
of the Council of State. Questions dealing with
political affairs in other countries revealed that
80 percent of the students could answer questions
about the United States and only 55 percent could
answer similar questions for West Germany. This is
particularly interesting in view of the fact that
the mass media and educational institutions give
much attention to political events in West Germany,
as a matter of course, and relatively little official notice is given to domestic political events
in the United States. When a similar group of students was asked who were their heros, John Kennedy,
Yuri Gagarin, Charles de Gaulle, Pope John XXIII,
and Karl Marx topped the list, in that order.[28]

    The best indications of the results of politi-
cal socialization efforts in secondary schools are
found in a 1959 nation-wide study of youths fifteen
to twenty-four. When asked how they would classify
their political views, only 2 percent of the sample
claimed to be Communist and 6 percent chose socialism. Three quarters, on the other hand, claimed
to have no political views or convictions.[29] The
introduction in the universities of the new four-
year political science curriculum consisting of
courses in Marxist philosophy, political economy,
the organization and sociology of labor, and foundations of political science will undoubtedly change
the outlook of some members of the growing intelligentsia, but for those who terminate their education
at the secondary level political education remains
problematic.

BRINGING UP THE INTELLIGENTSIA: THE UNIVERSITY

    Higher education is potentially one of the most
important and yet sensitive political mobilization

instruments in the Party's hands. Social and political change rarely originates in the masses but is
most generally spearheaded by the economic, political, and social elite. It is most important for
the Party to reach those who make the system work.
If members of the middle and upper levels of command in society accept the new system of values,
the decision-makers need have few worries about the
masses. Stripped of leaders, co-opted into the
managerial strata, the apathetic masses would be of
little importance. With continuing modernization,
those responsible for the successful functioning of
the socialist system will increasingly be products
of the universities and technical schools. Under
conditions where the number of applicants for higher education greatly exceeds the space available,
the Party closely manages the admission of students
to the universities and should be able to indirect-
ly control the development of ideologically qualified cadres of young technocrats.

Two categories of advanced studies are pursued
in socialist society. The more traditional approach
is represented by the universities, with a heavy emphasis on liberal arts subjects in addition to specialized courses of study. In this environment, the
student concentrates on humanist aspects of the creation of a "new socialist man," and it is here that
future developments in socialist humanism can be expected to occur. The other direction higher education has more recently taken is the development of
countless polytechnic institutes and training
schools designed to meet the need for more specialized patterns of training. Education in these institutions is narrow, specialized, and oriented
toward the development of functional skills required in the socialist economy.

As the socialist countries have become increasingly more industrialized, the universities
have become comparatively less important as the
needs for more technical personnel have greatly
increased. The universities have not decreased in
size, but rather their rate of enrollment increase

has not come close to matching the growth of the
technically oriented institutions. Between 1950
and 1966, the balance between university students
and students in other institutions of higher education shifted from 33 percent of the total in 1950
to 26 percent of the total in 1966. In raw figures,
the enrollment in the universities increased from
41,000 in 1950 to 65,000 in 1966; total higher educational enrollment jumped from 125,000 to 252,000.[30]
Technical education, increasingly devoid of humanistic emphasis, is the pattern for the future, and
knowledge of differences in ambitions, goals, and
ideological outlook between the products of the universities and technical schools is useful in pre-
dicting future developments in socialist societies.

Higher education is a prerequisite for involvement in any important aspect of the management of
an industrial society. As differences in privilege
have been minimized under socialism, the power and
prestige associated with a degree has become a basis
for a new system of stratification. In Poland, entrance into this "new class" is restricted by educational opportunities; management of admissions policies is used to build support for the established
politicians as well as to keep potential dissident
elements from reaching important positions. The
fact that it is not easy to identify potentially
dissident elements and that the selection procedure
has not worked very satisfactorily from the Party's
point of view was clearly demonstrated by the student uprisings in 1968 which led to the abolition
of whole university departments.

Theoretically the children of workers and peasants have first priority in obtaining admission to
institutions of higher education. Although the restrictive admission policies of the Stalinist era
have periodically been relaxed, sons and daughters
of those with ideologically correct class background are still favored by the awarding of extra
points on entrance examinations. Party leaders
reason that proletarian youth will be more thankful
for educational opportunities and easier to handle

ideologically. To some extent this has proved true,
but for many reasons admissions policies have not
worked exactly as planned. Proletarian students
are much more submissive and obedient than their
more sophisticated counterparts, but they often
lack the skills necessary to successfully complete
a university-level course of training; although
selective admissions policies can fulfill the goal
of keeping educational institutions filled with
children of workers and peasants, it is antithetical to the goal of turning out specialists capable
of assuming responsible positions in the modernizing
economy. A high proportion of those with "proper"
class background admitted because of the extra
points on their admission examinations fail to make
the grade and leave the institutions before com-
pleting their course of study. Such a selective
admission policy is self-defeating; poorly qualified students take up scarce space that could be
occupied by others and then drop their studies before receiving the credentials necessary to assume
an important role in the construction of socialist
society.

In addition, children of high-level officials
cannot be excluded from admission quotas; many practical pressures can be applied on their behalf.
Many of the leaders of the 1968 student disorders
were sons and daughters of those close to the centers of political power. Whereas technical schools
successfully turn out well-trained technocrats having very little concern with ideological matters,
the universities produce students well versed in
social and political matters. Even though universities are carefully managed by the Party, students
in courses in philosophy and the social sciences
often raise questions about the system that professors are hesitant to answer. The socialist university student, even though he may be the child of a
high party official, can be just as iconoclastic as
his Western counterparts. In this respect, the
university fulfills its liberal arts or broadening
functions too well. Students in the polytechnic,
on the other hand, receive an instrumental task-
oriented education and rarely consider ideological
questions.

Although data on university student composition and attitudes are not easily available, there
are a few studies that highlight some of the problems in education faced by the Party in Poland.
The monumental study of Warsaw students carried out
in 1957-61 has been made available in the West only
in small fragments. The study, initiated during the
period of the Polish thaw, didn't make it into print
in time to avoid the subsequent slow freeze. As a
result, it has never been published as a whole and
exists only as mimeographed and carefully numbered
manuscripts. In addition, the Public Opinion Research Center conducted a relevant national study
of youth in 1959, and there also have been several
smaller studies fragmentally reported in sources
available in the West.[31]

The study of Warsaw students completed between
1957 and 1961 is by far the most complete and useful study of the university student population.
The original study, completed in 1957-58, included
one of every forty students studying in Warsaw. At
that time, 26 percent of all university-level students were studying in Warsaw; this sample, then,
is fairly indicative of student attitudes in the
whole country. A follow-up study dealing with students in the polytechnics only was completed in
1961 to facilitate comparisons with the earlier
study. The choice of the nation's future elite
study in Warsaw; those studying in the provinces
are most likely to remain in less important positions. The structure of higher education in Warsaw
is similar to that of the entire country in that
the portion of students in teacher institutes, polytechnics, and the universities is nearly identical.
At the present time, about 24 percent of the country's students study in Warsaw and another 16 percent study in Krakow. Thus, almost half of Poland's
students pursuing a higher education study in one of
these two metropolitan areas.[32]

Admission to higher institutions is becoming
increasingly difficult, leaving the Party in an
ideal management position. In 1967 over 95,000
people took entrance examinations for 39,500 vacancies. The universities and technical schools in

Warsaw and the other large cities attract the greatest number of applicants; only the less qualified
settle for education in the provinces. Requests
for admission by departments are unbalanced and
often there are only slightly more applicants than
can be handled in the less prestigious fields such
as teachers' training and agricultural study.[33] At
the University of Warsaw, for example, there were
more than two candidates for every vacancy in
1967-68.

STUDENT COMPOSITION: THEORY VS. REALITY

One of the results of the proletarian revolution in socialist countries was supposedly to open
up channels of social mobility to segments of society that did not have their fair share of opportunities under the old system. This means that
ideally the children of workers and peasants will
be occupying more places in institutions of higher
education alongside the children of the intelligentsia, who have previously made up the bulk of
higher education enrollment. Realistically speaking, however, the added points for social background
on entrance examinations have not served to equalize
educational opportunities. Students from rural
areas receive a markedly inferior secondary education and in the absence of socialist "headstart"
programs there is little that can be done to truly
equalize opportunities. Rural and proletarian students score markedly lower on entrance examinations,
learn much more slowly, and as a result are less acceptable to university administrators. With "quotas"
for qualified graduates to be met, administrators
can't afford to waste time and space on those who
are not going to make the grade.

The educational training and limited horizons
of those from less affluent backgrounds block many
aspects of the Party's attempts to make educational
opportunities correspond to doctrinal precepts. Be-
sides the problem of admissions, those from less
fortunate environments tend to choose courses of

study that are easier, enroll in schools where
there is less competition, and generally become
more dissatisfied with their chosen plan of study
over time, if they survive at all. Data from the
Warsaw study reveal that the student body is mainly
composed of children with parents having at least a
complete secondary education. Only 35 percent of
the students are children of workers and peasants
(Table 1). More recent statistics for the country
as a whole show that only 42 percent of first-year
students were of worker or peasant background and
the percentage falls at advanced levels as a large
portion of these students flunk out over time.[34]

TABLE 1

Social Backgrounds of Students

Warsaw		Poland	
Worker	17%	Worker	27%
Peasant	18	Peasant	17
White-collar	32	White-collar	50
Crafts	8	Crafts	4
Intelligentsia (higher education)	13	(Intelligentsia merged with white collar)	

Sources: S. Nowak, J. Jasinski, A. Pawelczynska,
and B. Wilska, "Studenci Warszawy" (unpublished manuscript, University of Warsaw), p. 32; S. Nowak, "Social Attitudes of Warsaw Students," The Polish Sociological Bulletin, Nos. 1 and 2, 1962, pp. 91-103;
Rocznik Statystyczny (Warsaw: Glowny Urzad Statystyczny, 1966), p. 438.

It isn't possible to exactly pinpoint class recruitment differentials, but it is known that almost
half of all Polish families qualify as peasants;
this compares with the 17 percent university recruitment figure for peasant youth. Only 4 percent
of the socialist work force possess a university degree, although 13 percent of the Warsaw student
body comes from these families. Logic also leads
to the conclusion that children of working-class
families are heavily underrepresented as a much
greater portion of Polish youth is raised in blue-
collar families than the 27 percent admission figure
indicates. The heavy representation of children of
intelligentsia and the white-collar strata in universities gives evidence of a new self-perpetuating
class stratification based on education, about which
the Party has done little. Children from intellectual environments are much more likely to receive a
higher education than others.

Children of top-level decision-makers and the
intelligentsia are replacing their parents in key
positions, thereby cutting down on social mobility
possibilities for the young of peasant and working-
class background. As an example, between 1952 and
1961 the portion of students from working-class
backgrounds decreased from 36 to 26 percent, those
from peasant backgrounds from 23 to 18 percent,
whereas the white-collar representation rose from
36 to 49 percent.[35]

The state supports the educational efforts of
students from working-class backgrounds when it has
the opportunity. Additional data reveal that in
Warsaw 95 percent of the children of peasants receive a state stipend and 80 percent of students of
working-class background receive such, whereas only
71 percent of children of lower intelligentsia background and 51 percent of the children of parents
with a university degree are so rewarded.[36] Thus,
the state actively encourages the student from less
fortunate environments to complete his studies, but
even with this added support the children of the intelligentsia predominate among graduates.

Another barrier to true educational egalitarianism is the natural predilection of the less
gifted rural peasant and urban working-class students to seek out the easiest courses and the least
demanding schools for fear of not being able to compete. Table 2 illustrates the recruitment differentials in Poland by area of specialization. The
medical academies attract a striking proportion of
children of the intelligentsia, and the university
and technical schools also attract more than their
share. Teacher training institutes, schools of economics, and higher agricultural institutions attract
the greatest portion of youth from worker and peasant background. For the Warsaw sample it is obvious
that students of intelligentsia background heavily
overchoose the university and polytechnic. Although
only 13 percent of all Warsaw students come from
this social background, they compose 19 percent of
the university students and 15 percent of the polytechnic students. Students from white-collar families are oriented toward technical education; 37
percent of the polytechnic students come from these
families although they compose only 33 percent of
the general student population. Only 26 percent of
university students have white-collar backgrounds.
The working-class students reveal no particularly
interesting tendencies, and the children of peasants
overwhelmingly choose agricultural training.[37]

Additional data highlighting class differences
in educational choices reveal extreme differentials
in family income between students in different types
of educational institutions. Those in the Warsaw
School of Planning reported an average family monthly income of 1,427 zloties, the School of Medicine
2,138 zloties, and the University of Warsaw 2,211
zloties.[38] Those with the highest family incomes
are free to choose a humanistic model of education;
the less economically prosperous choose programs of
study most likely to yield highest economic returns
in the long run. It is clear that there are several factors determining one's choice of educational
institution including the ease of obtaining a place,
fear of competition, and desires for material

advantages. Working and peasant class youths have fewer educational opportunities and come from environments commonly associated with feelings of relative deprivation. Those students quite naturally have some doubts about their competitive abilities. They choose noncompetitive fields of study and select instrumental training in pursuit of economic goals internalized in their poorer environment.

TABLE 2

Class Recruitment in Higher Education
(percentage of total enrollment)

Schools	Worker	Peasant	White-Collar	Crafts
Medicine	24%	14%	56%	5%
Universities	26	14	53	5
Technical	30	15	51	4
Higher economics	34	18	43	4
Agricultural	21	34	40	5
Teacher institutes	36	21	39	4

Source: Rocznik Statystyczny (Warsaw: Glowny Urzad Statystyczny, 1966), p. 438.

Table 3 reveals that social and economic factors play a key role in determining reasons for choosing a career. The lower the average family monthly income the more likely that factors external to the family are important in motivating

the young in choosing a field of study. The influence of teachers, other students, as well as ease
of obtaining a place are important in career choice.
In the middle-income range, economic factors, prestige, and the importance of social role are important determining factors. Those from the most comfortable backgrounds are freer from economic need
and admit that family influence has often been most
important in career choice. This supports the observation that, especially among the intelligentsia,
the family remains a most important socialization
agent even among youth of university age.

TABLE 3

Family Income and Reasons for Choosing Careers

Average Family Income (zloties)	Reason for Career Choice
1,762	Influence of teacher
1,807	Ease of obtaining appointment
1,860	Contact with other students
1,907	Filling great social role
1,926	Prestige
1,928	Salary
2,058	Abilities and interests
2,469	Family influence

Source: S. Nowak, "Social Attitudes of Warsaw
Students," The Polish Sociological Bulletin, Nos. 1
and 2, 1962, pp. 91-103, Table 9.

The lack of proper guidance and motivation for
working-class and peasant youth means that most frequently they become dissatisfied with their fields
of study after entering the institutions. Select-
ing their goals on the advice of teacher or fellow
students and often choosing fields of study that
are easier to get into leads to trauma and misgiv-
ings later in their academic careers. The children
of the intelligentsia infrequently voice desires to
change their course of study, but those of worker
and peasant origin often voice displeasure with
original choices.[39] Those who approve of their
original course of study have an average family
monthly income of 2,054 zloties, those who would
make some changes have an average family income of
1,749 zloties, and those who want a complete change
of field have family incomes of only 1,664 zloties.[40]
The most alienated are those who were forced to make
choices on the basis of little information and often
are the students who chose the most expedient programs in terms of ease of admission.

The figures, broken down by discipline, indicate additional evidence that the more well-to-do
stick by original choices. Only 17 percent of the
students in the medical school, heavily populated
by offspring of the intelligentsia, would not make
the same choice again. The university, mainly a
white-collar institution, has a 29 percent dissatisfaction rate. Of those in the more proletarian
polytechnic, 31 percent are dissatisfied with their
choice of field, and two of every five in agricultural institutes express similar dissatisfaction.[41]
Exposure to a wider range of educational possibilities changes original goals among those from the
disadvantaged sectors of society. Those with better secondary educations and wider opportunities remain more satisfied with original choices.

The dynamics of educational development militate against the Party's attempts to use the universities for ideological mobilization. Youths

from worker and peasant families are natural allies
of the Party in constructing a new political, social,
and economic order, but many factors prevent the exploitation of this relationship. The Party would
like nothing better than to be able to follow doctrinal precepts and recruit working-class and peasant youth into higher educational institutions and
staff the more important sectors of society with
loyal followers. Party membership should present a
great opportunity to the upwardly mobile, and the
leaders would like to capitalize by increasing the
proportion of young technocrats of proletarian
background.

In addition to the systemic blocks to producing
more loyal technocrats from proletarian backgrounds,
however, data indicate that even the upwardly mobile
are not quite as loyal to party goals as the decision-
makers would like to believe. Proletarian youths in
the Warsaw sample clearly are much more accepting of
a socialist type of economic organization (Table 4),
yet attitudinal differences among students of different backgrounds are not extreme as measured by asking
them if they consider themselves to be Marxists
(Table 5). It is clear that those from intellectual
environments are not as clearly committed to Marxism
as other groups, but these are the more gifted students and the Party cannot afford to turn them away
from the universities.

Additional data indicate that worker and peasant children have not adjusted to de-Stalinization;
a greater proportion of their numbers are inclined
to view the period of the personality cult (1945-55)
somewhat positively. These figures can be taken as
indicative of working-class authoritarianism as well
as student perceptions that conditions among the
working class have been markedly improved by the
revolution. At any rate, they indicate that proletarian youth are more likely to support more
authoritarian elements in the party structure than
those coming from more intellectual families.

TABLE 4

Acceptance of Socialist Economy*

Social Background	Acceptance Score
Intelligentsia (higher education)	3.76
Intelligentsia (secondary education)	3.99
Crafts	3.81
Worker	4.10
Peasant	4.19

*Average figure based on scale constructed by University of Warsaw sociologists. The higher the scores the greater acceptance.

Source: S. Nowak, J. Jasinski, A. Pawelcz, and B. Wilska, "Studenci Warszawy" (unpublished manuscript, University of Warsaw).

TABLE 5

Attitudes on Selected Social and Political Issues

Family Background	Considers Self Marxist		Evaluation of 1945-55	
	Yes	No	Positive	Negative
Higher education	11%	46%	19%	17%
Secondary education	11	26	25	14
Worker	17	27	28	12
Peasant	15	25	33	10
Craft	12	33	33	16

Source: S. Nowak, J. Jasinski, A. Pawelcz, and B. Wilska, "Studenci Warszawy" (unpublished manuscript, University of Warsaw).

The small group of students from worker and peasant families that enters the university and succeeds is much more likely to become attached to party goals. These students consider themselves to be Marxists and remain extremely egalitarian compared to their proletarian peers in the polytechnic. Twenty-two percent of these students in the university consider themselves Marxists compared to only 9 percent undergoing polytechnic training.[42] From an ideological viewpoint, the rapidly expanding polytechnic institutes seem to exert a corrupting influence on all students enrolled and especially youth of working-class origin. Exposure to the polytechnic environment significantly decreases the egalitarianism of working-class and peasant youths. Scores on a scale designed to measure social egalitarianism reveal that youths of working-class origin in the polytechnic are less egalitarian than any other group and three times as likely to be nonegalitarian as counterparts in the university (Table 6).

Differences between the egalitarianism of students in the university and the polytechnic remain consistent for all class backgrounds--exposure to possibilities for greater earnings in the technical schools seems to change student values. Although the potential party allies among the students of worker and peasant origin in the university remain true to egalitarian beliefs, those in the polytechnic forsake such beliefs and become even less egalitarian than students from other classes.

When university students in the first two years of study are compared with those in the last three years, the average permitted monthly salary drops from 6,597 to 5,974 zloties, and the percentage scoring extremely nonegalitarian drops from 43 to 38. The opposite happens over time in the polytechnic. When the students in the first two years are compared with those in the last three years, the figures reveal that the average permitted maximum monthly salary increases from 6,826 to 7,804 zloties and the percentage that is extremely nonegalitarian rises from 50 to 67.[43]

TABLE 6

Social Background and Measures of Egalitarianism

Family Background	Highest Permitted Monthly Salary (in zloties)		Percent Extremely Nonegalitarian	
	University	Polytechnic	University	Polytechnic
Higher education	8,454	10,270	48%	63%
Lower education	6,298	7,298	44	59
Workers	5,433	6,027	26	70
Peasants	5,285	6,000	24	56
Crafts	6,125	7,578	44	50

Source: S. Nowak, J. Jasinski, A. Pawelcz, and B. Wilska, "Studenci Warszawy" (unpublished manuscript, University of Warsaw).

Thus, the socialist political managers are pursuing antithetical goals. The Party is interested
in industrialization in order to develop a society
of abundance. This leads to heavy investment in
polytechnic education which acts as a de-nivelizing
force and turns out nonegalitarian, privilege-
seeking young technocrats. The greater the number
of graduates produced by the polytechnics the less
likely that they will be willing to accept the
Party ideological programs.

University students, more willing to accept
egalitarian norms, attack the Party on theoretical
grounds and point to the many socialist differences
between theory and practice. Even if the Party desired to increase investments in university education, it actually is left with no choice. Increasing investments in polytechnic education are an
economic necessity although it means the creation
of a new privileged class not interested in party
goals. Ironically, it is these technocrats who
stand the best chance of being admitted to the
Party. This line of reasoning leads to the predic-
tion that mobilization fervor within the Party will
die out over time as the Party might well become
the instrument of those wishing to consolidate
their positions of privilege.

THE LIMITS OF CONTROLLED
POLITICAL SOCIALIZATION

Analysis of the Polish experience in ideological mobilization through the political socialization of youth suggests that several qualifications
should be made in any discussion of the limits of
political leaderships' potential to change societies. It is often assumed that control of the
agents of socialization gives the representatives
of change a nearly perfect weapon to use in mobilizing a hostile society. There are many obstacles
to the rapid implementation of plans for social and
political change even when all resources in a society can be concentrated on aspects of ideological
mobilization.

Values and goals are most easily changed when
societal primary relationships reinforce the changes
desired by representatives of a new system. Therefore, the first task of leadership interested in
change is to restructure the primary relationships
of the noncompliant sectors of society. As primordial or organic ties are broken by social mobilization and the ideological penetration of the periphery, an increasingly large portion of the population
becomes amenable to regime resocialization attempts.
The Party's difficulties in its attempts at penetration of the young as they move out from the primary
influences of family ties has been discussed above.
The more visible the state's attempts to structure
primary relationships the less likely they are to
succeed as people retreat from these pressures into
traditional primary groups. Mobilization by political leadership moves outward to the social periphery as well as downward to the young, and analysis
of the effects of resocialization of these less cosmopolitan citizens in the economic periphery begs
data similar to that available for students. The
data reveal certain facts about the socialization
of the rural young, but little information is available on the attitudes of their recently assimilated
parents.

In Eastern European socialist countries, the
family remains an important obstacle to the efforts
of the Party to resocialize the young. In an area
having a tradition of violence, the family is an
important source of stability and parents' influence over children remains great, even in the face
of the challenges presented by industrialization.
The Party would like to do away with the family,
but the strife and dislocation that would be caused
by such a rash action makes implementation impossible. The Church, still powerful in many areas of
Eastern Europe, buttresses the position of the
family and makes reshaping it even more difficult.

Control of secondary socialization agents is
easily obtained by representatives of the Party in
the socialist countries, but this control is much

less effective than control of primary agents.
Supervision of course content in the public school
system gives the decision-makers an opportunity to
reach the new generations, but staffing problems
preclude the optimum political use of schools.
Teachers cannot be removed from the influence of
the society in which they live. If the society at
large is alienated from the Party, the teachers are
not likely to be different. Teachers are in scarce
supply in all the modernizing socialist countries,
and campaigns to do away with the unfaithful would
undoubtedly set the educational system back many
years.

The universities and polytechnic institutes
represent a last chance for the Party to socialize
a portion of the young. It is the graduates of
these institutions who will be important figures in
the future socialist society. There are natural
affinities between the Party and the upwardly mobile
youths from working-class and peasant backgrounds,
but systemic factors prevent capitalizing on them.
Youths from poorer backgrounds less frequently maintain grades in the competitive higher educational
system; economic efficiency dictates that the best
prepared youths should be given advanced training.

Thus, there are limits to the power that the
state can employ in attempting to make allies.
Values inculcated by Church, family, and peer groups
are not easily thrown aside in favor of the party
line. When the true believers in the Party represent a small minority of society, even the clear
control of coercive forces and most of the secondary socialization agents cannot sway the masses.

NOTES

1. Put somewhat differently, this means the
reconstruction of the nations' political cultures.
For further explication, see S. Verba, "Comparative
Political Culture," ed. L. Pye and S. Verba, Politi-
cal Culture and Political Development (Princeton,
N.J.: Princeton University Press, 1965).

2. See A. Etzioni, A Comparative Analysis of Complex Organizations (New York: The Free Press, 1961), Chs. 3 and 4.

3. See, for example, D. Easton and J. Dennis, "The Child's Acquisition of Regime Norms: Political Efficacy," American Political Science Review, Vol. LXI, No. 1 (1967), p. 25.

4. These dynamics are also operative in some political subcultures in the United States. See D. Jaros, H. Hirsch, and F. J. Fleron, Jr., "The Malevolent Leader: Political Socialization in an American Sub-culture," American Political Science Review, Vol. LXII, No. 2 (1968), p. 564.

5. For a more detailed presentation concerning the importance of the covert political socialization of children, see F. E. Greenstein, Children and Politics (New Haven, Conn.: Yale University Press, 1968), Chs. 1 through 4.

6. Etzioni, op. cit., pp. 40-45.

7. R. E. Dawson and K. Prewitt, Political Socialization (Boston, Mass.: Little, Brown, 1969), pp. 99-103.

8. See S. Verba, "The Remaking of a Political Culture," Political Culture and Political Development, ed. L. Pye and S. Verba (Princeton, N.J.: Princeton University Press, 1965), pp. 162-68, for evidence of this phenomenon in German society.

9. A. Kassof, The Soviet Youth Program (Cambridge, Mass.: Harvard University Press, 1965), pp. 36-47.

10. See F. C. Barghoorn, Politics in the USSR (Boston, Mass.: Little, Brown, 1966), Ch. 3.

11. See Kassof, op. cit., Ch. 6. For a theoretical treatment of peer group importance in shaping political values, see K. P. Langton, "Peer

Group and School and the Political Socialization Process," American Political Science Review, Vol. LXI, No. 3 (1967), p. 751. See also U. Bronfenbrenner, Two Worlds of Childhood (New York: The Russell Sage Foundation, 1970).

12. See Rocznik Polityczny i Gospodarczy 1966 (Warsaw: Panstwowe Wydawnictwo Ekonomiczne, 1966), pp. 210-15.

13. Ibid., pp. 197-202.

14. Ibid., pp. 203-9.

15. "Youth Affairs: What are those young interested in," Zycie Partii, No. 2, 1967. For the sake of simplicity, when references are made to articles in small Polish newspapers and journals, page numbers will be omitted and only the translated title of the article given. Many of these periodicals are inaccessible to Western scholars, and the information presented is more than adequate to permit the specialist to find the article in question. Unlike their Western counterparts, Polish newspapers usually consist of only eight to ten pages.

16. Ibid.

17. These data come from an informal questionnaire administered, in collaboration with M. Simon, to a typical advanced undergraduate class (thirty-three students) in a major Polish university. These data are from a haphazard sample (students who signed up for the class made available to us), and inferences from it used here are limited.

18. Dawson and Prewitt, op. cit., pp. 107-8.

19. Ibid., pp. 121-216.

20. Again, these attitudes have very great similarities to those found in the United States in Appalachia. See Jaros, Hirsch, and Fleron, op. cit.

21. Dawson and Prewitt, op. cit., Ch. 8.

22. E. Ciupak, Kult Religijny i Jego Spoleczne Podloze (Warsaw: Ludowa Spoldzielnia Wydawnicza, 1965), p. 448.

23. Ibid., p. 445.

24. Studies of political attitudes and the political socialization of children are just beginning in Poland and are not readily available for analysis. Most of the insights into the attitudes of the young come from the author's own observations, aided by the enrollment of his son in a neighborhood "peoples' nursery school" during the 1966-67 academic year.

25. PZPR w 1961 (Warsaw: Polish United Workers' Party, 1962). This booklet is in numbered restricted circulation and most difficult to obtain.

26. Ibid., p. 18. Also H. Stehle, The Independent Satellite (New York: Frederick A. Praeger, Inc., 1965), p. 14.

27. For details, see "Political Training of Students," Zycie Literackie, No. 3, January 15, 1967. Mention should be made here of the great aid provided by the Polish News Bulletin, jointly published in mimeographed form by the American and British embassies, in locating and translating many such articles difficult for the individual to locate.

28. "Young People in Search of a Hero," Zycie Literackie, No. 45, November 6, 1966.

29. M. Szanawska, Swiatopoglad Mlodziezy [Youth's World View] (Warsaw: Osrodek Badania Opinii Publicznej, 1960), p. 4.

30. Rocznik Statystyczny (Warsaw: Glowny Urzad Statystyczny, 1966), p. 430.

31. See studies cited in <u>Spoleczenstwo Polskie</u> <u>w Badaniach Ankietowych</u> (Warsaw: Polskiej Akademii Nauk, 1966), pp. 57-59.

32. <u>Rocznik Statystyczny</u>, p. 431.

33. "Forty Thousand Places--Ninety-five Thousand Candidates," <u>Trybuna Ludu</u>, No. 101, April 13, 1967.

34. <u>Rocznik Statystyczny</u>, p. 438. Comparison of these figures with those available for other countries shows that the Party is making great progress in equalizing opportunities in comparison with others. In France, a European country at a development level fairly close to Poland, only 6 percent of students are from peasant background and only 9 percent are from working-class backgrounds. See H. W. Ehrmann, <u>Politics in France</u> (Boston, Mass.: Little, Brown, 1968), p. 71.

35. S. Nowak, J. Jasinski, A. Pawelczynska, and B. Wilska, "Studenci Warszawy" (unpublished manuscript, University of Warsaw), p. 40.

36. <u>Ibid.</u>, p. 45.

37. <u>Ibid.</u>, Table 6.

38. <u>Ibid.</u>, Table 7.

39. <u>Ibid.</u>, p. 81.

40. <u>Ibid.</u>, p. 82.

41. <u>Ibid.</u>, p. 88.

42. <u>Ibid.</u>, p. 197.

43. <u>Ibid.</u>, p. 209.

4

**TENSION
MANAGEMENT
AND ECONOMIC
PERFORMANCE:
THE WEAKEST LINK**

In modernizing societies, the developing economies are one of the main supports for political
organization. Complex economic organization has
made man much more dependent upon others for his
survival. No one any longer makes the argument
that man can secede from society, and no one in
control of his faculties would make such an attempt. In the course of becoming more modern, man
has become more dependent upon the machines he has
created as well as on the surplus economic product
the division of labor and economies of scale have
produced. The rationale for the continued support
of modern political leaders is found in the material benefits that accrue from their managerial
activities.

The tasks of political managers in industrial
societies more closely resemble those of their
counterparts in industry. Their main job is to
keep the economy productive, for if they fail the
economic lifeblood of society will not circulate
and political decay will be inevitable. Completely
centralized control over the productive processes
is more difficult to maintain in modern society.
Technocrats increasingly possess the expertise

required to keep the wheels of industry turning.[1]
An integral part of modernization is the willingness of central political actors to accept delegation of decision-making power. The society in
which the central political managers stubbornly re-
fuse to broaden the decision-making base is not going to move smoothly into advanced stages of industrialization.

Socialist party leaders cannot represent a
perfect reflection of desires of the industrial
structure and often interfere in the affairs of enterprise management. Pressures for decentralization are pressures to prevent central party figures
from interfering with those making decisions on the
lower levels. Technocrats and bureaucrats are
joining the parties in increasing numbers, but the
ideologically oriented party managers insist on
injecting nonpragmatic criteria into the economic
decision-making process. Lower-level decision-
makers in the industrial and economic structures
are closest to the problems of production and function best in all advanced economies when given
broad decision-making authority.[2]

HUMAN MOTIVATION IN THE ECONOMY

The close link between polity and economy in
the modern socialist society means that citizen
support for political leaders is predicated on
satisfaction with clearly defined exchange relationships with representatives of the party. People in all societies consciously or unconsciously
evaluate their relationships with others and certain institutions in exchange terms. Some people
are very conscious of exchange motives in associations, others don't consider them at all.[3]

Depicted clearly by the adage "a day's work
for a day's pay," this tendency to seek equity or
reciprocity in exchange relationships is nearly
universal. When one gives something valued to
others, he expects some equivalent return. If it

is not forthcoming, he is likely to withdraw from
associations with the nonreciprocating individuals
or institutions. In a society in which almost all
economic activities have been nationalized, the political leaders are responsible for one giant scale
of salaries and the socialist citizen visualizes
his relationship with the government in very direct
exchange terms. Socialist leaders are very clearly
responsible for allocating rewards and responsibilities. The socialist citizen expects his efforts
in support of political leaders to lead to reciprocal treatment.[4]

In pluralist societies, citizens can't directly calculate all economic transactions, because of
both their number and the extremely complex problem
of affixing responsibility in a society in which
the political managers are only held accountable
for a portion of economic welfare. A "free and independent economy" acts as a psychological buffer
between citizen and political leaders. If people
aren't receiving what they consider to be just compensation for their work, the discontent does not
necessarily become political. Blame is often placed
on the owners of enterprises who are recognized as
separate from political leaders. In monist society,
the relationship between economic, social, and political discontent is very close as citizens realize
that political managers closely regulate activity
in all of these sectors of society.

There are no universal rules for determining
fair exchange or equity in these relationships.
Political responses by societal managers are often
perceived differently by people in similar situations. Societal norms established over time are
one factor important in determining what one expects. The political culture helps shape the rules
governing citizen expectations. In societies that
have traditionally been ruled by autocrats, citizen
expectations are very small compared to countries
with more democratic political heritages. In addition, subcultures in a society develop their own
definitions of fair political exchange which may be

at odds with definitions commonly accepted. When
groups having semipolitical or political purpose
are allowed to form, the strength of numbers and
interaction among members can lead to internaliza-
tion of definitions of fair exchange that are more
demanding than those previously held. One of the
key aspects of political-tension management in non-
responsive political systems is to keep citizens
atomized and prohibit them from interacting and developing new definitions of fair exchange.[5]

    One of the key tension management problems
facing socialist political managers is motivating
workers to innovate and produce to their best ability. As the organization of production is becoming
an increasingly political problem in modern society
because of greater needs for innovation and decentralization, satisfaction with political leaders is
becoming essential in encouraging economic produc-
tivity--especially important in the socialist societies where the political managers both ideologically and practically justify their rule with economic performance. Marxist-Leninist economic and
social organization is based on the principle that
the overthrow of the owners of the means of production and their seizure by the proletariat leads to
a new era of abundance where production is oriented
to use rather than selfish profit. Socialist revolutions have enjoyed less than universal popularity
with the citizens; if they are to be justified to
workers, concrete results must be forthcoming.

    All aspects of life are politicized in social-
ist society in that the ruling party takes responsibility for economic productivity. Party con-
gresses are devoted to economic subjects, and problems of productivity occupy the attention of party
meetings in industrial cells. With the newspapers
brimming with economic headlines, there is little
doubt that the socialist leadership regards its
main function to be development of an economy of
abundance. This linkage between economic performance and political leadership is not necessarily
a liability considering the economic conditions in

which socialist revolutions have taken place. In
the Soviet Union, conditions among workers and
peasants were abysmal before the Revolution and any
increases in economic abundance were more than welcomed by the masses. In Eastern Europe, the extended period of destruction related to World War II
made economic reconstruction a goal of highest priority in the eyes of many citizens.

With the Workers' Party so clearly dominating
economic organization, it accepts all credit for
successes and is harnessed with the blame for all
setbacks. Thus, the price of meat in the neighborhood store, the availability of a flat, or the supply of consumer goods in the central department
store are political issues. The socialist citizen,
perhaps more clearly than his capitalist counterpart, recognizes that contemporary society is one
big organization with political figures playing
managerial roles. In the monist or socialist society, the effects of good or bad decision-making performances are much more directly linked to citizen
satisfaction and individual economic output than in
pluralist counterparts.[6]

Thus, socialist managers have been forced to
adopt piece-rate systems so that blue-collar workers feel rewards commensurate with productivity
rather than according to needs as judged by others.
The blue-collar masses have often been alienated
from the socialist political management during the
early stages of industrial transformation, but this
has largely been due to built-in limitations on the
system. During the immediate post-war period, the
available resources could barely provide for minimal
physiological needs. Under these conditions of
scarcity, there were no guaranteed base rates and
the worker was daily pitted against the machine.
Fear was most effective in motivating the worker to
produce for the system.[7]

Amending some of the most egalitarian features
of traditional Marxist-Leninist theory through the
installation of a piece-rate system has enabled

socialist political managers to overcome one of the
most difficult problems of socialist industrialization. All tasks that can be quantified are amenable to piece-rate rewards, and worker incentive
is built into this system. The harder one works
the more he receives. This calculative type of involvement has been sufficient to cement worker allegiance to the political system. The major problem still facing political managers is maintaining
commitment among blue-collar workers engaged in
activities that can't be quantified as well as
among the higher-level personnel where economic rewards assume less importance and production can't
easily be quantified.

White-collar and managerial personnel are much
harder to motivate than their less expectant blue-
collar comrades. The top echelons of factory management, high-level bureaucrats, technocrats, and
planners in the economy, as well as those employed
in the media have all made substantial educational
investments and their definitions of fair exchange
are based on much greater career preparation and
more universalistic standards of comparison. Although monetary rewards are still important, they
are of limited usefulness in dealing with higher-
level personnel no longer preoccupied with meeting
physiological needs. The more highly educated
specialists in socialist society have needs for esteem and self-actualization that have not developed
among the working class. Data indicate, for example, that in the Soviet Union blue-collar and
white-collar workers can be clearly separated according to the types of complaints they voice
against the system. Blue-collar workers complain
about salaries; white-collar employees complain
about a variety of other aspects of their jobs.[8]
Although pecuniary rewards are not completely unim-
portant for the technocratic stratum, especially in
Poland where the differences between workers' and
managers' salaries are so small, most white-collar
personnel need additional types of rewards to keep
them committed to the goals of the political managers.

Creativity, esteem, and self-actualization are a very important part of a high-level executive's life. Marx was among the first to clearly explicate a relationship between a man's work and happiness in life. The managerial strata must be coopted into the decision-making structure psychologically in order to motivate them to perform well. In the modern industrial state, individuals in important positions comply with decisions of political managers either because they believe in leadership goals or because they hope to change the goals to resemble their own by working within the system.[9] Without engendering a feeling of meaningful participation in societal decisions, it is impossible to motivate important strata of society to undertake difficult managerial tasks. Refusal to give participatory rewards along with heavier managerial responsibilities can mean problems for continued economic advancement.

The second aspect of political development, closely related to industrialization, is very complex in socialist society. The party managers have thus far been able to meet the rising expectations of the working class by elevating its economic rewards to the highest point in history relative to the intelligentsia. The working class has been appreciative, at least to the point that great numbers of workers could be mobilized in a counter demonstration against rebelling students in 1968. The period of industrialization is accompanied by rapidly fluctuating expectations of all types, not all of which are easily met. The upwardly mobile white-collar personnel, for example, must be rewarded adequately by their own definitions if they are to be maximally productive. This means that there are pressures for amendment of the overly egalitarian wage scales as well as for increasing responsibility in societal decision-making.

In these respects, the first round of industrialization in the Soviet Union and Eastern Europe has been a proletarian revolution. Workers and peasants have been squeezed into new roles in the

more complex economies, but the transition has not
been entirely without rewards. In relative terms,
the proletariat in Eastern Europe and the Soviet
Union now is in a much better position when compared to the intelligentsia than in any prior historical period. The key managerial problems in
these countries no longer involve solely the productivity of the blue-collar worker. Movement into
the second round of industrialization involves a
second stage of the socialist revolution in which a
real decentralization of decision-making responsibility from the hands of a narrow segment of party
members into the middle level of command closest to
everyday problems must take place. Without important changes in the structure of decision-making
the socialist society will have to face serious mo-
tivational problems.

FAIR EXCHANGE: PROBLEMS OF DEFINITION

Several issues undermine the relationship between the parties as economic managers and the
blue- and white-collar workers in Eastern Europe.
Because the socialist revolutions were not indigenous, party managers are still occasionally regarded as representatives of an occupying force. In
addition, the basic principle of Marxist theory,
that each should contribute to the whole according
to his abilities and receive from society according
to his needs does not find favor with the upwardly
mobile young socialist workers. The Party in Poland cannot do much to overcome the first problem
but, as in other socialist countries, workers are
now supposed to contribute according to their abilities and receive according to their work, a subtle
change in doctrine that permits employment of the
piece-rate system. The problem is far from solved,
however; there is a continuing debate over who
should receive greatest rewards for services and
how many times greater the maximum reward should be
when compared with the minimum. The debate is especially sharp in Poland because egalitarianism is
more pronounced there than in other socialist
countries.

One of the strengths of the reward system in capitalist society is the separation of economics and politics. In capitalist society, the distribution of rewards has rarely become an overt political issue. The myth of collective bargaining has held that workers can organize and bargain directly with employers for just rewards. There supposedly is a natural balance between supply and demand in the labor market, and the conventional wisdom holds that one will receive what his labor is worth at the going market price. The issue of wages becomes political only when employers attempt to keep employees from organizing and bargaining collectively. The battles for greater shares of privilege have largely been fought between workers and private corporations.

In socialist society, there is no folklore or myth surrounding the distribution of pecuniary rewards as powers over income are clearly in the hands of politicians who centrally determine salary levels. Any dissatisfaction with economic conditions is reflected directly in political discontent. The worker is not paid according to any mystical "going rate," but rather is compensated according to a pay scale set by political leaders far from the factory. Keeping everyone satisfied in the modernizing economy where citizen expectations rapidly increase is difficult enough without the added issue of establishing just criteria for reward distribution.

As one would expect, Polish citizens are far from unanimous in agreeing on criteria for the distribution of economic rewards. Very few people, even in socialist society, really believe that all should be treated equally. One study suggests five criteria that seem to be most relevant for the distribution of rewards; danger involved, qualifications required, responsibilities, working conditions, and national importance. A selected sample of Polish citizens in different economic strata was asked to select those of most importance. The selected criterion for distribution of salary varies considerably, but it is clear that the factor considered most important is determined by one's own occupation and reference groups. For example, miners' wives emphasize dangers involved in work as most important. Engineers feel that educational qualifications and responsibilities are most important; the bureaucrats in the Party (party activists) are quick to stress the responsibilities one has as well as the national importance of one's job.[10] With such clear divisions according to occupational group, the official determination of salaries continues to be an extremely touchy issue.

Perhaps the most complicated unsolved problem is the equation of academic training and physical effort in the hierarchy of rewards. The following excerpts taken from letters submitted to the editors of Polityka, a weekly political paper, illustrate these problems.

First a letter from a father of a laborer:

> The majority of skilled and unskilled manual workers . . . earn approximately 800 zloties a month. . . . Since he (a biologist) earns at least double what these people earn, he should have no cause for complaint, if that is any consolation to him. . . . As compared with laborers doing heavy manual work, the biologist uses half the calories and thus really earns more.

From a father of a college graduate:

> If some know-it-all thinks it is easy to get a degree because the state gives aid to students etc., why did he himself not go to a university, why has he been content to remain a semi-skilled worker? The answer is because he had no wish to study, because it would have meant too much effort, it would have demanded too

> many sacrifices of him. . . . When
> he (the student) finally graduates,
> it turns out that his younger brother
> that didn't even finish secondary
> school, earns much more than he does.[11]

These statements clearly illustrate the hostility surrounding the issue of compensation. The
situation is exacerbated, especially among the
technocrats, by Party reluctance to institute even
moderate gradations in rates of pay. Although this
may be in keeping with the wishes of the less ambitious blue-collar workers, it certainly meets with
disfavor among the educated and upwardly mobile
stratum of society. Table 7 illustrates the extreme egalitarianism pervading the Polish economy.
This pronounced lack of differentiation is at least
partially responsible for many problems of production discussed below.

TABLE 7

Distribution of Salaries in Poland, 1965

Zloties	Blue-Collar	White-Collar
700-1,000	11.0%	4.5%
1,000-1,500	21.5	22.6
1,500-2,000	25.4	26.5
2,000-2,500	18.8	17.5
2,500-3,000	11.1	11.3
3,000-5,000	11.2	14.7
5,000-	1.0	2.9

Source: Rocznik Statystyczny (Warsaw: Glowny
Urzad Statystyczny, 1966), pp. 499-500.

Two facts stand out very clearly. First,
there is an extreme homogeneity of salaries within
each functional stratum. The best-paid blue-collar
workers receive only about four times the rate of
pay received by the least well compensated. The
best-paid white-collar employees also receive little more than four times the pay of the least well
compensated. Most important, however, are the extremely small differences in rewards received by
white- and blue-collar employees. All across the
range of salaries the similarity in profiles is
very clear. It appears that Party managers neglect
educational investment as an important criterion in
determining just compensation.

A cursory examination of the wage scales leads
to the conclusion that those most unhappy with the
distribution of privilege in Polish society would
be the upwardly mobile white-collar workers. Survey evidence indicates that it is the white-collar
professionals who prefer both the greatest varia-
tion in salaries as well as the highest means.
Table 8 illustrates the average minimum and maximum
salary that surveyed members of the indicated occupational groups would permit in the Polish economy
and the suggested means. It is clear that those
with greatest responsibilities and investment in
education are in favor of a wide distribution of
privilege and high average salaries. Manual workers and unskilled laborers are most content with a
salary structure close to that which currently exists. Even Party activists, however, seem in favor
of salary schedules much less egalitarian than
those presently in force. Industrial managers, engineers and technicians, lawyers, physicians, professors, newsmen, and actors all demand a broadening of the wage scale. This corresponds to data in
Chapter 3 that illustrate nonegalitarian tendencies
among the young, especially among the graduates of
technical schools. It is also concrete evidence
that those bearing heavy responsibilities in the
middle level of command are less than satisfied
with the current rigid scale of rewards.

TABLE 8

Suggested Range of Socialist Compensation
(in zloties)

Profession	Minimum	Average*	Maximum
Typists	800	2,000	5,000
Farmers	1,200	2,200	3,400
Steelworkers	1,000	2,500	5,500
Party Activists	1,000	3,000	6,500
Newsmen	1,000	4,000	10,000
Industrial Managers	1,200	4,500	10,000
Mining Engineers	1,100	5,000	7,000
Lawyers	1,500	5,000	10,000
Professors	1,500	5,000	7,000
Actors	1,500	5,000	9,000

*Represents average of what one thinks is just
compensation in his own profession.

Source: A. Sarapata, "Justum Pretium," Polish
Sociological Bulletin, No. 1, 1963, p. 52.

DEPTH OF COMMITMENT

One of the most important aspects of political-
tension management and building commitment to leadership goals in modern society is using an intelligent distribution of economic rewards to meet
citizens' rising expectations. Favorable economic
experiences over time help cement allegiance with
even dictatorial political regimes. In Poland,

there is some evidence that continued reliance on
extreme egalitarianism magnify anti-Party tendencies
already a part of the Polish political culture.

Workers are clearly committed to the goal of
self-enrichment, but it is questionable whether
they produce because of commitment to wider social
goals. The enterprise in Poland is clearly linked
to the Workers' Party--Party members set the quotas
for the factories and determine rates of pay. The
managerial staff is most likely to be composed of
good Party members. Thus, political and economic
attitudes are inextricably intertwined at the enterprise level. Dissatisfaction with the scale of
rewards as well as dissatisfaction with decision-
making institutions is reflected in blue-collar attitudes toward socialist production and property.

The commitment of supervisory personnel to political goals is even more questionable. White-
collar workers on all levels certainly are not rewarded commensurate with their higher-skill levels
and greater responsibilities. The data show that
they would like greater rewards than they are now
receiving. Although one would expect white-collar
personnel to feel more responsible for the socialist economy than blue-collar workers, data reveal
that dissatisfaction with salaries and opportunities
to make one's voice heard are a cause of great
white-collar apathy and lack of concern for economic
production.

Data on citizen attitudes toward socialist
production and property is understandably difficult
to find. Few political leaders are willing to re-
lease data dealing with such touchy societal problems. Problems of production have become so pressing in Poland, however, that at least two studies
of worker and management attitudes in the enterprise have been completed--but not widely circulated. Both studies were carried out by the Public
Opinion Research Center. The first was a national
sample of 1,750 adult inhabitants of Poland's cities
employed in the socialist economy who were asked
about attitudes toward work and property.[12]   The

second study is less revealing, being composed of a
sample of only 720 workers and dealing exclusively
with opinions of supervisory personnel in different
work environments.[13]

Table 9 illustrates the level of concern with
private and public property in Poland. These figures indicate that there are two distinct attitudes
toward the two types of property. Offenses against
private property are subject to nearly universal
condemnation; offenses against socialist property
are not subject to the same type of condemnation.

TABLE 9

Attitudes Toward Property

	Condemn (percent)	Depends on Circumstances (percent)
Doing personal tasks during working hours	16	61
Riding public transportation without paying	39	53
Moonlighting on company time	41	39
Theft of small items from work	56	24
Failing to pay rent	61	33
Failure to return private loans	85	12
Damaging property borrowed from others	92	5

Source: A. Sicinski, "Postawy Wobec Pracy i
Wlasnosc" ["Attitudes About Work and Property"]
(Warsaw: Osrodek Badania Opinii Publicznej, 1961),
p. 22.

The people collectively own the means of production
as well as private possessions, but these data indicate that they don't feel that way. Only 41 percent condemn "moonlighting"--doing other jobs for
profit during working hours--and only about half
condemn the theft of items from enterprises.

Turning more specifically to affairs within the
state-operated place of work, Tables 10 and 11 illustrate the extent of worker apathy. Only a small
portion of the work force feels any moral responsibility for the fate of the government-run enterprises, and even among white-collar workers with
university education only half feel responsible.
Damaging tools and equipment and the theft of small
items from work would be criticized or reported only
by half the workers. The figures are very similar
for belief in the efficacy of criticism. Under
these conditions, it is most difficult to see how
deficiencies in production are to be remedied and
how innovation of new production techniques will
take place. Without worker commitment to managerial
goals, little can be economically accomplished.

TABLE 10

Involvement in Enterprise Affairs

	Feel Moral Responsibility for Enterprise (percent)	Believe in the Efficacy of Criticism (percent)
Unskilled blue-collar	22	37
Skilled blue-collar	37	46
White-collar (without higher education)	42	42
White-collar (with higher education)	51	59

Source: A. Sicinski, "Postawy Wobec Pracy i
Wlasnosc" ["Attitudes About Work and Property"]
(Warsaw: Osrodek Badanii Opinii Publicznej, 1961),
Table 4-B.

TABLE 11

Involvement in Enterprise Success

	Would Criticize or Report Colleagues for		
	Poor Work (percent)	Damage to Tools and Equipment (percent)	Theft of Small Items (percent)
Unskilled blue-collar	26	36	48
Skilled blue-collar	38	50	58
White-collar (without higher education)	39	50	63
White-collar (with higher education)	44	64	74

Source: A. Sicinski, "Postawy Wobec Pracy i Wlasnosc" ["Attitudes About Work and Property"] (Warsaw: Osrodek Badanii Opinii Publicznej, 1961), Table 5-C.

The data reveal that there is some division between white- and blue-collar attitudes toward the enterprise. In almost all cases, blue-collar workers feel less responsible than white-collar workers, who in turn feel more responsible if they possess a university degree. Supervisory personnel are more likely to feel moral responsibility than nonsupervisory personnel, but only 53 percent of the supervisory sample feel morally responsible for the enterprise.[14] Other figures indicate that especially among nonsupervisory personnel the greater an individual's pecuniary reward the more sensitive he is to protection of socialist property.[15] In general, however, both supervisory and nonsupervisory personnel have very little consideration for and involvement in enterprise affairs. This data does not necessarily prove a causal link between dissatisfaction with socialist politics, the egalitarian distribution of rewards, and lack of concern for productivity, but it does indicate a general lack of social consciousness, especially on the part of white-collar personnel.

Table 12 indicates that the situation is not likely to improve markedly in the near future inasmuch as there are very few differences in the level of social consciousness of different age groups. The clearest break in the data indicative of social consciousness occurs at age forty. This is extremely interesting as those under forty have for the most part been educated since the revolution whereas those who appear more socially conscious lived a good part of their lives under the old system. Lack of respect for private property remains constant across the generation gap; the young have been particularly insensitive to violation of socialist property. This is particularly important in light of the fact that the young have been socialized within the socialist system and have no personal recollections of the pre-war economy. This lack of concern among the young is additional evidence of the breakdown of patterns of political socialization in socialist society.

Although blue-collar workers in any society rarely become deeply involved in industrial affairs, white-collar workers and managerial personnel normally develop an involvement with their work and commitment to corporate goals. The data indicate that in Poland even the older, more highly educated, supervisory personnel are only half committed to the protection of socialist property and production. Inasmuch as continuing industrialization means greater pressures for the increasing delegation of power and responsibility to these members of the middle level of command, some changes will have to be made if the economy is to prosper.

TABLE 12

Age and Condemnation of Antisocial Behavior

Age	Failure to Pay on Public Transport (percent)	Moon-lighting (percent)	Theft (percent)	Failure to Repay Private Loans (percent)
18-24	31	36	54	86
25-29	39	40	52	85
30-39	39	36	53	87
40-49	42	50	61	84
50-59	43	48	63	86
60-	62	46	67	88

Source: A. Sicinski, "Postawy Wobec Pracy i Wlasnosc" ["Attitudes About Work and Property"] (Warsaw: Osrodek Badania Opinii Publicznej, 1961), Table 7-B.

PRODUCTION, INNOVATION, AND ALIENATION

Aside from the lack of interest in the protection of socialist property or commitment to Party goals, indirect evidence indicates that socialist workers don't produce near capacity outside of the piece-rate situation. Manifestations of lack of socialist productivity are obvious in Poland. In almost all sectors of the economy, it seems that workers are more frequently on breaks than on the job. Although this phenomenon is common in modernizing countries where formerly independent peasants are squeezed into the uncomfortable yoke of modern industrial production, the lack of incentives, lack of opportunities for advancement, and lack of

loyalty to the goals of the political leadership
all aggravate the problem in Poland.

Hardly a plenum passes without Party leadership spending the greatest portion of time discussing problems of production. This holds true in
Poland as well as the other Eastern European socialist countries. In a key speech at the Seventh
Party Plenum in 1966, Wladyslaw Gomulka spoke to
the Party about "negative phenomena in the various
branches of the processing industry" and a "poor
rate of productivity growth." He suggested setting
up enterprise commissions to evaluate the efficiency
of work in the enterprises. According to Gomulka,
irregularities in production are caused by "a bad
organization of production."[16]

The point to which Gomulka was speaking is
that the uncommitted managerial personnel are more
interested in looking out for their own welfare
than that of the state. The politicking and bargaining that goes on behind the scenes over enterprise quotas is only one example of how managerial
interests are put before those of the state. Gomulka castigated the fourth-quarter phenomenon that
results when enterprises keep down productivity
during the year so that low subsequent quotas will
be set and then break all records in the last quarter to insure that the enterprise will receive its
full bonus. In refuting attacks on the bonus and
incentive system, Gomulka frankly admitted that
"experience teaches us that it is necessary to use
stimuli. This is reality. We must use bonuses, reduce bonuses for bad work, slovenliness, negligence,
and indifference, and reward good work."[17] But with
only one third of the socialist labor force engaged
in actual productive work, the rest must be motivated with other means or not motivated at all.

The socialist countries generally exhibit
fairly high yearly growth in productivity, but in
Poland's case much of it has been paper growth.
The Polish economy has grown because there was so
much slack to be made up in recovering from the

destruction of war. Although apparent growth figures remain high, there is little real indication
of what economic growth potential would be available if the working force was truly dedicated to
societal goals. One only need refer to Czechoslovakia's economic collapse in the mid-1960's, after
a period of apparent continuous growth, for an example of how suddenly these problems can come to a
point of crisis.

Poland's economic crisis has developed more
slowly, although the outbreak of discontent in December of 1970 might indicate the situation is more
serious than Party officials believe. Gomulka had
finally become convinced that deliberate actions
needed to be taken to streamline the economy, but
he erred in underestimating the depth of worker
disenchantment. Raising consumer goods prices just
before Christmas without corresponding wage increases was a suicidal move. It remains to be seen
whether the Gierek regime will take a new look at
the old problem of worker motivation.

Inasmuch as there has been no violent or obvious economic collapse, as in Czechoslovakia, it
is difficult to estimate the resources lost through
poor worker commitment. One manifestation of poor
productivity is found in the merchandise produced
for domestic consumption. Tales of shortages of
key commodities, equipment that falls apart when
first used, wearing apparel that doesn't fit, and
poorly prepared foodstuffs are common. Hardly an
issue of the popular press appears without letters
to the editor complaining about the poor quality of
goods. Even the staid Party paper has printed many
complaints, including one particularly humorous in-
stallment concerning the quality of chocolates produced by the "July 22nd" candy factory. The angry
correspondent closed his letter of complaint by
offering the "last box of chocolate creams to the
management of 'July 22nd' with the request that
they eat them in (his) presence."[18] Express
Wieczorny, the major evening paper, has even gone
so far as to institute a public service campaign

against the production of shoddy merchanidse.
Tracing defective merchandise to the source, under
the motto "It Is Just a Waste of Time," the paper
pressured many establishments into changing their
methods in the consumers' interest in late 1966 and
early 1967.[19] Finally the huge surpluses of un-
wanted goods accumulated in the state warehouses,
twelve million zloties worth in 1960, further attests to both the production of defective goods and
poor planning by officials involved.[20]

Turning from statistics to other types of
analysis, this author's own contacts in Warsaw included clerks and technocrats describing the nature
of the working day in the socialist enterprise.
The typical day begins at 8:00 a.m. when office
workers straggle in to take their morning tea, read
the paper, and converse about the latest events.
This normally lasts until 8:45 when actual labor
commences. Then at 10:30 the morning break is
scheduled, which isn't over until well past 11:00.
Depending upon circumstances, workers are liable to
take their lunch break as early as noon and not return until 1:30 or 2:00. It is during this period
that employees do incidental shopping and take care
of personal matters on company time! The afternoon
break begins at 2:30 and is over at 3:00. An hour
of work is then accomplished before the workers begin cleaning up their things at 4:00 in preparation
for the hectic rush homeward on crowded trams.

This attitude toward work is also reflected in
delays and absenteeism. Effective production time
in the Polish enterprise varies between 70 and 80
percent of nominal work time due to delays and poor
planning. In addition, the average blue-collar
worker missed 300 hours of work in 1965, representing an increase of 10 percent over five years earlier. This indicates either that workers are becoming less healthy or lazier. These figures mean
that the average worker loses over one month of
time in each year, and the total of lost time represents over 12 percent of the aggregate possible
work time.[21]

Although no figures are available indicating
how alienated the work force actually is, one study
did put questions of this type to a selected sample
of white- and blue-collar workers. Of the general
sample, only 70 percent claimed that supervisory
personnel related well with employees and less than
two thirds claimed that men in managerial roles in
their sections were honest and knowledgeable.   On
the other hand, 37 percent accused managerial personnel of favoritism, 33 percent of arbitrariness,
and 42 percent of dogmatism.[22]

Much dissatisfaction arises from the role of
the Party in the office and enterprise.   Informants
stated that there are rigid dividing lines between
Party and non-Party members in the work place and
that many such charges against supervisors are related to this split.

Table 13 portrays worker attitudes in greater
detail.   There is a very clear difference in blue-
collar attitudes toward superiors and the superiors'
perceptions of themselves.   Even higher supervisory
personnel, however, admit that they feel that their
colleagues are arbitrary and dogmatic in nearly a
third of the cases.   Only half of the rank-and-file
workers feel that supervisors are honest and knowledgeable and almost as many accuse them of favoritism, dogmatism, and arbitrariness.   These attitudes
are far from functional for successful industrial
production and are undoubtedly indicative of more
widespread discontent on all levels.

To compensate for lack of efficiency at lower
levels of management, the Polish central administrative apparatus has developed a whole series of
inspections, reports, and inventories to keep track
of production in the economy.   The legal code has
been amended to stress responsibility and to discourage risk and innovation.   Under conditions
where personnel are not rewarded for taking chances,
the strict reliance on control serves only to more
deeply alienate supervisory and technocratic personnel and further discourage them from innovative
efforts.

TABLE 13

Employee Perceptions of Directing Personnel
(in percent attributing quality to
supervisory personnel)

| | As Perceived by | | |
	Blue-Collar (percent)	Lower Supervisor (percent)	Higher Supervisor (percent)
Relate favorably	63	76	76
Honest and knowledgeable	53	66	73
Favoritism	46	31	26
Arbitrary	41	28	22
Dogmatic	49	38	31

Source: L. Kaczmarczyk, "Niektore Uwarunkowania Opinii o Elicie Kierowniczej" ["Some Conditions of Opinions of Directing Elites"] (Warsaw: Osrodek Badania Opinii Publicznej, 1964), pp. 7-9.

The main Warsaw daily Zycie Warszawa ran a fourteen-part series on risk and responsibility in 1966. In search of answers to this dilemma, opinions about control varied from those of conservatives who were quick to stress the penal code and the social responsibility of factory management to those who clearly recognized the need for more incentives for innovation.[23] Perhaps the most startling revelation to come from the discussion was that the cult of mediocrity has become so embedded among managers that even they are not interested in changes that would permit them to take more risks and prefer to stick with established methods. Of the leading economic activists participating in a poll conducted by the department of penal law at

Warsaw University, over 70 percent considered ventures with any element of risk as being dangerous.
"It is characteristic of (managerial) employees
that they usually play safe, fearing responsibility
in case of failure."24   These conservative attitudes must be overcome if the modernizing Polish
society is to become truly active and innovative--
and live up to full economic potential.

ECONOMIC MODERNIZATION AND
TENSION MANAGEMENT

The socialist economy can be the greatest
strength or biggest weakness of the political-
tension management program.   In the face of the
limitations on the use of terror as a compliance-
insuring device as a result of the Twentieth Party
Congress in the Soviet Union, the main focus has
shifted to keeping the socialist citizen at least
calculatively involved with the system.   The Party
managers are controlling a society that has just
recovered from the destruction of war and in this
situation almost any type of economic development
has been welcomed.   The test of the strength of
this type of social cohesion will come when economic scarcity no longer is a pressing issue and when
other types of citizen needs become more manifest.

Although continued economic advancement is
definitely putting more resources in the political
managers' hands for distribution, there can be no
doubt that Polish citizens are less than happy with
their share.   Only blue-collar workers have a stake
in the overly egalitarian distribution of wages.
It is not a coincidence that factory workers were
called into the streets to demonstrate against rebelling students in 1968.   White-collar workers who
cannot be rewarded by the piece-rate method and
managerial personnel looking for other than economic satisfaction from their careers have much less
to retain by supporting the system.   Yet Poland is
a country in which even those most dissatisfied
have an interest in maintaining the established

order. Almost any type of political order appears
better than revolution to a war-weary citizenry.

Although resources increase and the managers
have a larger budget to allocate, the definitions
of fair exchange are changing as part of the developmental process. Demands for respect, esteem,
responsibility, and opportunities for self-
actualization can be expected from the educated
technocrats once the satisfaction of physiological
needs is relatively complete. Journals, newspapers, and face-to-face contacts at meetings and
conventions serve as a catalyst in organizing the
technocratic elements in demanding responsiveness
from Party leaders. Young writers, journalists,
planners, managerial personnel, academicians, and
even Party activists are making new demands based
on feelings of strength and unity.

These pressures and demands have become more
manifest in the Polish press in recent years.
Thus, Zbigniew Kwiatkowski freely writes about the
responsibilities of the journalist to inform the
people not only of events, but of the causes of
events, especially when a new figure appears on the
political scene to replace an old one. "The reader
. . . and the listener . . . and the television
spectator . . . has only one side of the Polish
reality to look at; its mechanism is shrouded in
darkness."[25] Pressures from interest groups have
become so intense that media managers have begun to
complain about the terror of opinion. These groups
are bringing political influence to bear in important positions and thereby restricting the freedom
of the press to criticize their groups:

> Once upon a time, any writer who
> dared to step on the national "corns"
> would be accused on the spot of
> "soiling the sanctities." Today
> such phenomena are sporadic and
> rare. . . . On the other hand, a
> new phenomenon has emerged. The
> phenomenon of "craft sanctity," or

almost caste-consciousness, falsely
understood esteem of an individual
profession.[26]

Thus, although there has not been a pronounced
broadening of the sanctioned decision-making structure in Polish society, the growth of the economy
has been accompanies by development of "group consciousness" accompanied by new and different demands. White-collar man does not live by bread
alone, although part of the technocrats' dissatisfaction has roots in the overly egalitarian wage
scales. Continued modernization means that a greater number of people assume responsibility in many
segments of the increasingly complex social organization. Whether this responsibility is officially
recognized by delegating different groups official
political representation or whether the broadening
of the structure takes place informally, socialist
economic man must be made to feel some loyalty to
the system during the second stage of industrialization when innovation and managerial motivation assume a much greater importance.

In this respect, the socialist economy has become "heavy" with interest groups and veto points
in the chain of command. The Party can make decisions and hand down orders from the top, but if an
increasing number of key personnel in the middle
level of command are dissatisfied, the order may be
ignored or poorly implemented. Affixing responsibility is most difficult. The socialist economy is
both the strongest and weakest link in the managing
of political tensions. Economic rewards have
largely been responsible for obtaining citizen compliance with the new political leadership during
the first stage of industrialization. Without
doubt, the greatest portion of Polish citizens calculate that it is in their own interest economically to cooperate with Party authorities based on
past economic performance. Yet the exercise of
this type of power is dangerous because of the possibilities of depression or the breakdown of economic production. The nature of the relationship

forged between the technocrats in the middle level of command and the Party authorities in the coming decade will be most important in determining whether Poland and other socialist societies will successfully move into a new stage of industrialization.

NOTES

1. J. K. Galbraith, The New Industrial State (Boston, Mass.: The New American Library, 1967), pp. 112-15.

2. Ibid., pp. 116-19.

3. For further explication of the exchange concept, see P M. Blau, Exchange and Power in Social Life (New York: John Wiley & Sons, 1964), Ch. 1; G. C. Homans, Social Behavior (New York: Harcourt, Brace, and World, 1961).

4. Blau, op. cit., pp. 25-31; A. W. Gouldner, "The Norm of Reciprocity," American Sociological Review, Vol. XXV (1960), pp. 161-78.

5. W. Kornhauser, The Politics of Mass Society (New York: The Free Press of Glencoe, 1961), Ch. 3; Blau, op. cit., Ch. 10. For applications of the exchange theory to political life, see R. L. Curry, Jr., and L. Wade, A Theory of Political Exchange (Englewood Cliffs, N J.: Prentice-Hall, 1968).

6. See R. E. Lane, Political Ideology (New York: The Free Press, 1962), pp. 91-92, and R. M. Merelman, "Learning and Legitimacy," American Political Science Review, Vol. LX (1966), No. 3.

7. A. Inkeles and R. Bauer, The Soviet Citizen (New York: Atheneum, 1968), pp. 110-12.

8. Ibid., pp. 117-20. See also the dynamic approach to a theory of human needs presented by

A. Maslow, "A Theory of Human Motivation," Twentieth Century Psychology, ed. P. I. Harriman (New
York: The Philosophical Library, 1946), pp. 11-12.

9. Galbraith, op. cit., Ch. 11.

10. A. Sarapata, "Justum Pretium," Polish Sociological Bulletin, No. 1 (1963), pp. 41-56;
Studia (Warsaw: Ksiazka i Wiedza, 1965), Ch. 10.

11. Sarapata, "Justum Pretium," pp. 41-52.

12. A. Sicinski, "Postawy Wobec Pracy i
Wlasnosc" ["Attitudes About Work and Property"]
(Warsaw: Osrodek Badania Opinii Publicznej, 1961).

13. L. Kaczmarczyk, "Niektore Uwarunkowania
Opinii o Elicie Kierowniczej" ["Some Conditions of
Opinions of Directing Elites'] (Warsaw: Osrodek
Badania Opinii Publicznej, 1964).

14. Sicinski, op. cit., p. 53.

15. Ibid., p. 46.

16. Trybuna Ludu, No. 304, November 3, 1966.

17. Ibid.

18. Trybuna Ludu, No. 279, October 9, 1966.

19. For examples, see Express Wieczorny, No.
302, December 20, 1966, or other issues of this
period.

20. H. Stehle, The Independent Satellite (New
York: Frederick A. Praeger, Inc., 1965), p. 154.

21. "In Search of Lost Time," Zagadnienia i
Materialy, No. 23, December, 1965, pp. 1-15.

22. Kaczmarczyk, op. cit., p. 6.

23. See S. Buczkowski, "Autonomy--a Principle

or a Cliche," _Zycie Warszawa_, No. 248, October 15, 1966; Z. Madej, "To Count and to Safeguard," _Zycie Warszawa_, No. 257, October 26, 1966; and other articles in the series of this period.

24.   Interview with J. Sawicki, _Zycie Warszawa_, No. 273, November 13, 1966.

25.   Z. Kwiatkowski, "In Whose Name," _Zycie Warszawa_, No. 9, February 26, 1967.

26.   W. Sokorski, "Against the Terror of Opinion," _Kultura_ (Warsaw), No. 19, May 7, 1967.

5

**STABILIZING
SOCIETY:
MEDIA VS. MESSAGE**

Modern mass communications give any political
leadership great tension-management potential. Control over the flow of information permits political
leaders to restructure citizens' worlds and enhance
their persuasive powers. The media must be handled
carefully, however; many images flow through communication channels and some can encourage an increase in expectations. The media have the potential to raise citizen expectations and aid the political managers in the creation of a new and dynamic culture as well as to create a distorted picture of reality or pacify the masses during periods
of conservative stabilization.

In the pre-industrial society, most communication takes place on a face-to-face basis. It is
not a highly differentiated function and there are
few who specialize in the transmission of messages.
Where only a small number of people share in an extremely limited division of labor, information flow
required to sustain the organization is small and
orders can be relayed face-to-face.

In complex modern societies, the exchange of
information has become crucial and the flow so
heavy that face-to-face contacts can no longer

begin to meet demands. Mass media have emerged as
a supplement overseen by a class of communication
specialists. Information now flows through the
printed word, the television picture, or the voice
on the radio. Elements of face-to-face communication still persist in even the most modern society;
much information citizens receive is relayed in interpersonal contacts rather than consumed directly
from organized media.[1] The sheer mass of information available in the media makes it impossible for
each person to keep up with all events of concern
to him, and informal opinion leaders select and
pass on information that is of interest.[2]

Modernization means both higher levels of education and literacy and greater potential for distribution of mass media. A larger proportion of
the population becomes tuned in to the information
flow and available to be mobilized by messages coming through the communications channels.[3] The dissemination of the mass media increases with modernization, but so do opportunities for face-to-face
contact. One of the crucial aspects of modernization is the movement to urban areas where an increasing density of population means each person
has a greater opportunity to communicate with
others. Greater numbers of information sources
increase the speed at which information moves
through society.

Although system stability and the division of
labor require that information be passed down from
decision points to those responsible for implement-
ing the decisions, information must also be fed
back to decision-makers if intelligent decisions
are to be made. The dissemination of information
through the mass media is only the first step in
communicating it to most citizens; the second step
in the information flow involves the abstraction
and retransmission of information by opinion leaders who are to a large degree responsible for what
is communicated to the masses. In the case of the
John F. Kennedy assassination, as an example, only
half of the adult population received the news from

the mass media and the rest received it through interpersonal contacts.[4]

Inasmuch as the organization of modern society depends heavily upon communication, it is impossible to study politics and tension management apart from the study of communication. Political decision-makers must have information from all segments of society if they are to successfully set goals and allocate resources and responsibility.

A vocational ethic is developing among professional communicators that messages relayed should resemble the objective truth as much as possible.[5] If messages are regularly distorted, the information is worthless to citizens as well as political managers. Although controlling the societal flow of information is an important tension management technique, keeping the media basically honest is in the long range interest of decision-makers. Feedback to the centers of decision is also likely to be distorted in a manipulated system.

The successful management of complex societies requires that decision-makers know the supportive and demanding predispositions of citizens in order to avoid violence and a possible overthrow of the system. The flow of information is so heavy in the advanced society that some decentralization of responsibility must take place in order to avoid chaos. This implies co-opting relevant people into the information net to act both as lower-level decision-makers and as sources of information close to the masses. Functionally speaking, an accessible decision-making elite dedicated to developing a free-flowing informational system characterized by truthful duo-directional communication seems necessary for the development of a modern stable society.[6]

The introduction of the media into a preindustrial society increases "psychic mobility" of citizens. In many cases, intellectual horizons in less industrial societies are limited to known people in known situations. The consumer becomes

an "empathetic" person through vicarious experience
gained through the media.[7] The empathetic person
is equipped with skills needed in a modern society,
the most important of which is the ability to adapt
to new situations and visualize oneself in the position of vicariously experienced others. No longer
limited to the directly experienced world, psychi-
cally mobile individuals contact different perspectives and values by confronting national or international standards through the media. One of the
most important consequences of greater mobility is
that the egalitarian and participatory values of
the world's industrial societies are internalized
by formerly nonexpectant peoples.

Thus, in the modernization process the media
can very well work against the message.[8] Even employing the best of personnel, messages relayed
through developing communications channels differ-
entially impact the key strata in a developing society. The constant changes in the media also
change the rules of communication. While the increasing volume of leadership messages assaults the
transitional citizen's ears, contact with media increases resistance to propaganda and develops audience sophistication. The ability of tension-
managing politicians to successfully exploit the
media as an instrument of stabilization is much
more problematic than it would at first appear.
No matter what the increase in message volume
directed by elites, if citizen sophistication develops commensurate with message volume the impact
of the additional communicatory channels may be no
greater.[9]

As the industrial revolution based on the efficiencies discovered in an increasingly complex
division of labor draws to a close in the more advanced economies, access to accurate information
is becoming a new source of power. Having milked
the division of labor and the economies of scale
for what they are worth, the complex industrial establishment needs increasingly sophisticated planning to progress. Just as a logic of division of

labor was related to industrialization of society,
the necessity for a division of decision-making
labor is impelling a cybernetic revolution in information storage and retrieval. In the long run,
the more successful decision-makers will be those
who are most conscious of problems in the societies
they manage. Self-understanding can only come
through the clearing of communication channels and
a smooth flow of accurate information both from decision centers to periphery and from the periphery
to decision-makers.

COMMUNICATION IN THE SOCIALIST SOCIETY

The party leaders in socialist societies recognize the media as an instrument to be used in a
struggle against hostile ideologies. The goal in
the Soviet Union, for example, is to develop a communication network geared to bringing the Party
message into the home of every Soviet citizen. Far
from being naive in their understanding of the
media, Party experts realize that all the vehicles
of communication, including face-to-face contacts,
are important potential agents of ideological mobilization. Not only is close attention paid to
the content of radio, television, and press, but
also the theatre, movies, and the arts receive careful scrutiny of interested officials.[10]

Control over media in socialist society reached
its apex during the excesses of the Stalinist period.
During the stresses of forced industrialization,
control of the media was very helpful to the Party
in restructuring attitudes and maintaining enthusiasm in the face of extreme hardships. Jamming of
Western radio broadcasts, restrictions on the introduction of reading matter from abroad, and limitations on foreign travel into the Soviet Union as
well as outside travel for Soviet citizens were effective in reducing citizen demands that might have
otherwise snowballed.

The control of mass media by the Party is assured through the allocation of top positions to

trusted Party figures. When Khrushchev was removed
from power, the ouster was quickly followed by the
dismissal of his trusted followers from the editor-
ships of _Izvestiya_ and _Pravda_.[11] In Poland the
purges of 1968 resulted in the dismissal of the editor of the Party paper as well as influential journalists from the less Party-oriented newspapers.[12]
Media personnel do not echo monolithic political
opinions and when political leaders perceive their
media activities as deviating from the party line
they are quick to take punitive action.

In the Soviet Union the development and control of communication has been pushed to extremes.
Not content with pouring resources only into mass
communication, a network of oral agitators, supple-
menting the more impersonal media, has been created
to make message transmission more effective. Taking
advantage of the natural two-step flow of communication, the Party has assigned over two million agitators to the task of making certain that messages
transmitted through the media don't get short-
circuited by opinion leaders. Ideally, with a
trusted Party worker relaying the message in every
factory, village, or shop, the messages reach the
citizen in undistorted form from Party sources.[13]

In many cases the strict control of the media
has been self-defeating in the Soviet Union--citi-
zens have learned to insulate themselves by reading
between the lines. In other cases, even employing
the best techniques of management, the Party's message has not always been received in the form anti-
cipated by the communicators.[14]

In other socialist countries, control of the
media has been less complete, especially since the
liberalization beginning with Stalin's death. In
Poland, although close Party attention has been
paid to the media, no oral agitation network has
been created to supplement the natural network of
opinion leadership. The social characteristics of
opinion leaders have come under close scrutiny,
however, indicating that Party officials are not

ignorant of the importance of face-to-face contacts,
but conditions in Poland and many of the other socialist states have not been conducive to strict
media controls.[15]

The Soviet leadership has been able to so
readily manipulate the media because Soviet society
has traditionally been isolated from extensive contact with Western philosophies. The imposition of
communication controls is not viewed as unnatural
by the Soviet citizen, historically subject to political controls, and in this environment the Party
has been able to recruit necessary trained and dedicated personnel. In Poland, however, the situation
in communication parallels that in education. In a
society physically and psychologically closer to
the West, the imposition of communication curbs is
viewed with suspicion and even hostility. Just as
it is difficult to control the substance of the
lessons imparted by the teacher in the classroom,
members of an oral agitation network would hardly
be any more loyal to the Party line than the average citizen. Thus, the degree of popular acceptance of political leaders sets parameters around
the potential for exploitation by Party-directed
communication networks.

In Poland, as in the Soviet Union, one citizen
respose to regime attempts to control information
sources has been growth in the importance of rumor
as well as face-to-face communication.[16] Data reveal that rumor is at least as important as a
source of information in Poland as in the Soviet
Union and probably even more so. Poles are especially sensitive to events affecting their delicate relationship with the Soviet Union. When any
top Soviet leader makes a "secret" visit to Warsaw,
the face-to-face rumor network is evidenced by the
lack of flour and bread in stores, all essential
goods having been purchased by anxious Polish house-
wives. The workings of this information system are
complex, but empty shelves attest to the fact that
the unofficial word has preceded the arrival of the
perplexed uninformed customer.

On occasions the influence of the informal
rumor network in Poland becomes so pervasive that
the press is forced to print denials of rumors that
develop. In November of 1966, for example, the
Party organ <u>Trybuna Ludu</u> was forced to issue a de-
nial that a vampire killer was loose and terrorizing
the countryside. After launching into an attack on
the rumor mechanism, the fairly lengthy article
went on to point out that "rumors . . . fall upon a
fertile soil" and "that it is sometimes necessary
to issue denials of such widespread rumors since
they provoke such anxiety." It closes by assuring
the readers that instances of robbery, murder, and
rape are currently reported by the press and that
it is unwise to rely on anxiety-building personal
conjectures as sources of information.[17]

Table 14 indicates that the press and radio
are most favored sources of information in Poland,
but that conversations with people run a respect-
able third. The data indicate that people are more
content to trust official sources as well as conversation on domestic matters as opposed to events
taking place abroad. These figures are roughly comparable to those reported by Inkeles and Bauer in
their study of Soviet refugees. It is reasonable
to assume that people in the refugee sample were
much more willing to report relying on word of
mouth for information than the Polish citizen being interviewed by representatives of the polling
agency. In either case, the figures point to the
large segment of the population that admits being
hooked into the face-to-face network.[18]

Two things in the table require special mention. The proportion of those dependent upon television as a source of information has skyrocketed
since television has more recently become more
widely available and currently offers more comprehensive news reporting. The format of the tele-
vised news is remarkably close to a face-to-face
conversation; easy face-to-face style, calm speaking manner, and little agitation or exhortation.
Second, a surprisingly large portion of the sample

of Warsaw adults admits preferring the foreign
press as a source of information about world affairs. These figures are especially significant
as this admission was made to representatives of
Polish media interests. They indicate that a significant proportion of the Warsaw population is in
contact with the foreign press. These people often
act as relay points for information from abroad in
a face-to-face information transfer.

TABLE 14

Preferred Information Sources
(in percent citing as important source)

Source	Foreign Events	Domestic Events
Polish radio	60	71
Polish papers	58	74
Conversations	38	44
Polish weeklies	29	34
Film chronicle	29	31
Television	14	16
Foreign press	10	4

Source: A. Sicinski, "Funkje Informacyjne
Prasy i Radia" ["The Information Functions of the
Press and Radio"] (Warsaw: Osrodek Banania Opinii
Publicznej, 1959), p. 6. The sample included 700
people.

A second response to media management in
Poland takes the form of reading between lines. A
whole special language has grown up in the media
that is an aid to people trying to interpret the

real significance of news stories. The meaning of
news items is not always found in the text but is
sometimes understood by placing the stories in the
context of other events and looking for changes in
phraseology and for significant omissions. Thus,
the more educated citizen reads two or more newspapers daily to help fill in limited information
and hopefully to glean slight differences in interpretation from newspapers representing different
interests.[19] People accept information in the press
only after checking with other reliable sources on
the plausibility of the story. When a sample of
Warsaw citizens was asked where they would turn for
authoritative information about economic difficulties, the same percentage of the sample said they
would turn to other people as would turn to any
official media source.[20]

The final response to the information hunger
that results from restricted circulation is turning
to outside sources as correctives on domestic information. When Stalin was in power, the "iron
curtain" was a key component of media management.
It kept contact with the outside to a minimum and
effectively excluded inputs of dissonant information. Radio jamming, refusal of requests for
travel abroad, limitations on visitors permitted to
travel in the socialist countries, restrictions on
the importation of literature from Western countries, and iron control of movies and the arts
served to severely restrict citizen contact with
ideas freely disseminated in other countries.

The removal of these restraints has created
severe media management problems in Poland; it is
now nearly impossible to keep out news of outside
events. Liberalization carried penalties in the
form of an increasing flow of information from visitors and outside media. The last barriers to direct
reception of foreign broadcasts fell with the end of
jamming of Western radio broadcasts. Now on any
clear night a typical listener in Warsaw can pick
up news from many foreign sources ranging from
Radio Free Europe to the British Broadcasting

Company. Few concerned Poles are limited to the
Polish language and broadcasts in English, French,
and German are also available. To make the life of
the political activist complete, there is also the
daily broadcast in Polish from Radio Tirana, which
compensates for any inaccuracies in domestic service, especially as they relate to Chinese affairs.

Liberalization has changed the media management rules considerably in the last few years. No
longer can political figures rely on outright distortion of reality in the media being accepted by
a noncritical public. Talents must be applied to
give the daily news a slant that will find acceptance among the masses. The critical citizen uses
the rumor network, reading between the lines, and
external sources to gather competing viewpoints
from which reasonably accurate opinions can be
formed. The Polish citizen doesn't listen to Radio
Free Europe to find truth, but rather to balance
the information presented in Trybuna Ludu, figuring
that objective reality lies someplace in between.

THE MEDIA: STRUCTURE AND AUDIENCE

The more structured a medium, the more easily
it can be subjected to centralized control. Live,
multidimensional (audio-visual, etc.) media, such
as television and theatre, can be controlled only
with difficulty inasmuch as action often takes
place on the spur of the moment. Formal content
can be controlled by precensorship, but facial expressions and subtle innuendoes are most difficult
to suppress in the finished product. The press,
movies, and radio are all easier to control either
because of the lapse in time between origin of a
message and its impact on the audience, or, in the
case of the radio, because of the single dimension
of contact between commentator and listener. Where
time is available to read scripts before they are
presented for mass consumption, individuals can be
held responsible for any lapses in social consciousness.

Increasing modernization in socialist society means that more resources are available for improving the impact of the media. Newspapers are available to more people, more television receivers are produced, new movie theatres are constructed, and radio receivers are now found in nearly all homes. The aim of political leaders is to make optimal use of resources and extract a maximum of tension management potential from each zloty invested. Media investment priorities are difficult to establish, and little concrete information is available to aid outsiders. Suffice it to say that reports exist, based on survey research, establishing "class" priorities for each type of media. Radio is regarded as an instrument through which to reach the working class, certain newspapers reach the intelligentsia, etc. In this way messages can be tempered to suit the audience that attends any particular medium. More sophisticated audiences must be reached by more sophisticated arguments; the less educated supposedly respond to simpler appeals.

The press is the most important and manageable of the media. In Warsaw 85 percent of the people read at least one paper daily and for the country as a whole the figures approach 80 percent.[21] It is often assumed that the party organs dominate in socialist countries, but this is not always the case. Trybuna Ludu, although obviously a most important paper to study because of its special relationship to the Party, is only one of several papers appearing daily on Warsaw newsstands. In fact, Table 15 reveals that even among a highly politicized Warsaw sample only 16 percent regularly read Trybuna Ludu. Express Wieczorny is the leading Warsaw daily in popularity followed by the more sophisticated Zycie Warszawa. To gain an understanding of the complicated role of the press in stabilization and tension management, it is not enough to study only the Party organ; careful attention must also be paid to the more popular mass circulation papers.

Most major newspapers are representative of some interest, or at least appeal to special groups

in a division of journalistic labor. Trybuna Ludu
is the source of the Party line and as such is read
more frequently by the highly educated and middle-
aged upwardly mobile bureaucrats and technocrats.
Express Wieczorny, on the other hand, is a tabloid-
type evening paper with widespread readership fall-
ing into almost every category of age and education.
The big exception is that the middle-aged shy away
in favor of more substantial journals. Slowo
Powszechne is representative of Catholic interests
and quite naturally is more heavily read by older
people.[22]

TABLE 15

Readership and Circulation of
Major Warsaw Dailies

	Readers	Circulation
Express Wieczorny (tabloid)	61%	420,000
Trybuna Ludu (Party)	16	310,000
Zycie Warszawa (upper-class general)	39	272,000
Kurier Polski (social democrats)	15	150,000
Sztandar Mlodych (youth)	10	133,000
Glos Pracy (labor)	1	120,000
Przeglad Sportowy (sports)	11	96,000
Slowo Powszechne (Catholic)	5	75,000

Sources: A. Sicinski, "Funkje Informacyjne
Prasy i Radia" ["The Information Functions of the
Press and Radio"] (Warsaw: Osrodek Badania Opinii
Publicznej, 1959), p. 12; Rocznik Polityczny i
Gospodarczy 1966 (Warsaw: Panstwowe Wydawnictwo
Ekonomiczne, 1966), p. 747.

The comparison of popularity with circulation
figures in the above table illustrates some pecu-
liarities of the Polish press. Many papers can always easily be bought on the newsstands whereas
there is a daily struggle for others because of
their small circulation. Trybuna Ludu is always
available the next day, but it is difficult any
time to find a copy of Slowo Powszechne on the newsstands. Those papers most clearly attached to the
Party are most likely to receive permission for
large printings. The figures are complicated by
the fact that several of the key papers are shipped
to the provinces where they are read later. A na-
tionwide sample of newspaper readers revealed, for
example, that nearly 40 percent of all papers read
originate in Warsaw.[23] In general, because of limited resources and paper shortages, the more popular journals are often in scarce supply while the
Party organs receive more than their share of the
available newsprint.

Because of the problem of allocating scarce
resources, Polish papers appear skimpy beside the
Sunday edition of The New York Times. To conserve
newsprint, the normal edition of a daily paper runs
from four to eight pages, which leaves the political managers a limited amount of space within which
to work. In a typical edition, two pages are reserved for international news, one page for editorials and comment, one page for domestic and local news, and the last two pages are devoted to
calendars of local events, radio schedules, what's
playing at the theatres, or in some papers death
notices and advertising. Lengthy and complicated
ideological articles or editorial harangues are
rare inasmuch as most space is reserved for current
events or briefer articles and editorials.

FUNCTIONS OF THE MEDIA

The restrictions imposed on possibilities for
slanting the news by renewed contacts with the non-
socialist world have meant that the job of the

journalist has become much more difficult. To get
the officially approved message accepted by the
citizens, it is not any longer possible to engage
in outright distortion of truth, which was common
in Stalinist times. Now insight and judgment must
be employed if newspapers are to function effectively as a tension management device. The news in the
Polish press is now "more or less" accurate, it being pointless to print stories that won't be accepted by the audience. The slanting that does
take place is more by omission or emphasis than by
outright distortion. Stories dealing with war
criminals or evidence of Nazi atrocities are always
picked up from wire services to reinforce citizen
fears of a resurgent Germany. Stories emphasizing
social decay in capitalist society are also particularly popular. The fears and prejudices of the
people are heightened by these items in the daily
press and a negative loyalty to the political regime is thereby fostered with no outright distortions.

The journalistic profession is one of the important pillars of the tension management system. The
editors and journalists are typical members of the
increasingly important middle level of command and
are responsible for dampening political and social
tension. Small misjudgments in newspaper policies
can lead to political violence. The number of journalists dismissed in recent purges testifies to the
scrutiny under which the profession works and the
importance the Party attaches to its loyalty.*

Evidence indicates that journalism in Poland
has been almost entirely restructured since World
War II--only 10 percent of active journalists began their career before 1944.[24] Today's journalist
is likely to be young (two thirds are between
twenty-five and forty years of age) and trained in

---

*In 1968, Leon Kassman was removed as editor
of Trybuna Ludu and four ranking journalists were
dismissed from Zycie Warszawa. Many lower-level
personnel were also sacked.

the university (83 percent have some type of higher educational experience).[25] Although 46 percent of all journalists belong to the Polish United Workers' Party, their social backgrounds betray a pattern that certainly should leave Party authorities uneasy. Nearly 60 percent of all contemporary journalists trace their family origin to the intelligentsia. Those of worker and peasant background don't acquire necessary skills; thus, the Party must rely on those whose loyalty to the Party line remains somewhat suspect.[26] Chief editors are more carefully selected, however; over 70 percent are members of the Polish United Workers' Party.[27]

It is false to assume that all journalists and editors are merely tools in the hands of politicians. Newspapers do serve functions of a representative nature through carefully controlled letters-to-the-editor campaigns as well as sporadic outbursts of concern for economic efficiency and consumer protection. Carefully worded letters to the editor are used to make political points when opportune moments arise. The printing of letters from readers on subjects of concern to all can act as a tension-relieving device. When correspondence complaining about certain activities begins to pile up, decisions can be made to print representative letters in the hopes that the message is not lost on those responsible, assuming those responsible are not pinpointed at the very highest levels. (For example, during 1966 and 1967 letters to the editor very critical of arbitrary actions by Warsaw police were printed. On one occasion police were accused of refusing to identify themselves to people being detained. On another, the Ministry of the Interior soccer team was accused of "kidnapping" a star soccer player from a provincial team.[28]

In economic affairs, for example, Express Wieczorny ran a successful campaign against the production and distribution of shoddy consumer goods in 1966. Under the banner of "It Is Just a Waste of Time," referring to results of citizen

complaints about poorly produced merchandise, the
paper tracked readers' complaints down to the people
responsible and in many cases brought lax management
to justice. Thus, in one edition the paper checked
out complaints involving the frozen egg industry,
textiles, hosiery, camping equipment, and women's
sweaters.[29] It would be a mistake to overestimate
the power of the pen, but the subtle and, in certain cases, rather overt pressures the daily press
can bring on fairly important political personnel
is a factor that should not be ignored in socialist
politics.

Radio is also used in the battle to manage political tensions and keep society stable. It is regarded by tension managers as a vehicle by which the
message can be relayed to those who do not regularly read the press. Nearly all Poles regularly listen to the radio, but the political message is
slanted to appeal to blue-collar groups not making
themselves accessible through the daily press.
Broadcasts are especially important in the countryside, where central newspapers are infrequently
read. People living in small cities and in the
country are more willing to listen to general and
political broadcasts and are least frequently critical of the completeness or honesty of radio reporting.[30]

Whether by design or because of lack of resources, the radio listener is faced with boring
and frustrating choices of programs. In Warsaw
there are only two stations to choose between at
any one time and the variety is most disappointing.
The broadcast day is perforated with news programs,
political specials, and historical dramas with
ideological messages. It is nearly impossible to
spend any length of time listening only to music or
entertainment; programs with political content pop
up at highly irregular intervals and are very difficult to avoid. Although the leadership may think
that this use of captive audience techniques is politically expedient, the listening audience has developed a resistance to this type of message. Many

Poles learn to treat the political message as Americans treat television commercials--a time to tune out and do the chores that have accumulated while listening to other programs.

Studies show that the radio audience has become so disinterested in political messages that "the number of daily listeners to the radio is two and one-half times greater among the blue-collar workers and two times higher among the white-collar workers than the number of people listening to political affairs broadcasts."[31] Even though political broadcasts are interspersed with more attractive programs, the audience claims to avoid listening to them. Data reveal that only 25 percent of the population listens to political broadcasts. Interest is highest in the "politicized" age grouping, thirty to forty-nine years of age, and greatest in the smaller Polish cities of less than 100,000 inhabitants.[32]

Television has grown rapidly as a medium to supplement radio broadcasts. Telecasts are designed to appeal to the more sophisticated strata both because the high price of a television set restricts viewing to the wealthier and because the range of television transmitters is limited to more urban areas. The resources available for investment in television have limited the construction of new stations to those heavily populated areas where more people can be reached for a given amount of money. Selection is limited to one channel because of the limited availability of resources and talent. Even with an abbreviated broadcast day, the television network often is reduced to showing dubbed foreign movies and American and British serials because of lack of domestically produced material.

In 1965, only eight television stations were operative in Poland, and the greatest share of programming was done in Warsaw studios and retransmitted on the other seven stations.[33] Although television is more an entertainment than political medium, it has certain advantages over press and

radio. The television commentator can provide a
substitute opinion leader for members of the television generation, and the presentation of the news
in a cool face-to-face manner is successful in encouraging audience identification. Television offers an opportunity to identify with a whole person,
rather than with just a voice, and the Party is
more than willing to exploit the cult of the television personality.

The movies and theatre are much less successful in shaping proper citizen opinions than the
other media. The theatre has been especially difficult to control and on more than one occasion official theatre and semi-official cabaret performances
have met with official disapproval. Theatres and
cabarets are very political and on occasion act as a
rallying point for those less than dedicated to regime programs. Official restrictions on theatre performances are not unknown in Poland, but the theatre
has been permitted indiscretions that would not be
tolerated in other media. Scripts can be carefully
supervised, but it is difficult to reprimand an
actor for speaking a line with too much gusto or
failing to exude enough enthusiasm in an approved
theatrical production. In addition, the theatre is
regularly attended by a small, exclusive segment of
the population; its messages don't reach the masses.
Thus, the regime has been content to permit the
staging of some ideologically questionable plays in
the interest of permitting a small group of the social elite to vent their frustrations without involving great numbers of people.

Movies present a challenge of a different nature. The construction of large numbers of movie
houses after World War II was undertaken in the
hope that they would act as another vehicle for the
promotion of rapid social change. The Stalinist
dream of people crowding into theatres on weekends
to receive the message of change has not borne fruit
for several reasons. Although the theatres have
been built and are kept busy on weekends, the fare
they offer is not exactly what would be prescribed

by a good Marxist-Leninist. Film production in the
socialist country is not sufficient to keep the
numerous theatres stocked. The Warsaw metropolitan
area, containing one million people, is serviced by
more than sixty movie theatres. To keep them
stocked with films capable of attracting an audience, the Polish film industry has been forced to
turn to the West for imports.

Unlike the press or radio--media upon which
people are highly dependent for information--movies
are a luxury that people need not attend if they
are dissatisfied. Knowing that people cannot be
forced to attend films and also realizing that to
cut back in the number of theatres would be tanta-
mount to instigating riots among an entertainment-
hungry people, those in charge of the movie industry have resigned themselves to salvaging what they
can from the ruins of the Stalinist dream. But
even attempts to screen more films made in the socialist countries have ended in partial failure in
that more successful film organizations have stopped
dealing with ideological topics in the quest for
hard currency and foreign markets. The Polish film
industry, before political pressures forced it into
decline, was highly successful in producing films
that had universal audience appeal but which were
light in political message. More recently the
Czech film industry produced films that also met
with public acceptance, but again changing political fortunes have destroyed the flourishing industry. Products from the more closely controlled
and politically oriented Soviet film industry meet
with less than popular acceptance in Poland.

The extent of the Polish film dilemma is reflected in the following figures. In 1965, Polish
theatres were showing 108 American films, 125
French productions, 81 British films, and 98 Czech
productions. American films made up only 14 percent of the total film showings, but they accounted
for 22 percent of all audiences. Soviet films also
composed 14 percent of all showings, but these
films attracted only 10 percent of the total audience. Faced with these statistics, it is difficult

for a motion picture industry conscious of attendance and profits to cut down on the importation of
popular films.[34]

Other types of communication are also important
in socialist society, but most of those not covered
above appeal to specialized audiences and are not
generally used as tension management devices. Professional journals and semiprofessional or political
reviews are important as foci around which pluralistic interests are aggregated and transmitted to members of specialized publics. In Poland the review
Po Prostu was used by a young group of liberal Party
members to crystallize opposition to the conservative and Stalinist forces within the Party. Once
the review was labelled as an opposition organ, it
was harassed by the Party and forced out of print.
The role it played in crystallizing opposition is
illustrative of the function journals can play;
their contents should also be closely analyzed as a
key to future trends in socialist society.[35]

MODERNIZATION AND THE MEDIA:
EXPECTATION VS. STABILIZATION

Continued modernization in Poland raises many
questions about the future role of the media in
political-tension management. Modernization means
more resources will be available to elements that
want to dampen expectations. More homes will have
television sets, newspaper readership will increase,
and attendance at movies and plays will undoubtedly
remain high. More highly skilled communications
personnel will be available in the communications
industry, and manipulation of the message will undoubtedly become a much more highly developed art.
Development of sophisticated survey research instruments, designed to ferret out and plot latent resistance to political messages, will aid in directing
appropriate content to the parts of the population
appearing in greatest need. On the other hand, the
nature of the Polish audience is also undergoing
substantial changes concomitant with the escalation
of resources and personnel. The mean level of

education of the audience will continue to rise and
much greater numbers of people will possess at least
some higher education.

The question is one of escalation. The resources that can be invested in the communication
industry to make it more effective in carrying the
controlled message to the citizens are increasing.
At the same time, the more sophisticated urbanites
are becoming more discriminating about accepting information from state-controlled sources. This will
increasingly be the case if socialist citizens are
normal human beings rather than "happy robots."

The information presented in Table 16 illustrates the differences in levels of communication
activity between urban and rural environments.
People in the cities turn to a greater variety of
information sources and can balance opinions with
information received from many directions. The ur-
banite more frequently turns to newspapers, radio,
and television, the more easily managed media, but
also has more opportunities to check his information
with friends in the know, the rumor network, or foreign press and radio.

Grouping data along occupational lines reveals
that white-collar workers much more frequently attend films and read books than their blue-collar
colleagues, in a nation-wide sample, but read newspapers more frequently only in Warsaw.[36] Other
studies show that the biggest differences in making
use of radio and press are based on educational and
rural-urban distinctions.[37]

Turning to more specific questions, education,
occupation, and age are most important in determining reading preferences. Table 17 reveals that
white-collar personnel are much more likely to take
interest in political news and economic affairs and
blue-collar readers show greater interests in accidents and announcements. Table 18 cites age as an
important variable; the data highlight the "politicization" of the middle-aged technocrats and bureaucrats.

TABLE 16

Communicatory Activity
(in percent reporting regular use)

	Urban	Rural
Newspapers	94	65
Movies	92	56
Radio	92	85
Weeklies	91	54
Books	84	51
Visits	80	32
Theatres	71	20
Television	53	15

Source: A. Sicinski, "Spoleczne Uwarunkowania Czytelnictwa Prasy i Sluchania Radia" ["Social Determinants of Press Readership and Radio Listening"] (Warsaw: Osrodek Badania Opinii Publicznej, 1962), p. 14. Data are from a national sample of over 3,000.

TABLE 17

Occupation and Reader Interests
(in percent claiming to be interested)

	White-Collar	Blue-Collar
Political news	76	57
Economic affairs	64	49
Accidents	55	65
City affairs	79	68
Sports	36	36
Announcements	26	33
Humor and satire	71	60

Source: A. Sicinski, "Rola Prasy i Radia w Kulturze Mosowej" ["The Role of the Press and Radio in a Mass Culture"] (Warsaw: Osrodek Badania Opinii Publicznej, 1959), Table 7.

TABLE 18

Age and Reader Interests
(in percent claiming to be interested)

	18-29	30-49	50-
Political news	56	65	60
Economic affairs	42	63	55
Accidents	58	54	51
City affairs	72	80	68
Sports	52	35	20
Announcements	24	28	29
Humor and satire	69	59	52

Source: A. Sicinski, "Funkje Informacyjne Prasy i Radia" ["The Information Functions of the Press and Radio"] (Warsaw: Osrodek Badania Opinii Publicznej, 1959), p. 44.

Interest in political and economic affairs is lowest among the apolitical young, moderate among the old, and greatest in the middle-aged category. The young are most interested in city affairs, the chronicle of accidents, sports, and satire. The middle-aged group pays closest attention to political and economic affairs because of their obvious importance for the upwardly mobile careerist. The profile of youth interests complements the apolitical picture painted in Chapter 3. Only half of the youngest group claims any interest in political affairs.

Education proves to be the best discriminator of reader interest (Table 19). The more highly educated are more interested in all subjects, but differences are especially pronounced in political affairs, economic affairs, and satire. Thus, occupational role, education, and age are important in

determining an interest in political and economic
news. The poorly educated, the young, and the blue-
collar workers are not exposed to the political message as frequently as their better educated counterparts. White-collar, highly educated, middle-aged
persons are much more frequently exposed to this information by choice, but this does not necessarily
mean they will become willing tools of the Party.

TABLE 19

Education and Reader Interests
(in percent claiming to be interested)

| | Attained Educational Level | | |
	Elementary	Secondary	College
Political news	40	61	87
Economic affairs	39	53	80
Accidents	41	68	48
City affairs	50	82	95
Sports	22	40	47
Announcements	21	33	25
Humor and satire	37	68	77

Source: A. Sicinski, "Funkje Informacjne
Prasy i Radia" ["The Information Functions of the
Press and Radio"] (Warsaw: Osrodek Badania Opinii
Publicznej, 1959), p. 45.

Additional data illustrate a tendency for
those who are more frequently exposed to media to
expect more from it and to be more critical of content. Table 20 reveals the relationship between
education and expressed desire to criticize the
press. There is a clear tendency for those

educationally more sophisticated, as measured in attained educational level, to be much more critical
of the press. Similar results are found when white-
collar workers are compared with their blue-collar
counterparts.[38] Statistics broken down according to
age reveal that the young (18-29 years) are most
likely to complain that the press is inadequate.
They are apolitical in their reading tastes but are
also most critical of press content. Other differences due to age are very slight.[39]

TABLE 20

Press Criticism and Education

	Attained Educational Level			
	Elementary	Some Secondary	Secondary	Higher
Frequently	22%	29%	31%	40%
Time to time	51	60	59	58
Never criticize	22	10	9	1
No response	5	1	1	1

Source: A. Sicinski, "Spoleczne Uwarunkowania
Czytelnictwa Prasy i Sluchania Radia" ["Social Determinants of Press Readership and Radio Listening"]
(Warsaw: Osrodek Badania Opinii Publicznej, 1962),
p. 38.

Although these results are far from conclusive,
especially if they are to be used for extrapolation
into the future when the educational level of society will be higher and the occupational structure
changed, they do indicate that those who are more

frequently exposed to the political message develop
immunities. The future may not belong to the media
managers; the struggle is far from over. The growing sophistication of the more highly educated
strata put limits on the political managers' ability to indiscriminately use news management to
dampen expectations.

On the other side of the question, however,
availability of survey research data on reading
habits attests to the diligence with which media
representatives are pressing attempts to make the
impact of the political message more effective. Between 1958 and 1964, at least ten different studies
were carried out by the Public Opinion Research Center dealing directly with problems of media interest.[40] In addition to the media studies, many other
studies designed to gauge public demands as well as
ideological proclivities were carried out under the
auspices of Polish Radio and Television.

Although concrete conclusions about the future
role of the media in Poland are premature, Table 21
gives some insight into the relationship between
communication development and other aspects of modernization (as derived from aggregate analysis in
Chapter 6). The figures illustrate that development
of an integrated communication network accompanies
the creation of a much more sophisticated working
force. The portion of the working force with a higher education increases concomitant with increase in
media saturation, as does the portion of the working force in economic planning, the portion working
in nonagricultural occupation, and expenditures for
education on a per capita basis.

It is clear from this and preceding data that
modernization leads to increasing mass and interpersonal communication, the formation of specialist
groups, possibilities for more frequent contact with
other societies, and higher educational levels. The
rumor network becomes more highly developed and privy
to more accurate information in the more urban setting. In brief, possibilities for the audience to

give a more sophisticated interpretation to media
content increase along with message volume. As the
managed society becomes more modern, the level of
sophistication among the audience can be expected to
rise, thereby forcing the political elite to esca-
late if the media is to continue to be effective in
constructing a picture of reality accepted by the
citizens and acceptable to Party leaders.

TABLE 21

Communication Development and
Highly Correlated Variables
(Pearson Product Moment Coefficients; n = 22)

Retail trade turnover	.99
Portion of work force economists	.95
Portion of population not in agriculture	.90
Portion of Party with higher education	.85
Portion of work force with higher education	.85
Educational expenditures per capita	.81
Intensity of industrial production	.79
Portion of Party joining before 1953	.77
Party organization size	.76
Alcohol consumption	.76

But even in the socialist society, the resources that can be devoted to media management are
limited, especially when the investment reaches the
point where little additional return can be developed by increasing levels of investments.[41] Attempts by the Party to control the information upon

which the socialist citizen makes his judgments
about the world will undoubtedly continue to be an
important part of the tension management program in
the future, although the impact in an increasingly
sophisticated audience is likely to be substantially
diminished.

NOTES

1. L. W. Pye, Communications and Political Development (Princeton, N.J.: Princeton University
Press, 1967), pp. 24-29.

2. K. W. Deutsch, The Nerves of Government
(New York: The Free Press of Glencoe, 1963), p. 152.

3. The factors affecting availability to leaders' messages are suggested in Deutsch, op. cit.,
pp. 146-49.

4. R. R. Fagen, Politics and Communication
(Boston, Mass.: Little, Brown, 1966), p. 80.

5. For deeper analysis of communication as a
political system function, see G. Almond, "Introduction: A Functional Approach to Comparative Politics," The Politics of the Developing Areas, ed.
G. Almond and J. S. Coleman (Princeton, N.J.:
Princeton University Press, 1960), pp. 45-52.

6. G. Almond and G. B. Powell, Jr., Comparative Politics: A Developmental Approach (Boston,
Mass.: Little, Brown, 1966), p. 180.

7. D. Lerner, The Passing of Traditional Society (New York: The Free Press of Glencoe, 1958),
pp. 47-52.

8. For further explication of usage of the
terms "media" and "message," see M. McLuhan, Understanding Media: The Extensions of Man (New York:
New American Library, 1964), Ch. 1.

9. Lerner, op. cit., pp. 52-55.

10. See A. Inkeles and R. Bauer, The Soviet Citizen (New York: Atheneum, 1968), p. 159; F. S. Siebert, T. Peterson, and W. Schramm, Four Theories of the Press (Urbana, Ill.: University of Illinois Press, 1963), Ch. 4; and M. Hopkins, Mass Media in the Soviet Union (New York: Pegasus, 1970).

11. F. C. Barghoorn, Politics in the USSR (Boston, Mass.: Little, Brown, 1966), pp. 158-59.

12. See East Europe, Vol. XVII, No. 8 (1968), pp. 50-51, for a complete list of important figures purged.

13. Inkeles and Bauer, op. cit., Ch. 7, passim.

14. For details of Soviet failures of this type, see Inkeles and Bauer, op. cit., p. 183. In one propaganda film on race, the audience claimed to know it was a fake because the shoes being worn by the blacks were of a superior quality that wouldn't be worn by the poor.

15. See A. Sicinski, "Przywodcy Opinii i Ich Rola w Procesie Obiegu Informacji" ["Opinion Leaders and Their Role in the Process of Circulating Information"] (Warsaw: Osrodek Badania Opinii Publicznej, 1961).

16. Inkeles and Bauer, op. cit., pp. 161-65.

17. Even after the article was printed, people refused to believe it and privately accused the government of withholding information. See "Untrue Rumors," Trybuna Ludu, No. 331, November 30, 1966.

18. For Soviet comparisons, see Inkeles and Bauer, op. cit., p. 163.

19. A. Sicinski, "Funkje Informacyjne Prasy i Radia" ["The Information Functions of the Press and Radio"] (Warsaw: Osrodek Badania Opinii Publicznej, 1959), p. 41.

20. Forty-five percent would turn to others,
44 percent to newspapers, and 41 percent to radio.
No other sources were frequently mentioned. A.
Sicinski, "Zasieg i Prestiz Informacji Gospodarczej
Prasy i Radia" ["Range and Prestige of Economic In-
formation in the Press and on Radio"] (Warsaw:
Osrodek Badania Opinii Publicznej, 1960), p. 17.
The sample consisted of 734 representative inhabi-
tants of Warsaw.

21. Sicinski, "Funkje Informacyjne Prasy i
Radia," p. 38; "Rola Prasy i Radia w Kulturze
Masowej" ["The Role of the Press and Radio in a
Mass Culture"] (Warsaw: Osrodek Badania Opinii
Publicznej, 1959), Tables 5 and 6. Sample consisted
of 1,800 city dwellers throughout Poland selected by
representative quota methods.

22. Sicinski, "Funkje Informacyjne Prasy i
Radia," p. 48.

23. Sicinski, "Rola Prasy i Radia w Kulturze,"
p. 6.

24. T. Kupis, Zawod Dziennikarza w Polsce
Ludowej (Warsaw: Ksiazka i Wiedza, 1966), p. 97.

25. Ibid., pp. 93, 116.

26. Ibid., pp. 101-4.

27. Ibid., p. 107.

28. "Kidnapping in Sports," Sztandar Ludu,
No. 73, March 28, 1967.

29. See Express Wieczorny, No. 302, December
20, 1966.

30. Sicinski, "Rola Prasy i Radia w Kulturze
Masowej," pp. 11-13.

31. Ibid., p. 11.

32. _Ibid._, p. 12.

33. _Rocznik Statystyczny_ (Warsaw: Glowny
Urzad Statystyczny, 1966), pp. 461-62.

34. _Ibid._, p. 460.

35. For more details, see G. Ionescu, _The
Politics of the European Communist States_ (New
York: Frederick A. Praeger, Inc., 1967), pp. 209-15.

36. Sicinski, "Rola Prasy i Radia w Kulturze
Masowej," pp. 20-26.

37. A. Sicinski, "Spoleczne Uwarunkowania
Czytelnictwa Prasy i Sluchania Radia" ["Social Determinants of Press Readership and Radio Listening"]
(Warsaw: Osrodek Badania Opinii Publicznej, 1962),
p. 32.

38. Sicinski, "Rola Prasy i Radia w Kulturze
Masowej," p. 13.

39. Sicinski, "Funkje Informacyjne Prasy i
Radia," p. 56.

40. See listings and brief descriptions in
Spoleczenstwo Polskie w Badaniach Ankietowych
[_Polish Society in Survey Research_] (Warsaw:
Polskiej Akademii Nauk, 1966), pp. 35-42.

41. See "Prasa and the Press," _Zycie Warszawa_,
No. 102, May 1, 1967.

6

**MODERNIZATION
AND TENSION
MANAGEMENT:
THE POLISH
DILEMMA**

Much of the available survey data relating to modernization and political-tension management has been analyzed in previous chapters. Here the emphasis shifts to aggregate data which also provides an interesting statistical portrait of modernization in contemporary Polish society. Industrialization, the core of the modernization process, is a goal continually pressed by the leadership of the Polish United Workers' Party. Industrial development is a key validator of governmental performance in Poland with the great emphasis on increasing material abundance. Industrialization leads to many changes in the economic, social, and political structure of society, many of which have been discussed in preceding chapters. These changes are all closely interrelated, and it is their relationship to aspects of political development and political-tension management that is of interest here. The theoretical discussion of modernization and politics in Chapter 2 provides the general framework for analyzing change in Polish society. This chapter presents empirical data in support of some propositions and rejection of others.

It is useful to conceive of a continuum of the countries of the world ranked according to the

degree of citizen mobilization attained by central
leadership. At the one end of the continuum are
found the industrial societies such as the United
States where most of society has been transformed
and citizens are directly involved in the central
political and economic systems. In these societies
the social structure is differentiated and the political system is usually egalitarian and stable.[1]
In the middle of this continuum are the nations in
which mobilization and industrialization are taking
place most rapidly. The social structure is in
flux as expectations increase and the types of political systems here are mixed.

Speaking of such a modernization continuum permits clarification of the concepts commonly used in
discussing societal transformation. Industrialization acts as a catalyst for changes in residence
patterns, a rise in education and literacy, attention to the mass and cultural media, increase in
societal wealth, and increasing participation in
politics. Together these form the core of the modernization process. Even in the most industrialized
countries, a large portion of the population lives
outside the direct influence of the central political authorities. Modernization refers to the movement along this continuum from the nonpenetrated
toward the mobilized end. The more modern societies
fall at the penetrated or mobilized end, and all nations are moving in the direction of greater mobilization by the political elite. Socioeconomic development and social mobilization refer to the increasing involvement of citizens with the central political and economic systems.

There is no reason to restrict use of such developmental concepts to descriptions of differences
among nation-states. Because of the peculiar problems of data collection in Poland, it is useful to
conceive of Poland's administrative units arrayed
along a similar modernization continuum.[2] Developmental data are available for seventeen Polish
"voivodships" ("states") and five separate urban
areas, permitting each of these units to be arrayed

along the continuum according to its level of mobilization relative to the other units.* The Polish
continuum ranges from the highly complex and mobilized society exemplified by Warsaw on the one end
to the simple, nonpoliticized agrarian regions represented by the Bialystock or Rzeszow voivodships
on the other.

Use of this type of model permits the aggregation of data according to administrative unit and
taken together with the preceding data permits a
summary description of modernization and its meaning in Poland. The use of quantitative data combined with survey research results aggregated by administrative unit help serve as a check on earlier
suppositions. The position of each Polish unit
along the dimensions of a modernization continuum
indicates the extent of societal mobilization and
side effects in each unit under consideration. In
the most modern units, indications of the effects
of socialist industrialization should be found.
The less modern units provide a portrait of the society yet to be mobilized by the political managers.

The type and quality of data available for
analysis is somewhat limited. Aggregate socioeconomic data are meticulously collected in the centralized economies because of their important implications for economic planning. Thus, raw industrial and sociocultural data provided by the Central
Statistical Agency (GUS) are of good quality. The
range of questions answered by these data is limited,
however, and other agencies are not so exacting in
data collection. Various central publications in
addition to the <u>Statistical Yearbook</u> are helpful,
and Party statistics--dated and not readily available--fill some gaps. Unfortunately the available
Party statistics are not broken down in the same

----

*The five urban areas treated as separate
states in data collection are the cities of Warsaw,
Lodz, Krakow, Wroclaw, and Poznan. The other units
used in analysis are the seventeen regular Polish
voivodships.

manner as the others and best estimates must be
made to use some of the data. The Party combines
three city units with their surrounding voivodships
and thus gives membership data for only nineteen
units. Secondary analysis of data, found in a more
recent study of foreign affairs attitudes among the
Polish population, provides additional data when
broken down according to administrative unit.[3]

This type of aggregate data analysis using
figures from several sources is far from ideal.
Especially in Poland, where administrative lines do
not always coincide with cultural or socioeconomic
regions, these types of data must be treated with
caution.[4] The study of socialist society presents
special problems, however, and a combination of
these data with the opinion studies examined in
previous chapters makes discovered relationships
much more meaningful. Although the range of questions asked and the type of aggregate data available necessarily restrict conclusions, we know so
little about the modernization of socialist societies that any type of hard data is preferable to
the speculation that has previously characterized
discussions of socialist modernization.

SOCIALIST MODERNIZATION:
TRADITIONAL CONCEPTS

Within these limits and with appropriate
caveats in mind, forty-five variables theoretically
related to aspects of modernization and political
development have been collected to test generalizations previously made. The core of modernization
is the change in the economic structure of society
referred to as industrialization. The increasingly
complex division of labor in society leads to
changes in the occupational and social structure as
a larger proportion of the citizenry moves to urban
areas. The need for specialists and technocrats increases the general level of education as well as
the portion of the work force directly involved in
planning activities. Consciousness of numbers and

functional importance, especially among white-collar industrial workers, aided by organization in the factories, is related to an increase in expectations by all segments of the industrial labor force. The five variables in Table 22 have been selected as indicators of the level of industrialization in each unit.

TABLE 22

Correlations: Indicators of Industrialization
(Pearson Product Moment Correlations; n = 22)

	2	3	4	5
Portion of population in the industrial work force	.93	.80	.67	.73
Industrial production per capita		.69	.54	.66
Portion not in agricultural occupation			.89	.91
Employees with higher education				.94
Portion of labor force in economic planning				

Sources: Rocznik Statystyczny (Warsaw: Glowny Urzad Statystyczny, 1966), pp. 19, 35, 146; Poziom Wyksztalcenia Zatrudnionych w Gospodarce Uspolecznionej w 1964 (Warsaw: Glowny Urzad Statystyczny, 1966), p. 10; Z. Grzelak, M. Roszkowska, J. Kluczynski, Z Badan nad Losami Absolmentow (Warsaw: Panstwowe Wydawnictwo Naukowe, 1966), p. 51.

Inspection of the small matrix reveals that selected indicators of industrialization are closely related in Polish society. As expected, the industrial productivity of a unit is related to the

portion of the population in the industrial work
force. Both in turn are tied to a smaller portion
of available labor force engaging in agricultural
occupations. Two additional measures, proportion
of economists in the work force and the proportion
of employees with higher educations, are also closely related to the increasing industrial complexity
of a unit. All the measures combined are indicative
of unit differences in the complexity of the industrial establishment. The increasing difficulty of
industrial roles played by the technocrats, as well
as the increasing class consciousness of the blue-
collar workers, indicate changes in citizen expectations. Industrialization should be the core of
many other related changes in the modernization
process including educational development, urbanization, growth of mass communications, and the emergence of united interest groups.

One unfortunate aspect of the mobilization of
society is the social dislocation that accompanies
the movement of large numbers of people from their
more traditional environments to the urban areas
during early stages. Measured by a variety of indicators including general criminality, juvenile delinquency, speculation, divorce, alcoholism, and
arson, social dislocation is both a reflection of
dissatisfaction with the rapidity of the transition
from rural to urban society as well as an indicator
of general social unrest (Table 23). In contrast
to Western sociological explanations for social
dislocation, the Party in Poland has developed some
of its own. Any indications of criminal activity
are "caused by backward segments of the population
that have not yet accepted the norms of socialism."
Political demonstrations and serious criminal acts
have been blamed on maladjusted Zionist cosmopoli-
tans and the lax discipline of youth. Little note
is taken of the possibility that social dislocation
is part of the penalty that must be paid for rapid
industrialization or that it is related to frustrations of living in an increasingly modern society
that rigidly restricts opportunities for personal
initiative and advancement.[5]

TABLE 23

Social Dislocation
(Pearson Product Moment Correlations; n = 22)

	2	3	4	5	6
Criminal offenses	.30	.71	.63	.65	-.28
Speculation offenses		.06	.60	.73	.23
Juvenile delinquency			.43	.29	-.40
Divorce				.83	.03
Alcohol consumption					-.01
Arson					

Sources: Rocznik Statystyczny (Warsaw: Glowny Urzad Statystyczny, 1966), pp. 50, 399, 548, 555; Spozycie Alkoholu w Polsce (Warsaw: Glowny Urzad Statystyczny, 1966), p. 19.

The correlations indicate that social dislocation is not quite the unidimensional concept at
first proposed. Arson is not significantly related
to any of the other indicators of social problems.
Speculation also seems to be a specialized type of
crime with a close relationship to alcoholism and
divorce rather than to more general measures of
criminality or juvenile delinquency. When discussing social dislocation further, arson is discarded
as an indicator and the special relationship of
speculation to the rest of the variables must be
kept in mind.

Just as social dislocation is a physical manifestation of discontent, social and economic dissatisfaction are the attitudinal components of
stress and tension. Dissatisfaction should not be

strongest in the least mobilized sections of society, but should be more closely linked to the revolution of rising expectations accompanying industrialization. Before citizens become dissatisfied
with existing social or economic conditions, it is
essential that they know what is available to others.
Feelings of deprivation are relative to an individual's reference group, and one of the most important
aspects of modernization is the widening of frames
of reference from the immediate village environment
to the entire society. The challenge modernization
presents to political leadership in all countries
is controlling the introduction of new wants and demands which keep leaping ahead of decision-makers'
ability to produce.

The first four indicators in Table 24 are derived from raw data collected by the Public Opinion
Research Center in Warsaw representing percentage
figures from the sample questioned. Dissatisfaction
is envisioned as a unified concept so that dissatisfaction with economic conditions should be related
to similar complaints about human behavior in general and political institutions, and even to psycho-
somatic complaints about health. If this is the
case, data should clarify the nature of this "halo
effect" by showing a close relationship between all
types of satisfaction or dissatisfaction, as the
case may be. An additional indicator, employment
turnover, is also included as potentially part of a
satisfaction-dissatisfaction cluster. It is reasonable to expect economic dissatisfaction to be reflected in frequent changing of jobs. One of the
major economic problems in socialist society is the
tremendous turnover of personnel resulting from disenchantment with available opportunities. In some
voivodships the turnover figure approaches three of
every ten employees annually.

The coefficients reveal that the indicators of
satisfaction cluster fairly well considering the
ecological problems of aggregating survey research

TABLE 24

Social Dissatisfaction
(Pearson Product Moment Correlations; n = 22)

	2	3	4	5
With salary	.36	.49	.45	.06
With behavior		.76	.53	-.19
With youth's behavior			.65	-.17
With health				.65
Employment turnover				

Sources: A. Sicinski, "Kraj, Swiat, Clowiek" (Warsaw: Osrodek Badania Opinii Publicznej, 1965); Rocznik Statystyczny (Warsaw: Glowny Urzad Statystyczny, 1966), p. 73.

data in this manner.* Dissatisfaction with the behavior of the younger generation forms the core of social discontent followed by dissatisfaction with health and dissatisfaction with human behavior in general. Salary dissatisfaction is much more peripheral. Most surprisingly, employment turnover correlates only with dissatisfaction with health and therefore is dropped from consideration as indicative of social dissatisfaction. Perhaps it is due simply to the generally high level of turnover in socialist society and is such a universal phenomenon that all relationships of significance are washed out.

----

*These types of correlations are undoubtedly artificially low because of problems of aggregation across voivodships instead of using individuals. Much of the sharpness of the relationship is undoubtedly lost by using this technique, but getting cooperation in even this type of analysis was most difficult.

Integrative message exchange refers to the
rapidity with which social and political ideas and
messages circulate through society.[6] Closely related to industrialization and social mobilization,
it is representative of elite ability to mobilize
society in times of crisis. In socialist society
integrative message exchange represents potential
ability to mobilize in pursuit of goals because, as
mentioned in Chapter 5, it is also important that
citizens learn to trust official messages that are
circulated. Increasing social communication is one
of the causes as well as effects of industrialization. It is a requisite for continuing development
of the complex social organization and is the by-
product of continuing urbanization with its increasing interpersonal and mediated contacts.

In the less developed units, the rural residence patterns and the isolated nature of the productive process restrict communication and the flow
of social and political ideas, economic demands,
and political ideologies. In urban Warsaw, on the
other hand, face-to-face communication still acts
as a supplement to the state press, but it is generally based on more accurate information which
travels much more quickly to all segments of society. One of the more important side effects of being linked into the urban communication network is
that the individuals involved gain a more accurate
picture of the thoughts and feelings of their fellow citizens. Table 25 contains six measures selected for relevance to integrative message exchange. Population density measures physical pro-
pinquity and is closely related to all the urbanization aspects of modernization. Newspaper sales,
radio receivers, and television receivers measured
on a per capita basis index mass media saturation.
Movie and theatre attendance are indicative of a
type of social communication. The power of these
latter media was emphasized by student demonstrations in 1968, which were partially sparked by con-
troversy over a line in a play that the authorities
felt was too potent for public consumption.

TABLE 25

Integrative Message Exchange
(Pearson Product Moment Correlations; n = 22)

	2	3	4	5	6
Population density	.85	.86	.81	.66	.85
Newspaper sales		.95	.91	.80	.95
Radio subscribers			.95	.71	.89
TV receivers				.74	.84
Movie attendance					.85
Theatrical and musical attendance					

Sources: Rocznik Statystyczny (Warsaw: Glowny
Urzad Statystyczny, 1966), pp. 15, 403, 452, 463;
20 Lat Kultury w Polsce Ludowej (Warsaw: Glowny
Urzad Statystyczny, 1966), pp. 63-64, 69.

According to Table 25, the indicators of integrative message exchange are all very highly correlated, indicating that this is one of the more pure-
ly definable aspects of the modernization process
in Polish society. Where population is densely
clustered around centers of industrialization, there
is also heavy saturation with the mass media and
heavy attendance at theatres and films. The development of one component of integrative message exchange implies the development of all others. The
only possible exception is movie attendance, which
seems less closely related to the core concept than
the other indicators. Perhaps this indicates the
role of movies as a mobilization device in Poland
inasmuch as attendance is least closely related to
population density.

The next grouping of variables (Table 26) represents an attempt to measure the rapidity of the transformation of society in each unit. Increases in industrial production and employment are indicative of the migration of large numbers of people lured to the city by promises of jobs, material benefits, and a more interesting life. The society being transformed is that in which social dislocation and dissatisfaction should be strongest according to generally accepted notions of social change.

TABLE 26

Social Transformation
(Pearson Product Moment Correlations; n = 22)

	2	3
Internal population movements	.32	.09
Industrial employment increase		.78
Industrial production increase		

Source: Rocznik Statystyczny (Warsaw: Glowny Urzad Statystyczny, 1966), pp. 59, 119, 146.

Logically and empirically, increases in industrial production are accompanied by increases in industrial employment. The high correlation between the two variables as well as subsequent analysis indicate that these increases are inseparable indicators of industrial activity; for this reason, industrial employment increase has been retained as the indicator of industrial expansion and production increase is dropped from further consideration. The measure of migration used does not correlate extremely well with industrial employment increase. This is undoubtedly the result of an early decision to define mobility both in terms of out- and in-migration. Although this more precisely defines

what is meant by transition, the inclusion of all
migration statistics lessens relationships between
industrial development and population mobility as
industrialization is closely connected with in-
migration. With these caveats in mind, the measure
of social transformation used below is a combination
of industrial employment increase and measures of
population mobility both in and out of an administrative unit. Hopefully this concept best measures
the heart of the social transformation idea, which
is that of a society in flux.

   Turning to more political indicators, one of
the most important aspects of modernization is the
increasing quantity of material benefits available
for distribution to citizens. An intelligent political leadership uses the distribution of benefits and social privileges to build supports in the
appropriate segments of society. In socialist society there are theoretically no partisan pressures
influencing the allocation of resources. It is obvious that this ideal is never approximated in reality, but to check for these demands and responses
requires indicators that are especially difficult
to find. Inasmuch as administrative areas in Poland
are represented by Party organizations with varying
degrees of power and influence, if there is a systematic distribution of demands as well as benefits
it should show up in aggregate indicators of demand
and response (Table 27).

   It is not easy to pick valid indicators of political responsiveness for a society in which any
political bargaining that takes place is unknown to
outside observers. Obviously there is much lobby-
ing in making investment plans and providing for
the distribution of tasks and benefits in the extended plans, but difficulties in determining what
objective nonpartisan needs of each area might be
limit the utility of certain types of response indicators. Per capita expenditures on education are
one measure of Party willingness to invest in the
young. Investment in education is very great in
Poland as the war-weary older generation seeks to

provide benefits for the young that have been denied in the past. A good educational system is one
of the firmest political demands.

TABLE 27

Political Response
(Pearson Product Moment Correlations; n = 22)

	2	3	4	5
Retail outlet density	.41	.46	.12	.27
Educational expenditures		.74	.36	.77
Wage increases			.35	.70
Wage levels				.76
Retail trade turnover				

Source: Rocznik Statystyczny (Warsaw: Glowny
Urzad Statystyczny, 1966), pp. 337, 342, 501, 528.

More common indicators of demand and response
are represented by average yearly wage increases as
well as average salaries in the socialized economy.
Retail trade turnover and retail outlet density
have also been included. The availability of consumer goods is one of the sore points in the socialist society; citizens wish to modify the current
heavy emphasis on capital goods. Even though salaries may be high, if there are few items to pur-
chase money cannot be sensibly spent. Similarly,
anyone who has spent long hours standing in line in
the freezing rain realizes the importance of response in the form of opening new retail outlets of
all types.

The figures indicate that political response is
a relevant concept for discussion. Wage increases

form the core of responsiveness with educational
expenditures and retail trade sales following closely behind. Absolute level of wages, on the other
hand, is a much weaker indicator of demand and response than wage increases. The density of population per retail outlet does not appear closely related to the rest of the indicators and has been
dropped from subsequent analysis. The correlations
within the matrix are far from perfect, but given
the nature of the data available and the complex
problem of conceptualizing political demands and responsiveness in socialist society, they indicate
that demands and responses are far from random.
Those areas receiving the greatest increases in
wages also have the highest wage levels, receive
the largest per capita investment in educational
facilities, and have the largest turnover in consumer goods.

POLITICS: STRUCTURE AND ACTIVITY

The theoretical relationship between modernization and aspects of political development were outlined in Chapter 2. In order to test the relevance
of the model developed there for the socialist society, several indicators of a political nature
have been included in this analysis.

Education, occupation, age, and date a member
joined the Party are all political variables that
should be related to the changing occupational
structure of society. There should also be close
relationships among these indicators as white-
collar Party units could be expected to be older on
the average and more conservative in outlook, having joined during the Stalinist period. The correlations reveal that there is some internal cohesion
within this group with closest relationships being
between blue-collar occupation and levels of education among Party members and date members joined
the Party and their average age (Table 28). Lesser
relationships are observed among the other indicators.

TABLE 28

Party Educational and Occupational Structure
(Pearson Product Moment Correlations; n = 22)

	2	3	4
Blue-collar membership	.89	-.06	-.45
Less than higher education		-.38	-.70
Membership over forty			.82
Membership pre-1953			

Source: PZPR w 1961 (Warsaw: Polish United
Workers' Party, 1962) (circulation restricted to
Party use).

Development of interest in political affairs
is another aspect of politicization that in Western
experience has been associated with modernization.
Table 29 is composed of five response items to the
survey questionnaire plus a measure of readership
of Polityka, an influential political weekly with
national circulation. Readership of Polityka is indicative of an interest in political events analogous to reading The New York Times in the United
States. Interest in affairs of the Sejm and perceived political efficacy in influencing leadership
behavior measure interest in and feelings of ability to influence domestic politics. Interest in
African independence struggles is a measure of interest in an ideological issue that received wide
press coverage at the time of the survey. Interest
in the British elections and interest in disarmament
negotiations that were taking place at the time of
the study probe respondent attention to international affairs.

The working assumption is that politicization
is a unidimensional concept reflected in rising

interest in both domestic and foreign affairs, readership of political journals, and growing feelings
of ability to influence the Party leadership. This
assumption is destroyed by the correlations in Table
29. They are much too low to substantiate the use
of political interest as a workable concept in discussing political development in Polish society.
Unlike the examples Western modernization provides,
Polish society is not characterized by a unidimensional increase of interest in political affairs.
Interest in the affairs of the Sejm is only slightly
related to interest in the British elections or with
readership of Polityka. Feelings of political efficacy are randomly distributed and are closely related only to interest in disarmament. The apparently random distribution of political efficacy is
extremely puzzling because the original data show
that the percentage of the sample that considers its
participation efficacious varies from a high of 63
percent in the Olstyn and Kielce voivodships to a
meagre 30 percent in the Koszalin voivodship. The
mechanism that leads to the development of efficacious feelings remains mysterious.

TABLE 29

Political Interest
(Pearson Product Moment Correlations; n = 22)

	2	3	4	5	6
Interest in African independence	-.17	.36	.43	.36	-.32
No interest in British elections		.05	-.20	-.17	-.10
In the disarmament negotiations			.36	.55	-.15
In the Sejm				.26	-.32
Perceived political efficacy					.02
Polityka readership					

Sources: Secondary analysis of A. Sicinski,
"Kraj, Swiat, Clowiek" (Warsaw: Osrodek Badania
Opinii Publicznej, 1965); "They're Reading Us,"
Polityka, No. 9, March 4, 1967).

The final collection of political variables is hopefully indicative of political activity (Table 30). Intense politicization is theoretically one of the important aspects of modernization. The political party acts as a mobilization device and helps to bring the citizen into contact with the national unit. It also aggregates interests during the early stages of industrial transformation. Unfortunately only data for the Polish United Workers' Party are available and analysis must proceed without comparable figures for the United Peasant Party and the Social Democrats. This is not deeply disturbing as the Workers' Party is clearly recognized as the leading and most important political force. In addition, a previous study on political mobilization has revealed that the three parties do not compete with each other in Poland. Where membership in the PUWP is high, it is accompanied by high membership in the Peasant Party and in the Social Democratic Party.[7]

TABLE 30

Political Activity
(Pearson Product Moment Correlations; n = 22)

	2	3	4	5
Membership increase	-.04	-.21	-.15	.06
Social acts		.02	.03	.08
Basic organization size			.64	.20
Proportion of citizens in Party				.22
Proportion in youth organizations				

Sources: PZPR w 1961 (Warsaw: Polish United Workers' Party, 1962) (circulation restricted to Party use); Czyny Spoleczne w PRL (Glowny Urzad Statystyczny, 1966), pp. 53, 70.

Social acts are a measure of voluntary contributions in money and labor to social projects. Similar to self-help programs, they represent one type of political and social mobilization. If the PUWP is truly the leading force in society, one would expect that the units having high PUWP membership would also have the highest per capita social acts. Size of the basic organizations is an indication of the depth of Party support as is the portion of eligible adults in each unit who are members of the Party. Membership in youth organizations on a percentage basis is a similar indicator of political mobilization and activity.

The data in Table 30 reveal that political activity in Poland is not unified; there is only one significant correlation in the entire matrix--between the proportion of citizens in the Party and the size of basic organizations. High Party membership does not imply high membership in youth groups or support of social acts. Growth of Party membership, although only measured over a brief span of time, is not significantly related to any other type of political activity. Where Party membership is already large, there are indications that the membership drives have tapered off perhaps as a hypothetical quota has been filled. The large established Party is not recruiting, devotes little attention to youth affairs, and does not direct participation in social acts.

In summary, most of the concepts used in discussing political and social development in Western societies are useful in discussing modernization in socialist society. Conventional indicators of industrialization, social dislocation, integrative message exchange, social mobilization, social satisfaction, and political response all cluster well enough to indicate that these concepts can successfully be used in describing the socialist transition. The political processes in socialist society, however, assume an unexpected structure. Political interest and activity are not unidimensional phenomena in the socialist transition. In an attempt to find some identifiable dimensions of political

activity, most of the variables defined as political have been regrouped and recorrelated.*

Inspection of this summary matrix yields two
clusters that make theoretical sense in describing
dimensions of political change. One cluster anchors
on what might be called proletarianism (Table 31).
The proletarian party structures are composed of
blue-collar workers and peasants, the level of member education is low, political sophistication as
represented by reading Polityka is very low, and interest in ideological issues as indexed by concern
with African independence struggles is high. This
is contrasted with the nonproletarian units in which
a good portion of Party members work in white-collar
occupations, as many as one in five Party members
have at least some higher education, there is little
concern with the African independence struggle, and
greater political sophistication among Party members
as indicated by heavy reading of Polityka.

TABLE 31

Party Proletarianism
(Pearson Product Moment Correlations; n = 22)

	2	3	4
Blue-collar membership	.89	.57	-.76
Less than higher education		.56	-.83
Interest in African independence struggle			-.35
Polityka readership			

*The size of this correlation matrix precludes
its publication here.

    A second empirical grouping of variables is
indicative of what can best be described as Party
conservatism (Table 32). The younger the members
in an administrative unit the less the proportion
of members remaining that entered the Party during
the Stalinist period. The younger and less "Stalinist" Party organizations are found where membership
figures are not high in proportion to population
and where basic Party units are small. In Party organizations where the membership is high and the
units are large, the average Party member is old
and a good portion of the membership is left over
from a more conservative era. It would seem that
having a high proportion of the population in the
Party is not really indicative of ideological fervor, but more closely related to conservative stabilization. Large Party membership figures mean
very large primary organizations. These organizations are dominated by old men who were more often
than not recruited into the Party during Stalinist
days and have remained ever since.

TABLE 32

Party Conservatism
(Pearson Product Moment Correlations; n = 22)

	2	3	4
Portion over forty	.82	.68	.64
Joined before 1953		.69	.65
Large basic organization			.64
Large Party membership			

    Along with these clarifications in political
structure and activity, the other refined concepts
permit a more accurate examination of socialist
modernization. Using the indicators for each of

the voivodships and city units, correlations have
been computed in an effort to ascertain dimensions
of modernization in contemporary Poland.

Table 33 reveals correlations among these selected dimensions of socialist modernization. Industrialization is virtually synonymous with increasing
integrative message exchange in society. Citizens
in an industrial environment have a much easier time
communicating and develop consciousness of their similarities and common problems. There also seems to
be a very clear political response accompanying industrialization. Response in the form of increasing
consumer goods, wage increases, and educational expenditures is forthcoming in the industrialized
units where one would predict heaviest demands from
the more expectant strata. There is no way to demonstrate whether this type of response is also linked
to responses to demands for increasing political participation which also should be heavy in industrial
areas.

TABLE 33

Socialist Modernization
(Pearson Product Moment Correlations; n = 22)

	2	3	4	5	6	7	8
Social dis- location	.50	.77	.73	-.29	.70	.51	-.79
Social dis- content		.50	.47	-.38	.56	.27	-.67
Integrative mes- sage exchange			.94	-.56	.95	.80	-.80
Political re- sponsiveness				-.45	.92	.72	-.74
Social trans- formation					-.67	-.71	.38
Industrialization						.80	-.78
Party conservatism							-.50
Party proletarianism							

Turning to other political concomitants of industrialization, the Party composition changes in
response to industrialization. The Party is shaped
by its environment, and where there are greater numbers of highly educated white-collar personnel this
is reflected in declining Party proletarianism.
The industrial Party is not the Party of the proletariat, but rather increasingly is the Party of the
specialists, undoubtedly seeking self-advancement.
There is little interest in ideology in the nonproletarian Party as the increasingly sophisticated
personnel regard ideological fervor as dispensable
and concentrate on more utilitarian aspects of politics. The industrial environment also supports a
more conservative Party organization. The members
are caught up in increasingly large and impersonal
local units, and members are older and were recruited
when the Party was more hierarchical and monolithic.
By contrast, the nonindustrial units support a more
proletarian Party with a young, small, and nonconservative membership.

Lesser but still significant correlations exist between industrialization and social dislocation, social discontent, and social transformation.
As the level of achieved industrialization increases,
measures of social transformation decline, indicating that transformation efforts are most intense in
the less modern areas and that this mobilization has
all but stopped in big urban areas. Indicators of
social dislocation are also closely linked to industrialization indicating that the modern industrial
socialist society is marked by frequent lapses in
social consciousness. The less mobilized areas are
characterized by less social dislocation, perhaps
indicating the strength of the old social fabric
and moral system. Social discontent exhibits the
weakest relationship with industrialization although
it is still significant. Thus, industrialization
and discontent are related in a U-shaped curve.
There is little evidence of discontent in the most
rural and the most urban areas, and it is heaviest
in the areas in transition.

Aside from the relationship between the variables and industrialization, there are other relationships of interest in the matrix. Social dislocation is highly correlated with integrative message exchange, indicating the possibility that feelings of relative deprivation engendered by close communicatory contact and the media are an important intervening variable in the relationship between modernization and dislocation. Party proletarianism is negatively related to social dislocation. Where the Party is basically blue-collar and not highly educated, there is little social dislocation. Again, however, these variables only modify the underlying relationship between industrialization and the transformation of all aspects of society.

EMPIRICAL ANALYSIS OF THE DATA

The structure imposed in the above analysis might justifiably leave one uneasy in light of political claims that the nature of the socialist transformation of society is significantly different from Western cases. Imposition of traditional concepts on the original indicators could very well restrict the findings unnecessarily. It is possible that there are more subtle and hidden relationships in the modernization process in Poland that would escape attention if analysis were so restricted.

An equally useful approach to the ordering of the data is factor analysis. The original collection of forty-five variables has been subjected to principle component factor analysis. The results represent a new approach to the original variables, describing them using a minimum number of dimensions.

Three separate analyses of the data were originally completed to check for consistency and to eliminate unrelated variables. Using the complete set of indicators, ten factors were originally extracted and rotated using an orthogonal rotation

with a varimax criterion. This type of solution
was selected because it results in the construction
of factors that are as nearly as possible distinct
from each other, defines each factor in terms of
the variables with which it is most strongly associated, and tends to produce factors of equal
strength in accounting for the total variance. All
of these were expected characteristics of the developmental data. The first six factors extracted
accounted for 80 percent of the unrotated variances
and the additional four factors added very little
in terms of explained variance or significant variable loadings. A check of the results, combined
with the earlier correlational analysis, led to a
decision to restrict further analysis to thirty-
eight variables and to extract only six factors.

    Two similar factor analyses were accomplished
with the reconstructed collection of variables.
Because of the nature of the units being analyzed,
two separate analyses were performed. The first
was an analysis of the seventeen voivodships exclusive of the city units. The second consisted of
all twenty-two units. In this manner a check was
run to see if the addition of the city units significantly distorted the nature of the factors that
were extracted. The comparisons of loadings for
the two sets of units was most interesting in terms
of shifts for some variables, but the basic factor
structure remained nearly the same for both sets of
units.

    The six factors resulting from the final analy-
sis of twenty-two units accounted for 85 percent of
the unrotated variance. The strongest factor accounted for 28 percent of the explained variance,
the second for 23 percent, and the third for 17
percent. The last three extracted factors accounted for only 32 percent of the explained variance among them and the nature of variable loadings
was such that little additional could be explained
by them. In accordance with theoretical speculation and the nature of the technique adopted,
three strong and interpretable factors emerged dis-
playing a small amount of variable overlap.

The emergent factors are treated both inferentially and descriptively in the following analysis. The clusterings of variables along the isolated dimensions are descriptive of the strongest empirical relationships in the larger correlation matrix. This type of summary is used to modify the conclusions reached in examining the earlier clusters. There is also a temptation to view the data inferentially and regard each of the isolated dimensions as unique aspects of modernization and political development in Poland.

The nature of the isolated factors encourages an interpretation somewhat in keeping with the relationship between modernization and aspects of political development discussed in Chapter 2. The strongest isolated factor seems akin to conservative stabilization (Table 34). The significant dimensions of this component concern the nature of the Party, which runs from the very large, old, fully structured, and conservative organizations on the one extreme to the small, young, loosely organized units with a membership largely recruited since 1953. Industrially there is a big share of output per person, little population movement, little agricultural employment, small increases in industrial employment, and a heavy concentration of planning specialists in the more stabilized units. This is opposed to the small productivity shares, heavy population flux, large agricultural employment, and low percentage of planning specialists in the least stabilized units. A third clear aspect of this factor is indicative of integrative message exchange; the units vary from those with high population density, heavy radio subscription, and high newspaper sales to those with low population density and little contact with the media.

Thus, the units vary from those that would be considered industrially and politically stable to those currently in flux. In the stable units the majority of the members of the Party joined before liberalization, a large portion of the membership is over forty years of age, is highly educated, and

TABLE 34

Industrial and Political Stabilization
(n = 22)

	Loading*
Basic organization size	.90
Population movement	-.81
Production share	.78
Portion of Party over forty	.75
Population density	.73
Radio subscribers	.73
Nonagricultural employment	.71
Industrial employment increase	-.68
Party membership density	.66
Newspaper sales	.65
Wage levels	.63
Party members before 1953	.63
Retail trade sales	.61
Interest in disarmament	-.61
Economist employment	.57
Portion of accounted for variance	28%

*In normal practice, loadings in the neighborhood of .40 are treated as significant. After much consultation with various experts, it was decided that in order to be safe with the extremely small "n" the minimum loading reported is .55.

is employed in white-collar occupations. Because
there is no problem in filling membership rolls,
close supervision is maintained over the admission
of younger members. The individual Party member is
likely to belong to an extremely large basic organization, probably at his place of work, where his
opinions count for very little. Population density
is high and stable and there is heavy mass media
saturation. Industrial productivity is intense and
retail trade sales and salaries are high, indicative of rewards commensurate with industrial output.
In the less stable voivodships the Party structure
is less rigid and exhibits a much younger member-
ship--joining after Stalin's death. There is less
emphasis on industrial production, little media
saturation, and correspondingly low levels of wages
and retail trade turnover. Stabilization represents a tendency common to all units regardless of
their stage of modernization, but the nature of the
highly loaded variables indicates that the more industrialized units are those in which a conservative stabilization is most pronounced.

Remaining close to the theoretical terminology
employed earlier, the second isolated factor might
best be labeled education and rising expectations
(Table 35). Dimensions of significance here are
related to investment in training and education
leading to changes in social and economic expectations. The Party structure ranges from those units
composed of highly educated white-collar workers to
the less educated blue-collar cells. There is a
large educational component--Polityka readership,
higher education, and economist employment are important. Theatre and movie attendance make another
contribution to expectation changes as they are
sources of vicarious experience leading to relative
deprivation and social frustration. Selected aspects of social dislocation form another part of
this factor. Alcoholism, divorce, and general
criminality result from stresses and strains of
rapid changes in expectations in industrial society.

TABLE 35

Education and Rising Expectations

	Loading
Polityka readers	.93
Party with less than higher education	-.80
Blue-collar Party membership	-.77
Economist employment	.67
Divorce	.66
Theatre attendance	.62
Movie attendance	.58
Higher education employment	.58
Party membership before 1953	.57
Alcohol consumption	.57
Retail trade sales	.56
Criminal offenses	.56
Wage levels	.55
Portion of accounted for variance	23%

The extremes of this dimension are denoted by units in which expectations are extremely high, on one hand, and units not characterized by changes in demands on the other. The Party reflects the educational level of the environment as well as the specialists required in the industrial society. Polityka readership, the most highly loaded variable, indicates attempts by young and upwardly mobile technocrats to keep up with political changes.

One unique aspect of this dimension is the role played by movie and theatre attendance. Earlier it was observed that media variables were part of a highly correlated cluster labeled integrative communication. Indications are that the media cluster splits into two factors. Mass media circulation is an aspect of stabilization whereas vicarious media attention represented by attendance at movies and theatrical attractions is related to growth of expectations. The aspects of media usage clustering along the industrial and social stabilization dimension can be taken as representing attention to political messages. The movies and theatres, on the other hand, are associated with increasing expectations as the media and the uncontrollable aspects of the message serve to raise rather than dim expectations.

The third important isolated factor accounts for a smaller portion of variance and might best be labeled mobilization and transformation (Table 36). Some of the variables are representative of the Party's penetration of the periphery; others seem to indicate attempts at political support building. Criminality and juvenile delinquency are traditionally associated with societal transformation and social mobilization. Movie attendance is closely related, and this indicates a role for films in awakening expectations in the more rural areas. Party membership is an important component, a direct indication of the Party role in political penetration.

On the support-building side, political response is indicated by density of retail outlets, educational expenditures, and wage increases. The areas being mobilized are favorably treated by Party leaders. Finally, the negative loading for arson activities indicates that initial mobilization does not lead to hostile actions against state-owned property.

When combined with the analysis in the early part of this chapter, factor analysis yields a fairly clear picture of aspects of modernization

and political development in Poland, at least in
terms of the available material. Interesting information is also provided by variables that were excluded. Seven variables were eliminated from final
consideration after earlier factor analysis--three
because they proved to be exact replications of
other variables and four because they proved irrele-
vant in the analysis. Media saturation as measured
by radio receivers per capita is almost exactly
duplicated by television sets per capita. Thus,
there is no large-scale division of communicatory
labor between radio and television, at least in
terms of ownership of radios and televisions. Similarly, measures of industrial production increases
mirrored indicators of industrial employment increases and the portion of the population in the
industrial work force compared with production intensity also yielded nearly identical results.

TABLE 36

Mobilization and Transformation

	Loading
Juvenile delinquency	.82
Educational expenditures	.79
Arson	-.73
Wage increases	.70
Movie attendance	.67
Criminal offenses	.61
People per retail outlet	-.61
Party membership	.58
Portion of accounted for variance	17%

The four indicators dropped for lack of relevance provide some surprising insights into socialist modernization. An indicator of perceived political efficacy proved almost randomly distributed in
relation to other modernization variables. Speculation led to hypotheses linking industrialization
with increased political response and eventually to
increased feelings of efficacy. On the other hand,
the inverse could also be true. Increasing sophistication of the various strata in the industrial
areas in the face of lack of decision-making decentralization could lead to political cynicism and
discontent. It may be that neither of these hypotheses holds for Polish society, or perhaps both
effects are operating and no conclusions can be
made about the distribution of political efficacy.

Two indicators selected as representing the
distribution of interest in political affairs provide similar peculiar results. Both interest in
the affairs of the Sejm, the official legislative
body, and interest in important British elections,
which were taking place at the time of the sampling,
showed little correlation with any other variables
and loaded significantly on none of the factors.
Employment turnover also correlated with nothing in
the matrix, undoubtedly because it is universally
so high in Poland. Thus, the politically cynical
and uninterested are as likely to be found in the
rural as in more urban areas. This undoubtedly results partially from the fact that these attitudes
result from political experiences and therefore may
not systematically relate to modernization. Interest in legislative affairs is known to be universally low. These peculiar variables indicate that
some aspects of modernization and the politicization of socialist society are less easily explained.

ASPECTS OF POLITICAL DEVELOPMENT

The first step in the transitional process is
the mobilization of peripheral societies by modernizing decision-makers. In Poland the Workers'

Party directs the mobilization process through planning and investment activities. The penetrations
are designed to minimize dislocation, which is prev-
alent in the less planned economies as people rapidly migrate from rural to industrial areas. Through
deliberate planning, decision-makers in socialist
society govern the rate of industrial development
and try to direct it away from the already industrialized areas.

Table 37 displays the eleven units that qualify as mobilized in Poland and the four others that
score high enough on this factor to be considered as
entering the mobilization stage. Those voivodships
with scores of thirteen or less can be regarded as
the sleeping countryside. In those voivodships production is mainly agricultural and the typical citizen lives on a small noncollectivized farm in isolation from the larger society. The Polish United
Workers' Party exists mostly in name only and the
proverbial stories of the difficulties the Party experiences in finding someone to elect as Powiat
(county) first secretary are close to truth. The
basic Party organizations are very small, and meetings are better characterized as neighborhood social
gatherings. In most of these still dormant areas
the typical basic organization has less than fifteen
members. Only 3 or 4 percent of the population be-
longs to the Party as contrasted with 7 or 8 percent
in the more industrial areas.

Life in these areas seems unchanging, especially for the young. There are very few cities of any
size, and even a movie theatre is rare in the most
primitive areas. Life on the small farm is harsh,
and there is little concern with events outside the
immediate environment. Folk Catholicism helps enforce traditional norms and standards of behavior.
This mutation of the Catholic religion consists of
irrational attachments to the outer trappings of
Catholicism with little concern for concrete doctrines. Worship centers around the "Black Madonna"
or other saints who miraculously intercede in
heaven. Although religion is beginning to lose its

tight grip on the young in the cities, a trip through
the villages on a Sunday morning reveals the still
strong role it plays in the countryside. Every
church is surrounded by parked horsecarts from which
peasants descend dressed in their Sunday best.

TABLE 37

Mobilization and Transformation
(in factor scores weighted according to loadings)

Not Mobilized		Social Mobilization		Mobilized	
Bydgoszca	17	Koszalin	22	Poznan (city)	25
Wroclaw	16	Zielona Gora	21	Wroclaw (city)	25
Rzeszow	15	Olstyn	21	Szczecin	25
Poznan	15	Gdansk	20	Lodz (city)	23
Lodz	13	Opole	19	Krakow (city)	23
Katowice	13			Warszawa (city)	23
Warszawa	12				
Bialystok	11				
Kielce	10				
Lublin	10				
Krakow	9				

Mobilization begins with a decision to locate
a large enterprise in a rural area. The construction of the new enterprise is typically accompanied
by the slipshod development of emergency housing
for the expected labor force. New drab apartment

complexes spring up suddenly near the villages and
the migration of labor from the countryside begins.
One of the peculiar features of socialist industrialization is the formation of a special class of
workers, best classified as farmer-laborers. Living on small private farms, these workers leave the
management of the farm in the hands of wives and
make a daily trip to the factory, often as much as
fifteen miles away. These combination workers are
undoubtedly spurred by the difficulties of making
ends meet on the inefficient small farms. This approach to manpower development is efficient in
utilizing untapped labor resources in the countryside, but has the distinct disadvantage that absenteeism is extremely high during the planting and
harvesting season.

     The mobilization of the countryside is accom-
panied by material responses as politicians attempt
to cement peasant allegiance to the Warsaw Government. Increases in wages, expenditures of new educational facilities, and greater numbers of retail
outlets accompany expenditure on new production
facilities. Juvenile delinquency and criminal offenses are substantial in the penetrated areas, and
movie attendance, with its attendant increases in
expectations, is also high. These social dislocation aspects of mobilization are undoubtedly related
to freeing of large numbers of workers and youths
from strictures of the traditional discipline of
family and Church. The factor scores indicate that
the activity represented by mobilization is still
being completed in most urban areas although urban
Warsaw, Lodz, and Krakow as well as the industrial
Katowice voivodship rank lower on the mobilization
factor than on others, indicating that this activity
is of relatively less importance in the most industrialized areas.

     A glance at a Polish map reveals that politi-
cal attention through social mobilization is based
on historical factors. With the exception of the
five large city units, which could be expected to
receive political attention, those areas classified

as in the early stages of mobilization are all areas
recovered from Germany after World War II. These
are areas in which a tremendous shift in population
occurred immediately after the War as large numbers
of Poles, displaced by the Russian incursions into
Poland's eastern territories, settled in the lands
vacated by the retreating Germans. Talking in terms
of objective need for political transformation and
response, it is precisely in these areas that it is
required. Conditions after the War were extremely
bad, the displaced citizens alienated, and demonstration of Polish intent to populate and develop
the area was needed.

Examination of the statistical profiles of the
five voivodships in the early stages of mobilization
reveals that criminality is very high. Four of the
voivodships rank in the top ten in criminality, and
Opole is thirteenth. Discontent as expressed to in-
terviewers is relatively low. It is moderately high
in Gdansk and Olstyn, perhaps predictive of the
riots of December, 1970, but is very low in Koszalin,
Zielona Gora, and Opole. As could be expected, all
these units score very high on measures of political
responsiveness and are right behind the five city
units. The Party structure in the changing areas
reveals most interesting characteristics. Whereas
Party conservatism is significantly negatively correlated with proletarianism for the whole sample of
units (-.50), in these areas the Party structure is
both nonconservative and nonproletarian, a significant departure from the general relationship. The
Party is likely to include a good portion of members
in white-collar occupations (45 percent of membership or more), there is a great interest in _Polityka_,
surprisingly small basic organizations, a very small
proportion of the Party membership over forty (36
percent), and a relatively small segment of the membership that was in the Party before 1953 (50 percent).

This mixture, peculiar to the mobilizing areas,
indicates that perhaps the young Party unit with few
old conservative Party members is the refuge of the

upwardly mobile young technocrats rather than the
bastion of the old guard. One could hypothesize on
the basis of this statistical profile that the
Party units are more responsive to members' demands
during the transition than either before industrialization takes place or after industry has become well
established.

The second aspect of modernization in Poland
is an intense rise in expectations accompanying
structural changes associated with industrial development (Table 38). Eight units rank very high
on the expectation factor and all, with the exception of Katowice, ranked at the top on the mobilization and transformation scale. The four units
judged entering the mobilization stage fall just
below the cutting point on the rising expectations
dimension. Katowice is especially interesting as a
deviant case. It is an industrial area that was
mobilized by modernizing leadership long before
World War II. Silesia has been a highly organized
area and perhaps the aspect of politics that has
been labeled mobilization has now declined to a
minimum in Katowice voivodship.

The rise in expectations and the development
of a new demand structure has been discussed in earlier chapters. The data presented in Tables 35 and
38 serve to statistically reinforce the arguments
made earlier. If not met with appropriate responses,
the rapid increase in expectations can lead to a
variety of social frustrations. Family problems of
increased tension lead to a divorce rate of two
thousand people each year in Warsaw as opposed to
only one-tenth that number in the rural Rzeszow
voivodship. Alcohol consumption increases along
with frustration; twice as much alcohol is consumed
in the units where industrialization has taken hold
than in the less modern units. Getting ahead at
all costs is emphasized in the urban society and is
reflected in the loading for criminal offenses.
Caught in the transition between the more primordial
values of youth and the new norms of the socialist
society, the expectant citizen often doesn't adhere

TABLE 38

Education and Rising Expectations
(in factor scores weighted according to loadings)

Low		High	
Koszalin	19	Warszawa (city)	39
Zielona Gora	18	Krakow (city)	28
Olstyn	18	Wroclaw (city)	27
Wroclaw	18	Lodz (city)	25
Opole	18	Poznan (city)	24
Krakow	17	Szczecin	23
Bydgoszcz	17	Gdansk	23
Warszawa	16	Katowice	22
Bialystok	16		
Lodz	16		
Lublin	16		
Rzeszow	16		
Kielce	16		
Poznan	15		

to any conventional codes of morality, and both un-
reported dishonesty and oficially reported criminality rise.[8]

The ranking of the voivodships indicates that
urbanization is the important element in setting
the stage for expectations. The professional strata
in the cities are most demanding in economic and political expectations and the most difficult for the

Party decision-makers to assuage. The integrative
message exchange structure of the urban areas is
more tightly knit and the reference groups that
help determine levels of expectations are much near-
er at hand. The especially high loadings for theatrical and movie attendance indicate a possible
expectation-raising role for the entertainment industries in the urban setting. The cosmopolitanism
of Warsaw stands out clearly on this dimension--
there is a large gap between Warsaw and the others.

     The third definable aspect of Polish moderniza-
tion seems related to freezing of political access
and attempts to stabilize rising expectations. In
Polish society as well as in the more pluralistic
varieties, there are continual pressures from those
holding power and privilege to stabilize the distribution of each. If the first and second aspects of
modernization are viewed as stages of development
(as suggested in the Guttmann interpretation of the
distribution of the units), they are the stages in
which the revolution of rising expectations is encouraged by political leaders attempting to lure
manpower into new industries and break the population away from local ties.* Social mobilization
creates political and social tensions, but during
early stages the status of politicians remains relatively secure as upwardly mobile citizens are paci-
fied by the benefits of a new life. When the well
appears to run dry in any society, those in positions of power and privilege increasingly recognize
continued social mobility as a zero sum game. Emphasis switches to the management of political tensions and the dampening of expectations among the

---

*A Guttmann distribution or scale refers to the
clear ordering of units along a series of items. In
this case it means that most voivodships scoring above
a cut-off point on stabilization will also be above
cut-off points on education-rising expectations as
well as mobilization. Those in a middle "developmental" state score above a cut-off on education-
rising expectations and mobilization but below the
cut-off for conservative stabilization, etc.

rising strata. This is a process that is always
taking place but which becomes more predominant as
scarcity of opportunity becomes apparent.

The theoretical aspects of the switch from the
revolution of rising expectations to industrial and
political stabilization and the management of political tensions have been discussed earlier. Table
39 reveals the ranking of the Polish units along
this dimension. The movement toward stabilization
is strongest in the urban units. The Katowice
voivodship, which was the only case showing little
mobilization activity along with high expectations,
is the only other unit to fall clearly above the
well-defined cutting point. This is in keeping
with the notion that its long industrial history
indicates that it was mobilized and stabilized well
before the Party-backed modernization began. It is
no secret that one of the main points of friction
between Gomulka and Gierek was a deliberate decision to downplay further economic investment in
Katowice because it was regarded by the Party as an
already suturated investment area.

As a unit begins to stabilize, population migration slows to a crawl although the interenter-
prise mobility of the labor force remains very high.
The Workers' Party reflects the move toward the cementing of privilege as technocrats and white-
collar officials scurry into its ranks to protect
their vital interests. Party membership is much
older and a larger portion joined when the hierarchical principles of control were much more pronounced. The leadership can afford to be increasingly concerned with elevating qualifications for
membership in the Party as greater numbers attempt
to enter. Most members are buried in large organizations where their voices are likely to be muffled
by an oligarchic leadership. The only significant
correlation between political efficacy and another
variable in the analysis was with the average size
of the basic organizations. The larger the average
basic organization size the less the feelings of
political efficacy. As mentioned earlier, there is
heavy investment in tension management activities
indicated by heavy saturation of the mass media.

TABLE 39

Industrial and Political Stabilization

Low		High	
Bydgoszcz	21	Warsaw (city)	33
Gdansk	20	Lodz (city)	31
Opole	20	Poznan (city)	30
Poznan	20	Krakow (city)	30
Lodz	18	Wroclaw (city)	27
Krakow	18	Katowice	26
Wroclaw	18		
Zielona Gora	18		
Szczecin	17		
Kielce	17		
Rzeszow	17		
Koszalin	17		
Warsaw	16		
Olstyn	15		
Lublin	15		
Bialystok	13		

Support by the average citizen for the Party could be expected to be minimal in areas where conservative stabilization becomes most apparent. As tension management increases in the slowing Polish economy, upward social mobility is dampened in the metropolitan areas and attempts are made to minimize discontent. Party leaders try to compensate for the closing of economic opportunities in the urban areas by sending many young specialists to more provincial locales to "serve time" before they are given jobs in the big cities. This method of removing opportunity congestion in the large cities leads to political discontent among those who are shipped to the provinces.

The emphasis on tension management with its resulting citizen dissatisfaction is reflected in extremely high rankings on discontent for all urban areas with only the exception of Poznan. In Warsaw, for example, 77 percent express dissatisfaction with salaries, 97 percent are dissatisfied with the behavior of people, and 50 percent say they are dissatisfied with the state of their health. These figures are duplicated in other urban areas and are exceeded in Krakow. There can be little doubt that this discontent is converted into dissatisfaction with the Workers' Party, held responsible for economic and social progress.

STAGES OF MODERNIZATION

The combined data lend support to an interpretation of socialist modernization in distinct stages similar to propositions theoretically suggested. The six areal units that rank very high on the industrial and political stabilization factor are all among the eight units having a high score on the education and rising expectation dimension. All these units in turn are found among those ranking highest in mobilization. The only exception to this perfect Guttmann arrangement is Katowice, a situation that has been explained in terms of the special historical modernization of this industrial voivodship.

The first stage involves the political and social mobilization of the sleeping countryside and
is followed by large-scale population mobility and
the beginnings of a revolution of rising expectations. Political response is part of the mobilization of society in which industrialization leads to
a change in the occupational structure of the countryside. As might be expected from a nation at an
intermediate level of development, only half of
Poland's administrative units are mobilized in terms
of the definitions used. Indications are that some
of the more industrial areas have passed the peak of
greatest mobilization; Warsaw and Krakow both rank
lower in terms of mobilization than they do on the
second and third factors representing advanced
stages of development.

The second socialist stage of development, only
analytically separated from the first and third, is
distinguished by a marked rise in expectations.
Technocrats and managers expect more in terms of
power, privilege, and prestige in return for their
perceived greater contributions to industrial production. Indications are that the Party responds
economically to these demands but that demands for
increased political power are ignored.

As industrial growth slows in the more advanced
sectors of Poland, the conservative stabilization
tendencies become much stronger as old leading figures struggle to maintain their privileged positions
in the face of the technocrat onslaught. The Party
leadership faces a dilemma. It needs certain of the
young technocrats to keep the economy functioning
but does not want to give up any measure of decisional control. Political-tension management becomes identified with politics in this situation as
the leaders attempt to strike a delicate balance between the exigencies of production, requiring some
broadening of the scope of decision-making, and the
realities of the political struggle. The use of
economic incentives, the mass media, and political
socialization as tension management devices are only
temporary solutions as conservative stabilization is
increasingly linked with high citizen discontent.

The leadership of the Polish United Workers'
Party has in the past reflected the views of the
most conservative elements in the organization.
Those in the Party Central Committee have worked
their way up through the conservative mass Party
organizations and they represent conservative interests. The younger Party units in less important
areas of the country are not well represented in
the Politburo and their role in the Central Committee is minor. It makes more sense to talk about
struggles in the Party being between the conservative, stabilizing representatives of the old style
of politics and the succeeding generations than as
a struggle between factions or cliques. The younger Party members are more aware of the importance
of innovation and pragmatism in making socialist
society work.[9]

If the Polish system is ever to be transformed,
the innovative pressures might very well come from
the areas now in transition. In these areas the
Party has a young, nonconservative membership and
citizen satisfaction seems high. Perhaps the Party
in these areas has a sound participatory base upon
which it can build a secure future. The young members in the mobilizing areas seem to be natural allies for the frustrated technocrats in the cities;
if innovation and change is to take place from
within the Workers' Party this coalition of forces
might well swing the balance.

Recent events have given cause for hope of
changes within the Party. Although the dominant
orientation in the powerful industrial areas and
therefore in the Party hierarchy has been one of
conservatism, the recent demonstrations and resulting shifts in top-level leadership may have provided
the spark necessary to initiate broad political
changes. Only time will tell whether or not the
Gierek regime has enough strength and initiative to
carry out needed reforms in the face of the conservative and partially discredited opposition. If
these reforms are not forthcoming, citizen discontent will undoubtedly increase and the Party will

move even further away from the people it is trying
to manage.[10]

Armed with data from the preceding chapters
and the developmental concepts derived above, some
conclusions about the future of political-tension
management can be attempted. Table 40 reveals
correlations between each of the modernization con-
structs discussed earlier and the dimensions representative of stages of political development. The
correlation coefficients are artificially high in
this case because some of the variables used to
create the concept scores also appear in the variables that produced the factor scores. The variable overlap is not great, however, and a safe
guess is that some of the correlations have been
enhanced by as much as .10.

It is readily apparent that this summary of
relationships also supports the stage thesis of
modernization. The mobilization dimension is most
closely related to the expectation syndrome, which
is the next state of development. Conservative
stabilization, on the other hand, is very closely
related to the expectation dimension, which precedes
it in the modernization process.

Industrialization is the key to the whole process. Industry is modestly correlated with social
mobilization. As the industrial establishment gets
larger, so do expectations. Finally, tendencies
toward stabilization are highly correlated with an
industrial establishment. The increasingly high
correlation coefficients between industrialization
and the three stages of development indicate this
progression.

Integrative message exchange is related to the
stages in a manner similar to industrialization ex-
cept for the fact that it splits into two clear
dimensions. During the period of penetration, the
aspiration-building arm of the media--motion pic-
tures and the theatre--is most important and thus a
fairly high correlation exists between integrative

TABLE 40

The Stages of Modernization
(Pearson Product Moment Correlations; n = 22)

	Mobilization	Expectation	Stabilization
Industrialization	.65	.90	.95
Social dislocation	.69	.84	.63
Social dissatisfaction	.27	.56	.45
Integrative message exchange	.77	.93	.91
Social transformation	-.09	-.44	-.80
Political response	.86	.86	.86
Party proletarianism	-.54	-.94	-.67
Party conservatism	.50	.70	.92
Mobilization	--	.66	.57
Rising expectations	.66	--	.82
Conservative stabilization	.57	.82	--

message exchange and social mobilization. When expectations have increased and conservative stabilization begins, both the aspirational and managerial
aspects of the media are important; this is reflected in the very high correlations between message exchange and the last two stages of Polish
modernization.

Indicators of social transformation, social
dislocation, and social discontent form peculiar
patterns. According to the measures of social
transformation used here, the greatest movement
should be taking place in voivodships in early
stages of mobilization as the mobile labor force
makes its way to the city. The lack of correlation
between transformation and the mobilization dimension is probably due to the fact that most mobility
activity is taking place in the rural units that
are only beginning to be penetrated. It is clear
that social transformation is strongly negatively
related to the other two aspects of political development.

Social dislocation and dissatisfaction are related to the developmental dimensions in different
ways. Criminal activities and other aspects of dislocation are highest where expectations are high.
Correlations are lower both in the mobilization
stage and when expectations have been dampened by
conservative stabilization. Expressed dissatisfaction, on the other hand, seems more randomly distributed in Poland. This perhaps indicates that
the citizens have a variety of grievances that are
not necessarily based on measured aspects of modernization. In the more rural areas dissatisfactions
can be based on religious or traditional grounds
rather than pragmatism. At any rate, expressed
discontent is highest in the voivodships characterized by the revolution of rising expectations. It
is fairly high under stabilized conditions and no
significant correlation is observed in the areas
that are being mobilized.

Turning to more political subjects, the indicators of political responsiveness are equally

related to all three dimensions of modernization.
This indicates that once an area is mobilized political responsiveness in the form of economic distribution begins and is forthcoming through the following stages of development. This reflects the common-
sense notion that once benefits are received it is
extremely difficult to stop providing them. Party
conservatism, an intimate part of conservative stabilization, increases steadily across the three
dimensions. Proletarianism is strangely related to
the modernization process. The Party in nonmobilized
areas is clearly proletarian as the negative correlations between the aspects of political development
and the proletarianism cluster indicate. The most
nonproletarian Party organizations are found in
those units where expectations are strongest.

MODERNIZATION AND POLITICAL-
TENSION MANAGEMENT

At this point some tentative conclusions about
the influence of modernization on Party prospects
for tension management in the future can be ven-
tured. Combining the more subjective secondary
analysis of available information in the early chapters with the aggregate data above yields a rather
unpleasant picture of future political development
in Poland. The Party has committed society to a
continuing program of economic development, but has
neglected to tend to political and social demands
of those upon whose shoulders the burdens of constructing the future socialist society rest. The
obvious tensions since retreat from the liberalization of 1956 indicate that this strategy is sound
in the short run if the maintenance of political
control is the only goal. There are other factors
involved that are every bit as important as maintaining control, however, not the least of which is
maintaining an active orientation toward the continued cultural, social, and economic development
of socialist society.[11]

There is little doubt after examining the data
in the preceding four chapters that industrialization

is synonymous with the formation of interest groups
demanding a greater share of power and more privileges. Although these growing intermediary strata
are becoming more demanding, they are also much
more hesitant to engage in any radical action that
might jeopardize the privileges already gained.
The Party, prior to Gierek, was not willing to take
the lead in expanding its base of support by expanding meaningful political participation. It remains
to be seen if he will initiate the much-needed reforms. One of the results of this stalemate is a
decline in economic and social innovation of the
type that forced Gomulka from office. As industry
continues to develop, pressures for change will increase and tensions will mount between the Party
and citizens.

Although there is every indication that Polish
society is still volatile, a complete overthrow of
the Workers' Party is a most unlikely prospect.
The recent shift in leadership in response to
Gomulka's December economic mistakes could possibly
lead to broad changes, but much depends on the wisdom of top leaders as well as their freedom of action. Yet, the conservative elements in the controlling city organizations are still very strong
in the Party, and it seems that some variant of the
hierarchical model of control combined with continued reliance on tension management devices is the
most likely course of future political development.
This means that the economy will continue to move
forward very slowly and citizen discontent will continue to grow. Because of the developing vested interests in Party control, the prospect of full-
blown revolution remains remote. In Poland, as in
most industrialized societies, people are content
to work within the established framework hoping for
change rather than trying to circumvent the established institutions openly. The Party's hope is
that the next generation of young Communists will
be suppliant and pliable and, therefore, less demanding. The data indicate that this is not a
likely prospect.

NOTES

1. Evidence also indicates, however, that at the most egalitarian extremes increasing societal wealth does not necessarily mean increasing democratization. See D. Neubauer, "Some Conditions of Democracy," American Political Science Review, Vol. LXI, No. 4 (December, 1967), p. 1002.

2. A similar technique has been used to analyze modernization in the United States. See J. Crittenden, "Dimensions of Modernization in the American States," American Political Science Review, Vol. LXI, No. 4 (December, 1967), p. 989.

3. The study "Kraj, Swiat, Clowiek" was carried out by A. Sicinski under the auspices of the Public Opinion Research Center in 1965 and consisted of a nation-wide random sample of 2,749 adults. After considerable negotiations I was able to obtain an aggregate voivodship breakdown which was then transformed into the data used here. I would like to thank those in Warsaw who were responsible, without mentioning them by name for obvious reasons.

4. A. Pawelczynska, Dynamika Przemian Kulturowych na Wsi (Warsaw: Panstwowe Wydawnictwo Naukowe, 1966), pp. 26-30, expresses many of these considerations in an analysis of Polish aggregate data.

5. Salary differentials in Poland, for example, are much smaller than in the Soviet Union. See S. Wellisz, Economies of the Soviet Bloc (New York: McGraw-Hill, 1964), pp. 71-72.

6. Crittenden, op. cit., pp. 994-97.

7. K. Ostrowski and A. Przeworski, "A Preliminary Inquiry into the Nature of Social Change: The Case of the Polish Countryside," Studies in Polish Political System, ed. J. Wiatr (Warsaw: Polish Academy of Sciences Press, 1967), p. 81.

8.   See H. Stehle, <u>The Independent Satellite</u>
(New York: Frederick A. Praeger, Inc., 1965), pp.
171-77, for examples of how one gets ahead in Polish
society.

9.   See A. Bromke, <u>Poland's Politics</u> (Cambridge,
Mass.:   Harvard University Press, 1967), <u>passim</u>, for
analysis of Polish politics in factional terms.
This is also the approach to political analysis of
Poland used by Radio Free Europe.

10.   This corresponds to the situation seen de-
veloping in the Soviet Union.   See Z. Brzezinski,
"Reflections on the Soviet System," <u>Problems of
Communism</u>, Vol. XVII, No. 3 (1968), pp. 44-48.

11.   For a precise explication of the meaning of
the term "active society," See A. Etzioni, <u>The Active Society</u> (New York: The Free Press, 1968),
Ch. 1.

7

**POSSIBILITIES
FOR CHANGE:
COMPLIANCE
WITHOUT
COMMITMENT**

The accumulated evidence makes it clear that no simplistic view of the political future of socialist societies is possible. It is obvious both from the evidence presented as well as from the record of recent events that the power position of the Party in Poland, as well as in the other industrialized Communist Party states, is sufficiently strong, when backed by Soviet power, to repulse any internal attempts at overthrow. Nor does it seem that any groups exhibit the commitment or numbers necessary to seriously disrupt internal politics. On the other hand, there are no indications that the heavy investment in tension management activities has made serious inroads into the traditional political culture or that they have substantially ameliorated the pressures created by industrialization and the concomitant revolution of rising expectations.

The dynamics of modernization appear to be much the same in monist and pluralist societies. Although the mobilization of the countryside takes place at a more controlled rate when a single party is responsible for industrialization, the rise in expectations, both economic and political, are very

much parallel to those found in developmental cases
with which we are more familiar. Although the
forces urging conservative stabilization in the socialist society may use different rhetoric than
their capitalist counterparts, their privilege-
cementing motives are much the same. As the data
indicate, this socialist "establishment" is an important force in Poland especially in the more urban areas where opportunities for social, political,
and economic mobility are becoming much more limited.

As for the future of political-tension management, continued modernization of the monist society
means that more resources, better personnel, and
more sophisticated managerial techniques are available for diminishing citizen expectations. On the
other hand, the modernization process itself con-
tributes to an increase in citizen sophistication
as well as expectations. The political leaders in
socialist countries have charted an unalterable
course, however, as they have staked their fortunes
on the continued development of the socialist economy as a legitimating device. They are going to be
forced to deal with more sophisticated and demanding
citizens in the near future unless they intend to
default in their program of economic development.
The political managers face a serious dilemma at
present because the benefits of a hierarchical
centrally controlled economy are becoming fewer as
the more developed socialist countries approach the
second round of industrialization. Apparently un-
willing to decentralize authority and responsibility for innovation, the managing parties increasingly think in terms of consolidating political and
economic gains.

In Poland it is clear that tension management
activities have been escalated in order to counter-
act increasing citizen discontent with economic and
political affairs. Polish economic growth, for
example, in comparison with other monist countries
is not great, indicative of the failure to commit
the economy to movement into the decentralizing

second round of industrialization.[1] Economic
growth that does take place is not readily visible
to the consumer who, because of the many slips between socialist cup and lip, often sees only rising
prices and constant salaries. Especially in the
urban areas one is faced with the alternative of
joining the Party in search of more privilege or
remaining outside and watching mobility opportunities become increasingly narrow as the stabilization proceeds. Key Party membership is old both in
actual years and in attitudes toward innovation and
social change. More recently, the intervention of
others in Eastern European affairs on the side of
orthodoxy only cemented these conservative tendencies. The Party purge in Poland in 1968 and the
recent internal turmoil give evidence that tension
management activities are being maintained and that
potential regime critics are being moved out of positions of power.[2]

TENSION MANAGEMENT AND
INTERNATIONAL PRESSURES

For analytic purposes it would be nice to continue with the assumption that political-tension
management in Poland takes place in a vacuum. Especially in the case of Poland this limiting assumption cannot be made. Geographical position that
has often left Poland as a European doormat is a
most important factor to be considered in any eval-
uation of her political future. The fear of a resurgent Germany combined with emphasis on the pro-
tective role played by the Soviet Union is a most
effective tension management technique that has
been carefully nurtured by the political leadership.
The fragmentation of the Iron Curtain due to developmental exigencies on the other hand has intro-
duced many important new variables into the tension
management equation.

Few countries in history have had the misfor-
tune of being located in such close proximity to so
many major enemies. Often partitioned and sometimes

failing to exist at all, Poland has been made pain-
fully aware of her exposed geographical position
and lack of defensible frontiers. With the outbreak of World War II, she was caught between two
major powers, both of whom demanded slices of her
territory. The Germans, seeking revenge for losses
after World War I, demanded that the frontiers of
1914 be established, thus depriving Poland of a
good deal of her western territory. The Russians,
on the other hand, demanded the restoration of the
frontiers of 1920, meaning that Poland would lose
some of her eastern territories. The result, of
course, was that Poland was devastated during the
War by the movements of troops from both sides as
alliances shifted. The Poland that emerged from
the struggle had shifted its boundaries approxi-
mately 150 miles to the west in deference to Soviet
demands.[3]

The contemporary Pole is quite naturally interested in international affairs and has a particularly deep interest in German affairs. Poland's
losses in World War II were heavier than those of
any other country. Over six million Poles lost
their lives, representing 22 percent of the population. Poland also lost an estimated 38 percent of
her material wealth as compared to only 1 or 2 percent in the case of France and Great Britain.[4] The
treatment the Poles received at the hands of the
Germans will not be easily forgotten.

Perhaps the most pressing problem in Poland's
international affairs derives from the settlements
following World War II. Under Soviet pressure,
immediately following the hostilities Poland's
eastern frontiers were moved nearly 200 miles west
and in return she was granted former German territory to the north and west. These transfers resulted in a net loss of nearly 30,000 square miles
of territory. Of greater importance is the fact
that Poland's western boundary on the Oder and
Neisse rivers has received only hesitant acknowl-
edgment by major powers although in fact there is
no doubt as to ownership. The territorial issue is

still politically sensitive in West Germany among
refugee groups forced to flee as a result of the
settlement. This leaves the Poles anxious lest the
Germans decide to take revenge for the loss of territory at some time in the future. This is particularly true among those now living in the new territories.[5]

Ignoring the fact that the Soviet Union took
more territory to the east than Poland received on
the west and that damage to Poland from Soviet occupation was also very heavy, political leaders
have seized upon the German issue as material that
can be exploited in building both loyalty to the
Polish United Workers' Party and its supporting
ally the Soviet Union. Trapped between the Soviet
Union and a possibly resurgent Germany, the Polish
citizen is told that the only certain way to avoid
a repetition of the German conquest is to cast Poland's lot with the Soviet ally. The Workers' Party is pictured as the only political group enjoying
the approval of Soviet authorities and thus the only
guarantee against a destructive revenge-minded West
Germany. To attack the Workers' Party is to risk
the disfavor or even the intervention of the Soviet
authorities, and the potentially disruptive citizen
is faced with this grim choice when contemplating
attacks on the political leadership. The lessons
of Hungary in 1956 and more recently of Czechoslovakia have not been lost on pragmatic Poles, nor
are the representatives of the media in a mood to
let them forget.

A recent national sample of Polish opinion revealed that among those having any interest in international affairs (three fourths of the sample)
the issue of German affairs and relations was by
far the most important.[6] This is both a product
and cause of the continuous round of attempts to
keep the fear of Germany foremost in the citizens'
minds by devoting a lion's share of media attention
to German affairs. When Kurt Kiesinger was elected
Chancellor in West Germany, the headlines in Warsaw
papers read "Hitlerite since 1933 a candidate for

Chancellor" in a continuing attempt to link contemporary German politics with the horrors of the War.
Rarely does a trial of a war criminal or an exposé
of this nature escape the front page of the press.
Even the Polish correspondent in Bonn in 1966 was
named R. Wojna, a Polish word for war. Rarely miss-
ing an opportunity to touch on the German threat, a
recent article criticizing the wave of Polish jokes
in the United States concludes as follows:

> The jokes mentioned in the introduc-
> tion have been spreading in the Amer-
> ican air a heavy stink not so much of
> Polish sausage with cabbage as of
> somewhat rotten German sauerkraut.
> The satirical style of the cartoons
> reminds one of the last page of
> Berliner Illustrieries from Hitler's
> time or of those racist cartoons from
> Sturmer.[7]

Whether the success of this type of campaign
is proportionate to the tremendous amount of energy
expended is questionable, but the data in Table 41
indicate that concern with German relations is high
among all Polish occupational groups. Using the
Germans to build a "negative" type of support for
the Party seems to be paying off. The data show
that skilled blue-collar and white-collar forces
are just as concerned, if not more so, than their
unskilled blue-collar or peasant counterparts. The
argument for supporting the program of the Polish
United Workers' Party on these pragmatic grounds is
a powerful one and explains a good deal of support
for the Party among white-collar segments. In the
long run, however, West Germany's policies of reconciliation with Eastern European countries is helping to destroy many of the arguments used by the
Party.

Thus, Poland and East Germany were the most
anxious among the Soviet Union's allies in crushing
the Czechoslovak liberalization. If Czechoslovakia
were permitted to develop independent from Soviet

TABLE 41

Interest in Foreign Affairs--Selected Aspects*
(in percent)

| | Blue-Collar | | White-Collar | | |
	Unskilled	Skilled	Less Educated	Highly Educated	Peasant
German affairs	77%	87%	83%	83%	79%
Disarmament	67	86	82	79	78
Western relations	45	55	53	53	42
Bloc politics and economics	40	54	54	55	41
Foreign cultures' life	31	43	50	66	30
Western politics and economics	37	49	52	49	41
Relations with socialist countries	34	47	44	36	34
Cooperation in economy and culture	19	31	34	45	21
Liberation movements	23	35	32	32	21
Workers' movements in other countries	16	27	19	6	15

*Among the 75 percent of sample interested in foreign affairs.

Source: A. Sicinski, "Spoleczenstwo Polskie a Polytika Miedzynarodowa" ["Polish Society and International Affairs"] (Warsaw: Osrodek Badania Opinii Publicznej, 1965), p. 63.

tutelage sharing a common border with West Germany,
the holes in the Party's propaganda would become
obvious to all concerned. Thus, the Workers' Party
has a great stake in preventing liberalization and
independence moves in the other countries of the
socialist bloc in that much support is derived from
the fact that the intelligent citizen perceives
himself as having no other choice. During the
events in Czechoslovakia the press went to great
pains to point out that the Leninist approach to
rights of self-determination "must be based pri-
marily on the interests of the working class as the
class most interested in the development of socialism. . . . An international dictatorship of the
proletariat in several countries, i.e. close unity
of the camp of socialist countries, thanks to which
their influence on world policy is possible, en-
sures the socialist character and national sover-
eignty; the leading role of the working class and
its party in every single socialist country is con-
ditional.[8] Complete with ideological justification,
the Party shatters hopes that Poland will in the
near future embark on an independent course apart
from that designated by the Soviet Union as leader
of the socialist bloc.

But Poland's geographical position is not the
only force complicating the problem of tension management. Contemporary Poland is a rapidly modernizing country having an increasing number of ties
to other countries with a variety of social, political, and economic systems. When the most odious
features of the Iron Curtain were removed following
Stalin's death, the resulting influx of information
did much to change citizen beliefs about the outside world as well as domestic expectations. Entering increasingly with foreign tourists, these
alternate views of the outside world put tight
strictures on the efforts of the propaganda machine
to portray the capitalist world as decaying. Although it still would be possible to exclude foreign
tourists from Poland, the Party is hesitant to do
so because each tourist is a source of foreign currency. In 1966 over one million foreign tourists

visited Poland, one fifth of that number coming
from capitalist countries, and the figures have
risen every year.[9]

Even the restriction of foreign tourism could
do little to restore the isolated conditions of the
era of the Iron Curtain. Many of the interests
listed in Table 41 indicate that the skilled workers and intelligentsia, forming an increasingly
larger part of the population, are interested in
cultural life in other countries as well as in
Western political and economic affairs. There is
extremely little interest in the workers' movements
and liberation movements, about which so much information is available. If desired information is
not forthcoming from official sources it is readily
available from foreign radio broadcasts or Poles
who have been in the West. Between 1956 and 1966
the number of Poles traveling abroad increased from
177,000 to more than 800,000 with over 100,000 in
the latter year going to capitalist countries.[10]
The Pole with a real interest in knowing what is
going on in the outside world no longer is isolated
from the information he seeks, and the propaganda
experts have had to adjust their tension management
strategies accordingly.

SOURCES OF DISSENT

In many respects the conservative stabilization taking place in Poland is symptomatic of processes taking place in the other developed socialist countries. Whether it is called the "routin-
ization of charisma" or the "end of ideology," it
is becoming increasingly clear that the dynamic
phase of socialist revolution is over in the more
modern socialist countries. Just as Lenin and
Trotsky gace way to Stalin, Khrushchev, and eventually Brezhnev and Kosygin, the early radicals in
the socialist countries with their visions of a
socialist utopia have given way to bureaucrats more
interested in consolidation and stability than innovation and ideological fervor. Perhaps the

"administered" society where the "management of political tensions" is the most important political
activity has already arrived in many of the socialist countries.[11]

The foregoing analysis presents a grim picture
of possibilities for rapid social and political
change in Poland. As in the other Eastern European
countries, there are very few forces that can be
mobilized in opposition to the dictates of the
Party. The United Peasant Party and the Social
Democrats coexist with the Polish United Workers'
Party, but they are poor competition and cooperate
with the leading party on all matters of importance.[12] The electoral system provides a method
whereby some independents get elected to the Sejm,
but their powers are limited as are the powers of
the Sejm.

Outside of politics there are some groups that
profit least from the stabilization under Party
guidance; it is from them that dissent is most likely to come. These include the Catholic Church,
which normally profits most from stabilization but
as yet has been unable to reach an understanding
with the Party. In addition, university students
and other discontented elements among the young see
the stabilization as directly affecting their
chances for social mobility and the good life. The
intelligentsia suffers most from the heavy emphasis
on egalitarian distributions of benefits under the
current system and also has to be looked upon as a
source of possible dissent.

At least nine out of ten Poles have some con-
nection with the Church ranging from baptism
through regular attendance at services. Religious
attendance outside of the most urban areas is
heavy; nearly three quarters of parishioners regis-
tered attend mass on any given Sunday.[13] Among the
young the pattern is very similar. A nation-wide
survey reported that 78 percent consider themselves
to be Catholic, indicating that religion is going
to be an important influence in Poland in the

future.[14] What is more interesting, however, is
that among the portion of the sample that gave
their political views as "Communist," 30 percent
also claimed that they were Catholic.[15] Only 35
percent of the Communists claimed to be atheists.
Almost all the Communist Catholics in the sample
believed in the Creation, voiced their intention
to have church weddings, and said that they would
raise their children in a religious manner.[16] Although hard data is difficult to come by, a good
share of adult Party members are found in church on
Sunday morning.[17]

Although the potential power of the Church is
very great, the influence the Church currently has
in political affairs is not proportionate to its
following. The Church's power is mainly normative
in nature. The people can be persuaded from the
pulpit on Sunday to take certain actions but otherwise the Church has few economic or political weapons to direct at the Party. Nor do church leaders
give any indication that they are willing to take
the Party on in head-to-head combat. This would
not be in the interest of either; the Church would
face destruction of its physical facilities and the
Party would find that such conflict would certainly
further alienate a greater portion of the citizens.
The Church is not interested in the overthrow of
the political system as long as it has reasonable
facilities for caring for the spiritual needs of
Poles. The fact that a member of the Polish Workers' Party should technically regard religion as
the opiate of the people does not have much meaning
for a clergy which recognizes that the congregation
is composed of large numbers of nominal Party members.

Thus, the Church has been actively seeking a
modus vivendi with the representatives of the state.
An agreement signed in 1950 has served as the basic
pattern for church-state relations and, depending
on the constellations of political forces at any
particular time, has been violated by both sides.
Freedom of worship is still guaranteed and there is

little harassment of people attending services.
The Church has also been permitted to maintain a
Catholic university at Lublin and a number of associations of a religious nature. The building of
new churches and religious structures has been a
point of friction as the state has been loath to
permit scarce building material to be converted
into houses of worship. The Church has contracted
to limit its activities to the spiritual needs of
Poles and condemns any acts that are hostile to the
state.

The more recent frictions between Church and
state can be best described as skirmishes rather
than battles. In 1966 both the Church and state
celebrated their respective "milleniums"; the
Church celebrated 1,000 years in Poland and the
state celebrated 1,000 years of the Polish nation.
Much pettiness was obvious on both sides, often
taking the form of scheduling political celebrations at the same hour as church dedications. Many
American postage stamps printed in honor of the
millenium were confiscated because the eagle on the
stamps wore a crown not found on the current Polish
State Seal, indicating that the stamp was considered to have been printed more in honor of the religious millenium than the state celebrations.[18]

The Church as a force potentially disruptive
of the tension management program need give the
Party little serious concern. In the future any
disruptions of the understandings will come from
the government. In terms of potentially fomenting
opposition, the Church has been "managed" right out
of the political arena. If the Party wishes to
make any drastic changes that affect Church interests, the believers can be mobilized to resist
state actions. It is virtually impossible for the
Church to initiate action programs on its own, however. In this respect the Church's power is mainly
negative, as is its attitude toward Church reforms.

The other major source of dissenting opinions
in Poland is the intelligentsia. The universities

are becoming more important centers of dissent in
all societies and this tendency is also found in
the socialist countries. In Poland it is not only
students who act as critics of the political managers. Professors and instructors have recently
been outspoken in their criticism of the direction
of social and political development and have in
many cases helped initiate dissent. Students and
faculty at the University of Warsaw were important
in the events of 1956 which led to the Polish "thaw"
but remained quiet until 1968 when new outbreaks
against the Party were reported.

Universities are by nature centers of dissent
in that students are trained to analyze social
problems and suggest alternate solutions. There
are times, however, when the questioning student is
not welcomed by political leaders. This is especially true in periods of stabilization when the
political leadership is not willing to have the established goals and methods questioned. Students
are caught in a dilemma because their training and
ideals lead them to challenge many existing practices whereas the political authorities desire to
crush dissent.

In Poland, the result has been that many of
the leading and internationally respected scholars
have been the first to feel the brunt of Party attacks on intellectuals. Marxist philosopher Leszek
Kolokowski was first to feel the effects of Party
disfavor. His "crimes" were writings regarded by
some high in the Party as criticisms of the existing system. It is indisputable that there is criticism in his writings, but the question is how to
make political leaders aware of societal problems
if intellectuals aren't allowed to criticize.

The student uprising in 1968 is illustrative
of many problems facing contemporary student movements. The demonstrations erupted at the University
of Warsaw with a long period elapsing before the
aspiring technocrats in training at the Polytechnic
Institute could be coaxed into joining. Once the

demonstrations started, the leaders were at a loss
to explain exactly for what they were demonstrating.
There is no question that the majority of the dem-
onstrators were alienated from the Polish "establishment," but they offered various solutions to
Poland's problems based on their own interpretations
of Marxism. "We live by the utopia of Marxism-
Leninism, therefore, we want to open people's eyes."
"Under the present conditions only cowards, boot-
lickers, and passive executors of orders can achieve
promotion; it will never be achieved by educated
people with open minds and initiative."[19] These
words, spoken by leaders of the movement, are remarkably similar to the cries uttered by revolutionary student groups in the United States, France,
and other countries struck by protest movements.
In Poland, the students were equipped with powerful
slogans but little in the way of concrete political
solutions or support.

In the reaction following the student outbursts, the department of philosophy at the University was shattered by Party officials as professors
were dismissed along with all students in the department, to be re-admitted only upon application.
In this manner the student body has been purged;
potentially disruptive elements were denied re-
admission. Those professors who had given impetus
to the student revolt by encouraging the questioning of the system were released from academic positions. Thus, Adam Schaff, Zygmunt Bauman, Maria
Hirszowicz and Nina Assordobraj, in addition to
Kolokowski and others, were removed from positions
in which they could influence future students.

Thus, the university has been eliminated as a
potential future source of disruption in the managed Polish society. The "reactionary" professors
and students have been removed from the environment
within which they were dangerous to the Party.
This is not to suggest that the university has been
permanently eliminated as a source of discontent.
Education is by nature opposed to movements stress-
ing conservative stabilization. It would take a

return to outmoded Stalinist educational practices,
amounting to nothing more than technical training
and mouthing proper doctrine, to permanently stifle
dissent in the university. This is no longer a
realistic alternative for the political leaders;
successful tension management itself requires the
training of people in social and behavioral sciences to aid the Party managers.

The Party, having learned its lesson in 1968,
has taken steps to closely control the universities
by increasing the portion of sons and daughters of
workers and peasants accepted. It is unlikely that
an open challenge from the students will be mounted
against the Party in the near future. Operating
under the watchful eye of the Party, the dissenters
are most likely to retreat into silent opposition.
Even if the students as a whole are committed to
the overthrow of the Party, they have little power
of their own and enjoy little sympathy in the society as a whole. The 1968 events revealed that
the working class can easily be mobilized against
the students in time of crisis. Furthermore, there
are no indications that the great majority of the
students are totally alienated from the Party and
its program. The available data indicates that
students desire incremental changes within the system rather than its complete abolition.

It is most difficult to form a coherent picture of student demands and programs in Poland.
For every student there seems to be a different
revolutionary prospectus. In this author's own
experience in the "notorious" department of philosophy at the University of Warsaw, there was little
exposure to the extreme radical rhetoric that char-
acterizes student movements in Poland. It was
clear that students in the department were more
than mildly alienated from a leadership that gave
social scientists little voice and few rewards, but
the arguments had much in common with those made in
graduate seminars in the United States. The Party
is clearly regarded as a reactionary establishment
that is unnecessarily restricting advancement

opportunities, possibilities for trips abroad, and
cross-national research and in general is not encouraging the advancement of bright young people
with new ideas. Aside from general agreement on
these points, however, there seemed to be little
coherence in plans for the society of the future.
The dissenters represented a coalition of most di-
verse interests.[20]

The available empirical evidence portrays Polish youth as basically apolitical. Only 3 percent
of a national sample of youth aged fifteen to
twenty-four said they were Communists and nearly
two thirds claimed that they were "comfortable"
with the current system or had no particular political opinions.[21] The young resemble their more
aged counterparts in their level of social honesty
as only 65 percent condemn the theft of social
property and 57 percent condemn dishonesty in professional work. These figures contrast sharply
with the 79 percent that condemn the theft of private property.[22] When asked reasons for choosing a
career, nearly half the sample was most interested
in good pay, one third would pick a job because it
was interesting, and less than 12 percent would
pick a career for its social usefulness.[23]

Additional data pertaining directly to Warsaw
University students reveal that a third consider
themselves definitely not Marxists, 12 percent
claim to definitely be Marxists, and the majority
voice no opinion on the matter.[24] Although family
income has no influence on whether one considers
himself to be a Marxist (average family income of
the Marxists is nearly the same as the non-Marxists),
social origin is important in determining whether a
student wants the world to move toward some form of
socialism. The average family income of those who
answered this question by checking "yes" is 1,800
zloties monthly; those who answered "no" have an
average family income of 2,600 zloties.[25]

Two thirds of the sample would prefer that the
world move in the direction of socialism, but the

students are not unanimous in their opinion of what
constitutes socialism. When asked to fill in the
names of two or three countries that in their opinion come closest to what they understand as socialist, Yugoslavia received more than twice as many
votes as the nearest competitor indicating that
students prefer Poland to move closer to the innovative and pragmatic form of socialism practiced in
that country. The Soviet Union and Poland were
next popular as examples of the students' ideal,
but they were followed by Sweden and China, representatives of two very different types of political
and economic systems. Polish students have definitely accepted some form of socialism as a goal
for all countries, but they have no clear definition of what it means.

In addition to the tendency to remain apolitical, when questioned about their aims in life, the
sample of Warsaw students voiced very privatistic
and noncontroversial choices. Two thirds of the
sample chose "attaining a decent position and living a relatively peaceful and comfortable life while
realizing personal and private interests." "Influencing human values by personal attitudes and
work activities," a worthy but safe and comfortable
choice, was second in popularity and selected by
half the students. "Living life in a circle of
friends that you like and that like you" appealed
to two fifths of those polled. More innovative or
controversial styles of life such as "living a
colorful life full of impressions" or "realizing
ideological or social values" were shunned by a
majority of students who apparently prefer stability and material comforts.[26]

Mention should be made of a small deviant
group characterized by attitudes substantially different from the majority. Many students coming
from peasant and worker backgrounds are more patri-
otic than their counterparts, are much more strongly attached to the socialist system, consider themselves Marxists, and evaluatethe 1945-55 Stalinist
period positively.[27] This indicates that the

appeals of socialism are stronger among upwardly
mobile students from lower-class backgrounds who
have profited from the socialist revolution.   In
this and other respects, the Party is really a party of workers and peasants and, at least by some in
the younger age groups, is perceived as a positive
force.   It is no wonder that the Party raised the
quota of worker and peasant children to be admitted
to the universities after the 1968 disturbances or
that it had little trouble organizing counterdemon-
strations from among young workers in opposition to
the students.

     The threat posed by the university to political
leaders has been neutralized by Party actions and
by apathy and lack of direction among the students.
Alienation stemming from the more odious and restrictive features of tension management policies
is coupled with diffuse support of socialist ideals.
Even were opposition to the regime or the system to
crystallize on any particular issue, there is little students can do to threaten the political leadership.   Like their counterparts in other countries,
Polish students have little power to affect the
course of political events due to their vulnerabil-
ity.   They are admitted to the university and supported by the state and have few allies outside the
university community.

     Aside from the Church and the universities,
there are very few other possibilities for the generation of political change in Poland.   G. Ionescu
lists reviews, armies and partisans, and personal-
ities as possible sources of change pressures and
dissent in Eastern Europe, but in Poland they seem
of little importance.[28] Since the 1957 closing of
<u>Po Prostu</u>, one of the most active and critical of
the Polish journals, the reviews as political tools
have been in decline. Apart from the criticisms
voiced by ambitious journalists in the press, there
is little indication that the printed word is a
real threat to the Party.

     The army is clearly under Party control; al-
though the partisans are an active political force

in Poland, their pressures are felt within the Party and not from the outside. Gomulka was swept from power by a coalition of younger, technocratic, nationalistic, but careful leaders and there is little indication of massive transformations of the Party from the top. Gierek must pursue reformist policies unless he wishes to suffer Gomulka's fate, but there have as yet been few clues that major departures from Gomulka's politics of stabilization will be forthcoming. Thus, after evaluating the tension management possibilities and threats to the conservative stabilization that is precluding political, social, and economic innovation, it seems that there is little hope for rapid change in the near future. The Party is quite capable of insuring citizen compliance without commitment. The potential opposition is held in check and political opponents and interest groups have only negative power to keep the Party from making drastic changes affecting them--especially in Church affairs and the collectivization of agriculture. No one, aside from the Party, possesses the positive power to initiate new reforms and programs that seem to be necessary if the current impasse in economic and political affairs is to be overcome. If conservative stabilization in Poland is to be halted, the impetus must come from within the Party and not from the outside.

THE PARTY

With minor exceptions, the Polish United Workers' Party is typical of the ruling parties in the more economically developed socialist countries. It differs from the normal pattern of control by permitting two alternate sources of interest articulation--the United Peasant Party and the Social Democrats. As in other countries the Party is the sole repository of power and in reality the only source of social change. Dominated by a conservative group of leaders, the Party is responsible for the present economic stagnation. Allied with Moscow and aging leaders in other socialist countries, Polish leaders continue to invest their resources

in managerial activities and consolidating their
power rather than taking innovative risks that
might conceivably rejuvenate the Party.

The Western view of typical Party members is,
however, unfortunately limited because of their extremely low visibility. We know very little about
the characteristics of other than the top 5 percent
of Party membership because little information is
available and there has been little reason to study
this subject. It is easy to forget that those at
the top in Party affairs are mostly members of one
generation--the revolutionary forces that joined
the Party before or during World War II. They have
suffered the excesses of the Stalinist period, and
their survival makes them members of a very select
group. They have worked their way into positions
of power over a long period of time, especially in
the more urban areas where the Party has been an
important force for over two decades. The domination of the Party by urban organizations with high
concentrations of population has insured that these
conservative elements maintain political power.
Members of this group are quite old, however, and
they are beginning to rapidly disappear from the
scene. As their numbers diminish it will become
increasingly important to know something about
their subordinates in the Party ranks.

Making accurate and concrete statements about
the "typical" Party member is difficult. In Poland
all the more important and revealing data about
Party membership is restricted. Even the most innocent Party publication, The Party in Figures, is
restricted to internal Party use. One of the potentially most revealing studies was launched in
1968 and covers the ideological preparedness of
Party members. Although the data has now been analyzed, it is highly unlikely that more than a carefully selected portion will ever be made public.

The best approach to the study of Party members' attitudes is available in a composite picture
from questions asked of both Party and non-Party
members in public opinion surveys. These permit

comparisons between the non-Party and Party members
questioned. In addition, other purportedly secret
and admittedly dated materials combined with theoretical perspectives on Polish politics yield some
hints about the current values and beliefs of rank-
and-file members.

It is clear that the Party program has different appeals to various segments of the population.
The Party is in reality a party for the workers,
and they seem to be responding with support. The
extremely egalitarian approach to wages undoubtedly
distributes a greater segment of the national income to the working class than in any other contemporary or historical society. Seeking to cement
the image of the Workers' Party as such, there are
continuous drives to recruit workers into the Party.
Workers and peasants make up the majority of candidates recruited and composed 60 percent of the total admitted in 1960-61. Because of both higher
attrition in the worker ranks and promotion of Party members from blue-collar to white-collar occupations, the actual composition of the Party reflected
50 to 55 percent workers and peasants over the period 1961-66. Workers made up a constant 40 percent
of the Party over the same period.[29]

Peasants make up a very small proportion of
Party membership for several reasons. They have
their own party which acts as an adjunct to the
PUWP and thus consumes much peasant interest. In
addition, political interest and activity among the
peasantry is extremely small. The rare peasant who
wants to get ahead in politics will of course join
the important dominating party. Men spending most
of their time cultivating the soil are not noted
for political activities. Finally, the peasants
and the Party have been traditional enemies and
many long battles have been fought over the collectivization issue. The bulk of the peasantry is not
in a hurry to obtain a Party card.

White-collar segments of Polish society have
been most neglected by the socialist distribution
of rewards and are most disgruntled about Party

policies. Opportunism keeps white-collar personnel
joining the Party; a constant 43 percent of the
Party membership has been classified as white-
collar from 1961 to the present. A Party card
helps one move up the managerial ladder. In 1961
one quarter of the white-collar Party membership
was classified as "officials," indicating bureaucrats who found it either necessary to join the
Party to maintain their positions or advisable in
order to obtain promotions. Technicians and teachers were next important in membership portion as
the Party has been especially interested in enrol-
ling the latter for obvious reasons. In 1961 over
28 percent of all teachers were enrolled in the
Party.[30]

Additional data indicate that the calibre of
the average Party member is getting better over
time although the class composition remains much
the same. The portion of the Party holding university degrees increased from 5 to 7 percent between
1961 and 1966. At the same time, the portion that
hadn't finished grade school declined from 24 to 15
percent and the portion of high school graduates in
the ranks increased from 21 to 24 percent.[31] The
age structure of the Party changed very little during this period of time, another indication of un-
willingness to yield responsibilities to the young.
In the earlier year 42 percent of the membership
was over forty and the figure remained exactly the
same five years later. There was a 1 percent increase in the under twenty-four category.[32]

With heavy emphasis on recruitment of the
working class, the Party does have some difficulty
in keeping the quality of the membership high. In
1961, for example, nearly 2,000 workers were expelled for bribery and theft and 1,000 were removed
for immoral behavior and drunkenness. Another
12,000 workers were deleted from the rolls, the
majority of these for lack of interest and neglect
of Party duties. White-collar personnel expelled
from the Party were most often guilty of financial
irregularities and theft and very infrequently of
drunkenness and immoral behavior.[33]

Turning to survey data for further information,
Party members differ very significantly from non-
Party members in information on international affairs and attitudes toward social and political
problems. The 540 Party members in a sample of
3,000 Poles in a recent study scored significantly
higher on an international affairs quiz included
with the questionnaire. Out of the twelve questions asked, Party members averaged 9.4 correct re-
plies, members of the other two political parties
averaged 8.8 correct answers, and the rest of the
sample averaged 7.8 correct answers.[34] Especially
among people with little education, Party membership clearly differentiates the more from the less
politically informed.[35] Party members are almost
universally more interested in all aspects of international affairs than their non-Party counterparts. The differences are greatest in expressed
interest in Soviet politics and in the West, in international cooperation in economics and culture,
and in relations between Poland and the developing
areas.[36]

Table 42 presents some major differences between Party and non-Party members in compact form.
It is clear that Party members take a greater interest in foreign affairs and more frequently believe that the information in the Polish media is
basically true. In this respect being a member of
the Party to some extent is correlated with trust-
ing the leadership and their representatives although less than half of the Party members express
this belief in the truth of media information.
Surprisingly, Party members more frequently believe
that avoiding war is possible and in possibilities
for peaceful coexistence. Most interesting is the
fact that a substantially greater portion of Party
members believe that the common man can influence
the affairs of government, an indication that Party
membership carries feelings of political efficacy
with it.

The statistical picture of the Party member
created by this type of data is much at variance
with the nonsophisticated Party hack image so

popular in the West. There is nothing in the data
to dispel the picture of many Party members joining
for opportunistic reasons, but it is clear that
they are informed politically and interested in
world affairs and to a certain extent feel that
they can do something about them. It is very possible that the rank-and-file members of the Party
might differ from those in positions of authority
in these matters, as the younger Party members are
more educated and more active.

TABLE 42

Attitude Differences--PUWP Members and Others

	Rural		Urban	
	PUWP	Non-PUWP	PUWP	Non-PUWP
Interested in international affairs	68%	37%	70%	42%
Believe information honest	47	29	49	27
Peaceful coexistence possible	59	49	64	55
People can influence government	50	30	50	35
Avoiding war is possible	15	11	23	13

Source: A. Sicinski, "Spoleczenstwo Polskie
a Polytika Miedzynarodowa" ["Polish Society and
International Affairs"] (Warsaw: Osrodek Badania
Opinii Publicznej, 1965), Table 12.

     The data also help highlight one of the big-
gest dilemmas facing the citizens in many Party
states. To join the Party is to help legitimate an

institution that is unpopular with the majority and
bitterly opposed by a substantial minority. To remain outside the Party, on the other hand, is to
remain apart from the only organization that seems
capable of bringing about substantial changes. The
politically concerned socialist citizen is caught
in intense cross-pressures; whichever decision he
makes he is likely to have his opinions polarized
by the dynamics of cognitive dissonance.[37] If he
joins the Party, he must live with his decision and
will see the good points in Party membership as
justifying his decision. If he decides to remain
outside, he will gravitate into the company of
those who hate the Party. These dynamics help explain a peculiar phenomenon in socialist countries.
In the neighborhood, in the factory, or in the university, there is often most intense hatred between
Party and non-Party members. This is made all the
more intriguing in that the sociological profiles
of the Party and non-Party members are often so
similar that there are very few variables that can
account for these differences.

     The data do indicate that there is some hope
for changes within Poland in the future. The leading figures within the Party have the political
situation well in hand for the present, but it is
going to be difficult to maintain tight control
over the membership when the old members begin to
disappear. Although it is not clear how the more
concerned, educated, and progressive forces in the
Party will move into positions of power, or even
whether they will be able to, it is certain that
future tension management attention in Poland will
have to be directed at the Party ranks rather than
those outside.

             THE POLISH LESSON: OTHER PARTY STATES

     If the path political development is taking in
Poland is so unique that little can be learned
about other political systems or modernization and
politics in general, this study will play the role

of a historical curiosity. Many of Poland's problems, however, result from the fact that she is not
so isolated but rather is closely allied to the
Soviet Union and other socialist countries facing
similar problems. The Soviet Union sets the pace
for the members of the socialist camp, and those
ruling parties closest and most important to the
Soviet leadership are more exposed to Soviet pressure. The current tone that the Soviet leaders are
setting for the other ruling parties is one of conservative stabilization. Thus, the problems in Poland have parallels in other industrial socialist
countries. Although pressures for change in Czechoslovakia became manifest in a much more violent manner than they have in Poland, a good case can be
made that the basic dynamics of the situation are
the same.

Conservative stabilization is becoming the accepted pattern in the socialist countries. Those
that are not "managerially" oriented are roundly
condemned by Soviet leaders. Thus, the Chinese
were accused of trying to disrupt the "business-
like atmosphere" of the meeting of world Communist
parties in Moscow. The innovators who might
threaten the power position of the dominant party
are regarded as primitives in today's stable and
orderly socialist world. The gerontocracy in the
Kremlin, having survived the years of scarcity and
turmoil, is not about to let anyone rock the socialist boat now that Russian society has become
stable and reasonably productive.

The problems this attitude creates for the
leaders of the other socialist countries vary with
societal levels of modernization and a country's
historical heritage and political culture. Pressures for decentralization of decision-making are
strongest in countries where citizens have reached
a level of awareness that leads them to become actively involved in political affairs. In those
countries with traditions of autocracy, citizens
have very low levels of political expectations.
Czechoslovakia, a country with a fairly democratic

heritage and a high level of development, was the
first to feel revolutionary pressures directed
against the tension managers.

Pressures for change have mounted much more
slowly in East Germany than one would predict judg-
ing solely from level of economic development.
Historical and cultural factors, isolation from the
Western world since World War II, and the traditional authoritarianism of the Prussian people have
helped to limit citizen expectations. Although
there are growing indications of discontent with
leadership policies in East Germany, particularly
among intellectuals, meaningful changes in leadership orientations will be slow in coming. East
Germany is likely to remain Moscow's most faithful
ally in suppressing innovative challenges to the
accepted methods of socialist societal management.

Hungary still suffers from the effects of the
suppression of the Revolution. Hungarian political
culture is one of violence and action, factors
which help explain why the liberalization in Hungary took such a radical and dangerous turn in 1956.
The loss of revolutionary leadership connected with
the events of this period diminished many overt
pressures for political change. With the bloody
events still in many Hungarians' minds, direct challenges to Soviet policies are not likely to be
forthcoming in the near future.

The Soviet Union is the key to continued emphasis on conservative stabilization and political-
tension management in the other countries. Political expectations have traditionally been low in
this country dominated by autocratic government for
so much of its history. The Soviet citizen is currently enjoying the fruits of one of the longest
periods of stability in recent Soviet history. Under these conditions, citizen discontents are not
likely to become a serious problem in the near future. Inasmuch as the Soviets are setting parameters around actions that others may take in meeting citizen demands, it is unfortunate that this

"leading" party has not experienced the problems facing the leadership in countries where citizen discontent is much higher. In this respect the Soviet lack of understanding makes the leading party an anchor on future innovation and progress in the other countries in the Communist system.

Bulgaria and Rumania are countries with very poorly developed economies and less than democratic political traditions. Under these conditions, citizen demands have been few as there is little indigenous citizen interest in politics and few opportunities for contact with other societies and different values. The mobilization model of decision-making was developed for this type of society as very few people demand a voice in decision-making. Most of their time is taken up in the daily struggle for existence. Indeed, these two countries have exhibited extremely high rates of economic growth over the past few years indicating that the tight centralized control indicative of the first round of industrialization is still very functional in economies this poorly developed.[38]

The other socialist countries cannot be as easily analyzed within the framework developed above for many reasons. They all are much farther from Moscow's control and thus much less bound to follow the Soviet patterns with all their consequences. In addition, these countries are very poorly developed industrially and have different cultural heritages than those of the Party states of Eastern Europe. They are much more likely to carve out their own paths of modernization and perhaps avoid the problems now being faced in the other member states.

Thus, the lessons learned from an analysis of modernization in Poland are more or less applicable to all socialist countries depending upon developmental level and potential independence from Soviet control. In many respects the problems that have become so obvious in Poland are faced to a lesser but still important degree by the citizens in all

industrial nations.   In complex societies, decision-
making power must be delegated.   It is hard to keep
those who have power accountable for their actions.
As long as the system remains fairly productive and
reasonably stable, it is difficult for both the
rulers and the often apathetic masses to maintain
an active orientation toward problem solving.   The
conservative stabilization of society always lurks
as a threat to the exploitation of full potential.
Those who stress satisfaction with system performance and eagerly cement their positions of privilege are society's worst enemies.   Settling for
less than an active and innovative leadership keeps
all segments of society from profiting from full
productive potential.

NOTES

1.   See the comparative figures in S. Zemelka,
"The Problem of Specialization in Comecon," East
Europe, Vol. XVIII, No. 5 (May, 1969), p. 9.

2.   For a list of those purged, see East Europe, Vol. XVII, No. 8 (June, 1968), pp. 50-51.

3.   A good discussion of the territorial issue
is found in H. Stehle, The Independent Satellite
(New York: Frederick A. Praeger, Inc., 1965),
Ch. 5.

4.   Ibid., pp. 247-48.

5.   Ibid., pp. 268-80.

6.   A. Sicinski, "Spoleczenstwo Polskie a
Polytika Miedzynarodowa" ["Polish Society and In-
ternational Affairs"] (Warsaw: Osrodek Badania
Opinii Publicznej, 1965), p. 63.

7.   "Free Jokes in a Free Country," Zycie
Warszawy, No. 52, March 2, 1967.

8.   J. Waclawek, "Leninist and Petty Bourgeois

Approach to the Right to Self-Determination,"
Trybuna Ludu, No. 331, December 1, 1968.

9.   "Poland Increasingly Attractive to Tourists," Kurier Polski, No. 85, April 11, 1967.

10. J. Bryniarski, "Travel Without Colli-
sions," Polytika, No. 14, April 8, 1967, and "Tourist News: Polish People Abroad," Trybuna Ludu, No.
357, December 28, 1966.

11. See A. Kassof, "The Administered Society,"
World Politics, July, 1964, pp. 558-75.

12. For a more complete discussion of the
party system, see J. Wiatr, "The Hegemonic Party
System in Poland," Studies in Polish Political System, ed. J. Wiatr (Warsaw: Polish Academy of Sciences' Press, 1967), p. 108.

13. G. Ionescu, The Politics of the European
Communist States (New York: Frederick A. Praeger,
Inc., 1967), p. 196.

14. M. Szanawska, Swiatopoglad Modziezy
[Youth's World View] (Warsaw: Osrodek Badania
Opinii Publicznej, 1960), p. 27.

15. Ibid., p. 15.

16. Ibid., p. 16.

17. The role of the Church in manufacturing
dissent is further discussed in Ionescu, op. cit.,
pp. 190-203.

18. For more details, see Stehle, op. cit.,
Ch. 3 and Appendix 3.

19. A. Reutt and Z. Andruszkiewicz, "Alliance
of Hatred," Walka Mlodych, No. 47, November 24,
1968.

20. For greater detail, see ibid.; also R.

Gontarz, "Shut Up or Lie," Pravo i Zycie, No. 23, November 23, 1968; and G. Mond, "The Student Rebels in Poland," East Europe, Vol. XVIII, No. 7 (July, 1969), pp. 2-7.

21. Szanawska, op. cit., p. 14.

22. Ibid., pp. 20-21.

23. Ibid., p. 25.

24. S. Nowak, J. Jasinski, A. Pawelczynska, and B. Wilska, "Studenci Warszawy" ["Warsaw Students"] (unpublished manuscript, University of Warsaw), p. 181.

25. Ibid., pp. 185-86.

26. Ibid., Table 21. See also Z. Bauman, "Values and Standards of Success of the Warsaw Youth," The Polish Sociological Bulletin, No. 3-4 (January-June, 1962), pp. 77-91; S. Nowak, "Social Attitudes of Warsaw Students," The Polish Sociological Bulletin, No. 3-4 (January-June, 1962), pp. 91-104.

27. Nowak et al., op. cit., pp. 123-25.

28. For greater detail, see Ionescu, op. cit., Ch. 3.

29. "The PUWP in Figures," Zagadnienia i Materialy No. 9, May, 1967, pp. 1-15; and PZPR w 1961 (Warsaw: Polish United Workers' Party, 1962) (for internal Party use only).

30. PZPR w 1961, p. 17.

31. Ibid., p. 9; "The PUWP in Figures."

32. PZPR w 1961, pp. 3-5; "The PUWP in Figures."

33. PZPR w 1961, pp. 11-12.

34.   Sicinski, op. cit., p. 70.

35.   Ibid., p. 60.

36.   Ibid., p. 65.

37.   See L. Festinger, A Theory of Cognitive Dissonance (Evanston, Ill.: Row-Peterson, 1957).

38.   For differential growth rates, see S. Zemelka, op. cit., p. 11.

BIBLIOGRAPHY

General References

Almond, G., and Verba S. *The Civic Culture*. Princeton, N.J.: Princeton University Press, 1963.

Barghoorn, F. *Politics in the USSR*. Boston, Mass.: Little, Brown, 1966.

Blau, P. M. *Exchange and Power in Social Life*. New York: John Wiley & Sons, 1964.

Bronfenbrenner, U. *Two Worlds of Childhood*. New York: The Russell Sage Foundation, 1970.

Brzezinski, A., and Friederick, C. *Totalitarian Dictatorship and Autocracy*. New York: Frederick A. Praeger, Inc., 1961.

Coser, L. *The Functions of Social Conflict*. New York: The Free Press, 1964.

Curry, R., and Wade, L. *A Theory of Political Exchange*. Englewood Cliffs, N.J.: Prentice-Hall, 1968.

Dahrendorf, R. *Class and Class Conflict in Industrial Society*. Stanford, Calif.: Stanford University Press, 1966.

Dawson, R., and Prewitt, K. *Political Socialization*. Boston, Mass.: Little, Brown, 1969.

Dentler, R., Polsby, N., and Smith, P. (eds.). *Politics and Social Life*. Boston, Mass.: Houghton Mifflin, 1963.

Deutsch, K. W. *The Nerves of Government*. New York: The Free Press of Glencoe, 1963.

Domhoff. G. W. Who Rules America? Englewood Cliffs, N.J.: Prentice-Hall, 1967.

Easton, D. A Framework for Political Analysis.
     Englewood Cliffs, N.J.: Prentice-Hall, 1968.

Etzioni, A. The Active Society. New York: The
     Free Press, 1968.

_____. A Comparative Analysis of Complex Organiza-
     tions. New York: The Free Press, 1961.

Fagen, R. Politics and Communication. Boston,
     Mass.: Little, Brown, 1966.

Festinger, L. A Theory of Cognitive Dissonance.
     Evanston, Ill.: Row-Peterson, 1957.

Greenstein, F. Children and Politics. New Haven,
     Conn.: Yale University Press, 1968.

Harriman, P. I. (ed.). Twentieth Century Psychology.
     New York: The Philosophical Library, 1946.

Homans, G. C. Social Behavior. New York: Harcourt,
     Brace, and World, 1961.

Hopkins, M. Mass Media in the Soviet Union. New
     York: Pegasus, 1970.

Huizinga, J. The Waning of the Middle Ages. Garden
     City, N.Y.: Doubleday, 1954.

Inkeles, A., and Bauer, R. The Soviet Citizen.
     Cambridge, Mass.: Harvard University Press,
     1959.

Ionescu, G. The Politics of the European Communist
     States. New York: Frederick A. Praeger, Inc.,
     1967.

Jacob, P., and Toscano, J. (eds.). The Integration
     of Political Communities. New York: J. B.
     Lippincott, 1964.

Kassof, A. The Soviet Youth Program. Cambridge,
     Mass.: Harvard University Press, 1965.

Kornhauser, W. The Politics of Mass Society. New
    York: The Free Press of Glencoe, 1961.

Lane, R. E. Political Ideology. New York: The
    Free Press, 1962.

Lenski, G. Power and Privilege. New York: McGraw-
    Hill, 1966.

Lipset, S. Political Man. Garden City, N.Y.:
    Doubleday, 1960.

Lipset, S., and Rokkan, S. Party Systems and Voter
    Alignments. New York: The Free Press, 1967.

McLuhan, M. Understanding Media: The Extensions
    of Man. New York: New American Library, 1964.

Marcuse, H. One-Dimensional Man. Boston, Mass.:
    Beacon Press, 1968.

Mills, C. W. The Power Elite. New York: Oxford
    University Press, 1956.

Parsons, T. The Social System. New York: The
    Free Press of Glencoe, 1951.

Siebert, F. S., Peterson, T., and Schramm, W. Four
    Theories of the Press. Urbana, Ill.: Univer-
    sity of Illinois Press, 1963.

Triska, J. (ed.). Communist Party States: Compara-
    tive and International Studies. Indianapolis,
    Ind.: Bobbs-Merrill, 1969.

_____. Soviet Communism: Programs and Rules. San
    Francisco, Calif.: Chandler Publishing Co.,
    1962.

Von Bertalanffy, L. Robots, Men, and Minds. New
    York: George Braziller, 1967.

Wellisz, S. Economies of the Soviet Bloc. New
    York: McGraw-Hill, 1964.

Modernization

Almond, G., and Coleman, J. S. (eds.). The Politics of Developing Areas. Princeton, N.J.: Princeton University Press, 1960.

Almond, G., and Powell, G. B., Jr. Comparative Politics: A Developmental Approach. Boston, Mass.: Little, Brown, 1966.

Black, C. The Dynamics of Modernization: A Study in Comparative History. New York: Harper and Row, 1966.

Ehrmann, H. Politics in France. Boston, Mass.: Little, Brown, 1968.

Farrel, R. (ed.). Leadership Change in Eastern Europe and the Soviet Union. Chicago, Ill.: Aldine Publishing Co., 1969.

Fischer, G. The Soviet System and Modern Society. New York: Atherton Press, 1968.

Galbraith, J. K. The New Industrial State. Boston, Mass.: The New American Library, 1967.

Geertz, C. (ed.). Old Societies and New States. New York: The Free Press, 1963.

Hagen, E. On the Theory of Social Change. Homewood, Ill.: The Dorsey Press, 1962.

Holt, R. T., and Turner, J. E. The Political Basis of Economic Development. Princeton, N.J.: D. Van Nostrand, 1966.

Huntington, S. Political Order in Changing Societies. New Haven, Conn.: Yale University Press, 1968.

Johnson, C. Revolutionary Change. Boston, Mass.: Little, Brown, 1966.

Lerner, D. The Passing of Traditional Society. New York: The Free Press of Glencoe, 1958.

Moore, B., Jr. Social Origins of Dictatorship and Democracy. Boston, Mass.: Beacon Press, 1967.

Organski, A. F. K. The Stages of Political Development. New York: Alfred A. Knopf, 1965.

Pawelczynska, A. Dynamika Przemian Kulturowych na Wsi. Warsaw: Panstwowe Wydawnictwo Naukowe, 1966.

Pye, L. Politics, Personality, and Nation-Building: Burma's Search for Identity. New Haven, Conn.: Yale University Press, 1962.

Pye, L. (ed.). Communications and Political Development. Princeton, N.J.: Princeton University Press, 1967.

Pye, L., and Verba, S. (eds.). Political Culture and Political Development. Princeton, N.J.: Princeton University Press, 1965.

de Schweinitz, K., Jr. Industrialization and Democracy. New York: The Free Press of Glencoe, 1964.

Poland

Bromke, A. Poland's Politics. Cambridge, Mass.: Harvard University Press, 1967.

Lendvai, P. Anti-Semitism without Jews. Garden City, N.Y.: Doubleday, 1971.

Morrison, J. The Polish People's Republic. Baltimore, Md.: The Johns Hopkins Press, 1969.

Stehle, H. The Independent Satellite. New York: Frederick A. Praeger, Inc., 1965.

Szczepanski, J. Polish Society. New York: Random House, 1970.

Wiatr, J. (ed.). Studies in Polish Political System. Warsaw: Ossolineum, 1967.

Special Studies - Poland

Ciupak, E. Kult Religijny i Jego Spoleczne Podloze [Religious Cult and Its Social Base]. Warsaw: Ludowa Spoldielnia Wydawnicza, 1965.

Grzelak, Z., Kluczynski, J., Roszkowska, M. Z Badan nad Losami Absolmentow [Studies on the Fate of Graduates]. Warsaw: Panstwowe Wydawnictwo Naukowe, 1966.

Kaczmarczyk, L. "Niektore Uwarunkowanie Opinii o Elicie Kierowniczej" ["Some Conditions of Opinions of Directing Elites"]. Warsaw: Osrodek Badania Opinii Publicznej, 1964.

Kupis, T. Zawod Dziennikarza w Polsce Ludowej [Journalism as an Occupation in the Polish Republic]. Warsaw: Ksiazka i Wiedza, 1966.

Nowak, S., Jasinski, J., Pawelczynska, A., Wilska, B. "Studenci Warszawy" ["Warsaw Students"]. Unpublished Manuscript, University of Warsaw,

Sicinski, A. "Spoleczenstwo Polskie a Polytika Miedzynarodowa" ["Polish Society and International Affairs"]. Warsaw: Osrodek Badania Opinii Publicznej, 1965.

_____. "Postawy Wobec Pracy i Wlasnosc" ["Attitudes About Work and Property"]. Warsaw: Osrodek Badania Opinii Publicznej, 1961.

_____. "Przywodcy Opinii i Ich Rola w Procesie Obiegu Informacji" ["Opinion Leaders and Their Role in the Process of Circulating Information"]. Warsaw: Osrodek Badania Opinii Publicznej, 1961.

_____. "Funkje Informacyjne Prasy i Radia" ["The
Information Functions of Press and Radio"].
Warsaw: Osrodek Badania Opinii Publicznej,
1959.

_____. "Zasieg i Prestiz Informacji Gospodarczy
Prasy i Radia" ["Range and Prestige of Eco-
nomic Information in the Press and on the
Radio"]. Warsaw: Osrodek Badania Opinii
Publicznej, 1960.

_____. "Rola Prasy i Radia w Kulturze Masowej"
["The Role of the Press and Radio in a Mass
Culture"]. Warsaw: Osrodek Badania Opinii
Publicznej, 1959.

_____. "Spoleczne Uwarunkowania Czytelnictwa Prasy
i Sluchania Radia" ["Social Determinants of
Press Readership and Radio Listening"]. Warsaw:
Osrodek Badania Opinii Publicznej, 1962.

Spoleczenstowo Polskie w Badaniach Ankietowych.
    [Polish Society in Survey Research]. Warsaw:
    Polskiej Akademii Nauk, 1966.

Szanawska, M. Swiatopoglad Mlodziezy [Youth's World
    View]. Warsaw: Osrodek Badania Opinii
    Publicznej, 1960.

Statistical References

Czyny Spoleczne w PRL. Warsaw: Glowny Urzad
    Statystyczny, 1966.

Poziom Wyksztalcenia Zatrudnionych w Gospodarce
    Uspolecznionej w 1964. Warsaw: Glowny Urzad
    Statystyczny, 1966.

PZPR w 1961. Warsaw: Polish United Workers' Party,
    1962. Restricted circulation of this document.

Rocznik Polyticzny i Gospodarcy 1966. Warsaw:
    Panstwowe Wydawnictwo Ekonomiczne, 1966.

Rocznik Statystyczny. Warsaw: Glowny Urzad
    Statystyczny, 1966.

Russet, B., et al. World Handbook of Political and
    Social Indicators. New Haven, Conn.: Yale
    University Press, 1964.

Spozycie Alkoholu w Polsce. Warsaw: Glowny Urzad
    Statystyczny, 1966.

20 Lat Kultury w Polsce Ludowej. Warsaw: Glowny
    Urzad Statystyczny, 1966.

                    Journals and Newspapers

English:

        The American Political Science Review
        The American Sociological Review
        Comparative Politics
        East Europe
        Polish Sociological Bulletin (Warsaw)
        Problems of Communism
        World Politics

Polish:

        Express Wieczorny
        Kulture (Warsaw)
        Kurier Polski
        Polytika
        Pravo i Zycie
        Sztandar Ludu
        Trybuna Ludu
        Walka Mlodych
        Zagadnienia i Materialy
        Zycie Literackie
        Zycie Partii
        Zycie Warszawa

Dennis Pirages received a bachelor's degree
with honors from The State University of Iowa in
1964 and a doctorate from Stanford University in
1968. During the academic year 1966-67, he was a
student at the University of Warsaw and gained much
of the first-hand experience that went into the
writing of this book. Since receiving his degree,
he has taught at the University of Connecticut and
the University of Georgia.

Professor Pirages has contributed chapters to
Communist Party States: International and Comparative Studies (ed. Jan F. Triska), and Political
Leadership in Eastern Europe and the Soviet Union
(ed. R. Barry Farrell), and has recently edited
Alternatives for Addison Wesley. He is currently
working on a book on societal survival with Paul
Ehrlich. His work reflects a diversity of interests centered around an attempt to bring the knowledge generated by the comparative study of societies
to focus on current critical problems.

In keeping with these interests, Professor
Pirages is currently working with a Stanford University interdisciplinary group devoted to analyzing current social and environmental problems that
will have a serious impact on man's political future. He believes that much meaningful work can
now be done by combining the talents of biologists,
economists, engineers, and political scientists in
approaching social and political questions with a
broad focus.